M000113904

LEADING THE ROMAN ARMY

LEADING THE ROMAN ARMY

Soldiers & Emperors
31 BC – AD 235

Jonathan Eaton

Pen & Sword
MILITARY
AN IMPRINT OF PEN & SWORD BOOKS LTD.
YORKSHIRE – PHILADELPHIA

First published in Great Britain in 2020 by
Pen & Sword Military
An imprint of
Pen & Sword Books Ltd
Yorkshire - Philadelphia

Copyright © Jonathan Eaton, 2020

ISBN 978 1 47385 563 2

The right of Jonathan Eaton to be identified as the Author of this work
has been asserted by him in accordance with the Copyright, Designs and
Patents Act 1988.

A CIP catalogue record for this book is available from the British Library.

All rights reserved. No part of this book may be reproduced or transmitted
in any form or by any means, electronic or mechanical including
photocopying, recording or by any information storage and retrieval
system, without permission from the Publisher in writing.

Printed and bound in England
By TJ International Ltd.

MIX
Paper from
responsible sources
FSC® C013056

Pen & Sword Books Ltd incorporates the Imprints of Pen & Sword
Archaeology, Atlas, Aviation, Battleground, Discovery, Family History,
History, Maritime, Military, Naval, Politics, Railways, Select, Transport,
True Crime, Fiction, Frontline Books, Leo Cooper, Praetorian Press,
Seaforth Publishing, Wharncliffe and White Owl.

For a complete list of Pen & Sword titles please contact

PEN & SWORD BOOKS LIMITED
47 Church Street, Barnsley, South Yorkshire, S70 2AS, England
E-mail: enquiries@pen-and-sword.co.uk
Website: www.pen-and-sword.co.uk

or

PEN AND SWORD BOOKS
1950 Lawrence Rd, Havertown, PA 19083, USA
E-mail: uspen-and-sword@casematepublishers.com
Website: www.penandswordbooks.com

Contents

Preface

This book has enjoyed a long gestation. Its genesis lies in a childhood fascination with the Roman army, encouraged by family holidays to Hadrian's Wall and weekend visits to Ribchester. My interest in the command structures of the Roman imperial army was further developed during undergraduate and postgraduate study. In particular, it was encouraged by reading the classic work *The Emperor and the Roman Army: 31 BC – AD 235.*[1] I subsequently had the opportunity to study under the supervision of Professor Brian Campbell at the Queen's University, Belfast. The research undertaken during this period, supported by funding from the Northern Ireland Department for Employment and Learning, shaped the development of this book.

My passion for the management and operation of the Roman army has been shaped by two extraordinary teachers. Derek Slater introduced me to the rigorous academic study of ancient history based upon a close reading of the classical sources, and believed in me when few others did. Professor Brian Campbell shaped my thinking as a researcher, while advocating a critical approach to the established scholarly literature and encouraging me to situate my own work within its contemporary academic context.

With any piece of writing, it is often the author's family who pay the highest price in the form of lost time. For this reason, this book is dedicated to Jake, Millie, Heidi and Penny, of whom I am more proud than they will ever know.

Introduction

Many dire events, and particularly those which befell the Romans after the death of Nero, bear witness to this and show plainly that an empire has nothing more fearful to show than a military force given over to untrained and unreasoning impulses.[1]

The Empire arose out of a violent usurpation that was the culmination of a series of destructive civil wars waged by rival army commanders. Augustus was the last survivor of a line of generals who used military support to enforce their political will. In securing his pre-eminent position, it was imperative that Augustus prevent his troops from being used against him by ambitious army commanders. In this he was remarkably successful. Over the next two centuries, there would be only two periods of prolonged civil conflict and, in both cases, these were the result of the sudden demise of an established dynasty. Augustus' army reforms represent his greatest achievement.

During the late Republic, soldiers participated in the political machinations of their commanders, to whom they were bound by personal oaths of allegiance. This process began with Marius' enlistment of the *capite censi*, who were reliant on him to provide them with land on their discharge from active service.[2] The civil wars between Marius and Sulla and later between Caesar and Pompey were symptomatic of the soldiers' availability as a political weapon. The troops were not silent partners in this relationship and indeed used their military strength to further their own self-interest.[3] But personal loyalty also influenced their actions. It is noteworthy that by the end of the Republic, soldiers viewed their allegiance as belonging to individual generals rather than to the *res publica*. A Pompeian deserter lamented to Julius Caesar: 'I wish that the immortal gods had made it that I were your soldier rather than Gnaeus Pompey's, and that I were showing my constancy of courage in your victory rather than his defeat'.[4]

In the aftermath of the assassination of Caesar, soldiers took an active role in influencing the political scene.[5] His veterans were eager to avenge their fallen leader and looked to Octavian to fulfil this expectation.[6] Self-interest also motivated their desire to avenge Caesar as they wanted the land rights, which he had granted to them, to be upheld by his successors. For this reason, the soldiers were concerned about the solidarity of the Caesarian faction.[7] Veterans and centurions, in particular, emphasized the need for reconciliation between Antonius and Octavian.[8] As Caesar's adopted son,

Octavian could claim the loyalty of the veterans as the successor of their patron.[9] Yet the soldiers had extremely limited aims and lacked any long-term political vision. Their eagerness to achieve a united front between Antonius and Octavian evaporated once their needs had been met, and they had no qualms about fighting their former comrades when the split between them later became irrevocable. Soldiers' actions under the late Republic created a clear precedent for troops to intervene politically to further their own aims.

After Actium and the final defeat of Antonius, Octavian oversaw the return of political stability and peace across the empire, as symbolized by the closing of the Gates of Janus, for only the third time in Roman history, in 29 BC.[10] Alongside the necessary demobilization and settlement of Triumviral veterans was a pressing need for the depoliticization of the remaining military formations. Octavian accomplished this by instituting sweeping army reforms that ensured that the privileges and terms of army service would henceforth be under the control of the emperor rather than individual army commanders. Lengths of service, pay and discharge privileges for the various branches of the military were standardized. Soldiers' salaries and discharge benefits would now be dispensed from the *aerarium militare*, which was created out of a significant portion of the emperor's personal fortune and supplemented through the raising of new taxes.[11] The temporary armies of the Republic were comprehensively replaced by a permanent imperial institution, which owed its existence and status solely to the emperor.

After the civil wars, Augustus maintained a standing army of twenty-eight legions. Three legions were catastrophically lost with Quinctilius Varus, but more were raised by later emperors. The army consisted of thirty-three legions by the second century AD.[12] Additionally, Augustus began to incorporate native levies into the army as auxiliary units. Auxiliary units eventually made up around half of the total military forces.[13] A permanent naval fleet was also established, with bases at Misenum and Ravenna. Additional fleets were later created in the provinces.[14] With the exception of the units based in Rome for the emperor's personal protection, the army was scattered across the frontier regions of the empire, both to deal with the general strategic situation and to displace the threat posed by the concentration of the military in a single area.[15] Regional army groups developed in areas of particular military importance. In the first century, legions were concentrated in Spain, Britain and on the Rhine. By the reign of Marcus Aurelius, the emphasis had shifted to the Danubian provinces, in light of hostile incursions across the river. In the third century, there were increasing military deployments in the Eastern provinces, which reflected the growing status of the Sasanian dynasty and their hostility to Rome.

The purpose of this book is to examine the problems and possible solutions in the management of the Roman army under the Principate. This topic is important because the high value that the emperors placed upon their personal relationships with the soldiers reveals the crucial importance of the management of the army within the workings of the empire as a whole. Although the Augustan army reforms were successful in establishing an effective framework for military service, maintaining the continued allegiance of the soldiers required eternal vigilance by the emperor. We can have sympathy with Domitian's claim that no one believes in a conspiracy until it is successful.[16] The army always posed a potential threat to the safety and stability of the emperor. I will examine how the command hierarchy and structure of the army were specifically designed to prevent potential rivals from subverting the loyalty of the troops. The overriding factor in ensuring the political allegiance of the soldiers was their relationship with the emperor and this rapport will loom ever present in my study. Given that over twenty years have elapsed since the publication of the fundamental treatment of this theme, a fresh look at the subject is in order.[17] I aim to supplement this work by using archaeological and epigraphic evidence to examine the viewpoint of the soldiers themselves.

Research on the role of soldiers in imperial politics has tended to be constricted by narrow chronological limits, often focussing on the well recorded events of AD 69, rather than the broad thematic overview that I propose.[18] Anthony Birley has described the political involvement of the imperial army using a narrative format and, in doing so, inadvertently revealed the acute limitations of such an approach, in that it highlights the rare occasions that the system broke down rather than the normal circumstances under which it worked.[19] I have chosen to follow a thematic approach to this problem as the recurring forces at work in both securing and subverting the allegiance of the soldiers can be most clearly understood by deconstructing the various managerial layers within the army. This approach demonstrates the gradual adaptation of the army to changing political and strategic circumstances by analysing, both individually and collectively, the evolution of different methods of managing the troops.

My research is not limited to the relationship between the emperor and the soldiers but rather aims to encompass the power relationships which existed between the different levels of command within the army, notably the centurions, equestrians and senatorial officers. Research on these groups has been limited to a prosopographical approach dealing mainly with their origins, careers and promotion structures. Eric Birley and Brian Dobson, in particular, concentrated on the career structures of centurions and *primipilares* as a means of understanding how the army was run, in terms of promotions and transfers.[20] Work on the equestrian officers has also focussed upon their career patterns and later political success, as exemplified by Devijer's vast catalogue of their military careers.[21] The army careers of members of the senatorial order have tended to be examined on a narrow chronological or geographical basis.[22] My work aims to transcend these limitations by analysing the political importance of these men and, in particular, their role in managing the army. This approach demands a broad synthesis of much of the existing research on various aspects of the Roman army, which allows me to put forward original insights into the political management of soldiers under the Principate.

A problematic legacy left by Augustus was the permanent deployment of soldiers in and around Rome. A number of different military and paramilitary units were present in Rome throughout this period and their presence at the centre of power necessitated that they be carefully managed. The emperor was forced to delegate the immediate command of these units to carefully chosen individuals, the most important of whom were the Praetorian prefects. Chapter 1 examines the political importance of the various military units in Rome. It will assess the extent to which the Praetorian Guard in particular was able to play a decisive role in imperial politics. It will also look at the role of the Praetorian prefects, their relationships with both the soldiers and the emperor and the criteria by which they were selected for this role. As a key component in his personal security, the emperor was undoubtedly keen to maintain the allegiance of the Rome cohorts and prevent it being subverted by potential rivals. The methods which emperors and usurpers used to win the loyalty of the city units are described in detail.

Augustus ensured that army units outside of Rome were scattered strategically across the empire in order to serve as an effective means of defence. In Chapter 2, I suggest that this led to the fragmentation of the army into different divided elements, which led to some provincial armies developing and expressing their own individual sense of identity. This fragmentation endangered the unity of the army as a whole. Divisions within the army were combated by the spread of customs common to all soldiers across the empire, which, in turn, created a unique military identity separate to and above that of a civilian. The *sacramentum*, military religious calendar and the transfer of personnel between the provincial armies maintained the unity of the army as a whole. I will explore the various methods used to maintain discipline and morale, which also reinforced the military identity. The breakdown of discipline and a failure in the cohesion of the army could result in a mutiny. The causes and consequences of mutinies under the Principate will be analysed in the context of the potential for small scale disturbance to escalate into direct threats against the stability of the emperor.

Another revolutionary aspect of the new imperial army was the increased importance and enhanced career path open to centurions. Although the increasing status of centurions is evident in Julius Caesar's commentaries, it was only under the Principate that they were able to reach the senior levels of the imperial administration. Emperors aimed to control their soldiers through the legionary and, to a lesser extent, auxiliary centurions, who functioned as infantry leaders and the primary instigators of military discipline. For the most part these were highly experienced soldiers and provided an invaluable source of military knowledge. Equestrians could receive direct commissions into the centurionate often via the patronage of more senior individuals, if not the emperor himself. Former members of the praetorian cohorts could also be transferred as centurions into the legions. The careers of these men, coupled with the frequent transfers of centurions between provincial armies, ensured that the legionary centurions functioned as a focus of political loyalty towards the emperor and imperial house. In particular, the irregular transfers of groups of centurions during times of political crisis may indicate their use as a stabilizing factor in otherwise rebellious units. This theme is examined in my third chapter.

The sheer size of the empire and the deployment of the imperial army in distinct regional groups forced the emperor to delegate command of his soldiers to his army commanders. Members of the senatorial order usually commanded legions and provincial armies, whereas equestrians could serve as officers in the legions and commanded auxiliary units. These individuals had to build a good working relationship with the soldiers under their command, which gave them the ability to influence their soldiers. This fact forced the emperor to be extremely careful in selecting the men he sent out to command the troops. These commanders and officers had the resources to attempt to seize power for themselves, yet the vast majority remained loyal to their emperor. The attitude of the upper classes towards military service and soldiers in general is valuable for understanding how Augustus was able to exclude members of prestigious senatorial families from important military commands. This is reflected in shifting concepts of the meaning of *virtus* and the appearance of alternative legitimate avenues for displaying it. My fourth chapter explores the importance of the senatorial and equestrian officers in controlling the troops and the means by which the emperor was able to control their activities.

My final two chapters act in unison to form a coherent whole in analysing the bond between the emperor and his army. As mentioned above, during the late Republic the soldiers began to become politically aware and this continued under Augustus. This awareness created problems in that the formation of military political opinion had to be carefully managed to ensure that they remained loyal to the reigning imperial family. My fifth chapter therefore examines the soldiers' level of political awareness and the means by which this was controlled. A particular emphasis is placed on the differentiation between formal and informal methods of communication open to the troops, although much depended on levels of literacy within the army. Assessing levels of political awareness for any section of Roman society is difficult, but I will describe three specific cases where the reaction of soldiers to events within the imperial family demonstrates their grasp of political events, namely the deaths of the elder Drusus, Germanicus and Geta.

The central figure in the management of the Roman army was the emperor himself and my final chapter focuses on his personal relationship with his soldiers. His role was predominant in maintaining the political loyalty of the army as a whole and his persona as *commilito* (or 'fellow soldier') was expressed through his conduct towards individual soldiers and behaviour on campaign. I examine the gradual inclusion of members of the imperial family in dynastic propaganda aimed at the army, which is expressed through imagery relating to important individuals on the material culture used by ordinary soldiers. Finally, I discuss a specific image on imperial reliefs to symbolize the relationship between the emperor and his soldiers which has, until now, been overlooked by modern scholars.

In this book I have utilized material from three main fields: epigraphy, numismatics and the surviving literary texts. Each of these sources poses specific pitfalls for the historian. I have relied heavily on five main authors during my research: Pliny the Younger, Tacitus, Suetonius, Cassius Dio and Herodian.[23] These authors were writing from the viewpoint of the upper classes. They did not share the same feelings and opinions as the soldiers; indeed in some cases they despised the army. But all of them had access, through their own rank and status, to information about some, if not all, of the events they described. Pliny, Tacitus and Dio all held consulships and Suetonius served as imperial secretary to Hadrian. Herodian's career is less clear, but he states that he had witnessed some of the events he describes during his imperial service.[24] Nevertheless, as in any era, many of the important issues of state were decided in secret behind closed doors.[25] Furthermore, when historians wrote about events outside their own experience, they must have utilized other sources. The reliability of these missing texts cannot be tested and the process of 'Quellenforschung' is often highly speculative.

The historian must certainly be alert to possible bias in his sources, but there are also other potential problems lurking in wait for the unwary scholar. The author's purpose in constructing a particular narrative is often unclear. Was it intended to be a reliable description of events or an exercise in eloquence? In comparing their texts, we must take account of differing intentions and styles. These authors were not writing in the same genre. Pliny the Younger's works, for example, consist of his published letters and his speech in praise of Trajan. It would be unrealistic to expect to find any criticism of the new regime in his writings. Finally, the political context within which the author worked must be considered. Under the Principate, the writing of history was potentially subversive, as criticism (real or implied) of previous emperors could threaten the prestige of the incumbent *princeps*. When composing his account of Roman history, the future emperor Claudius wisely chose to include the assassination of Julius Caesar and its immediate aftermath, but exclude the civil wars that followed.[26] Some things were best forgotten.

I have also used, to a lesser extent, other classical authors including Velleius Paterculus, whose career I discuss elsewhere.[27] The most difficult text to which I have referred is undoubtedly the *Historia Augusta*. This infuriating mixture of fact, fiction and outright falsehood has been the subject of heated discussion. The current consensus amongst modern scholars is that these imperial biographies were written by a single author towards the end of the fourth century. His motive in writing the work and disguising his identity behind a number of pseudonyms is unknown, but it is clear that the *Historia Augusta* is a dangerous text for the unwary reader. The life of Severus Alexander, for example, contains a great deal of information about the emperor's attitude towards his soldiers. However, many of the details are a fraudulent invention and the depiction of Severus Alexander corresponds to the image of an ideal emperor from a fourth-century perspective, rather than the reality of the Severan emperor whose reign was dominated by military ill-discipline.[28] For this reason, I have used the text with extreme caution. At no point in this book have I based a supposition solely on evidence from the *Historia Augusta*, using it instead to supply supplementary material to elucidate an argument further.

Epigraphic material or inscriptions will feature heavily throughout this study. There are a number of factors that must be considered when dealing with inscriptions.[29] Epigraphy does not allow us to study the total population, only the individuals who chose to erect inscriptions which were fortunate enough to survive until the present day.[30] The 'epigraphic habit' reached a peak towards the end of the second century with a quite rapid decline thereafter.[31] For these reasons, any statistical analysis using epigraphic material can only be of a speculative nature. Like all archaeological material, inscriptions are vulnerable to loss, destruction or reuse. Furthermore, the use of epigraphy varied between provinces. Fortunately, military units and individual soldiers were heavily imbued with the 'epigraphic habit' and it is possible to trace the movements of formations and officers through the inscriptions they left behind. However, epigraphy does not represent a source of pure unbiased material. Inscriptions were costly and therefore they were erected for a purpose. Very often they represent the status of the individual concerned, or the status that they wished to be perceived to possess. They do not explain why a particular individual held a specific post and often obscure the correct order in which offices were held. Dating is also problematic, as few inscriptions include a specific consular year. Inscriptions are usually assigned a date on the basis of their style or connection to a known historical event. Historians working with inscriptions usually refer to epigraphic commentaries published in relevant journals and catalogues. This invariably involves placing a degree of trust in the competence and judgement of the published text and commentary. Moreover, care must be taken in separating the actual preserved text from the reconstructions proposed by the epigrapher. There is an inherent danger in viewing history through square brackets.[32]

For all its familiarity, there is much about the imperial coinage that we do not know.[33] Any attempt to trace propagandistic themes through numismatic images is plagued by doubts about the validity of the imperial coinage as evidence. It is not clear for whom specific designs were produced. Nor is evidence forthcoming as to how the images on the imperial coinage were received by ordinary people or specific sectors of society. We may assume that the emperor had a level of oversight over the design and production of his coins, but even this point has been debated by modern scholars. Another factor worthy of consideration is the speed and efficiency of coin circulation. How fast would a coin of relevance to the military reach the purse of a Batavian serving at Vindolanda in northern Britain, or an Egyptian auxiliary serving in the Fayum? Slow circulation speeds would inevitably result in coin imagery being of limited political value. These factors are of direct relevance to my study and I have explored them in detail elsewhere.[34]

On a number of points I suggest parallels from the military history of the modern era. This has enabled me to illustrate particular ideas that may have a universal application. In doing so, I am not suggesting that the Roman army was equivalent to the military forces of the twentieth and twenty-first centuries. On the contrary, I view the Roman army as a unique institution that was remarkably alien from modern concepts of what constitutes a military force. However, I perceive aspects of modern soldierly behaviour which can be applied successfully to the ancient world. In every case, comparative material is used to reinforce an argument, rather than make one.

Throughout this book, I have weighed the ancient evidence judiciously and exercised considerable caution in selecting relevant material. When the sources are problematic, as in passages from the *Historia Augusta*, or the chronological framework unclear, as in certain inscriptions, I have informed the reader. Despite the challenging legacy of much of the ancient evidence, there is a great deal to be learned from applying it to the problem of the political management of the Roman army. In the words of Syme's maxim: 'One uses what one has, and there is work to be done.'[35]

Chapter 1

The Political Influence of the Rome Garrison

The presence of armed soldiers in Rome added an extra dimension to the politics of the Principate. In contrast to the usual situation under the Republic, the inhabitants of imperial Rome would have been familiar with the sight of troops on the streets. This military presence emphasized the power of the emperor and acted as both a deterrent and a threat to his potential opponents. The impact of the soldiery on the social fabric of the city can be demonstrated by the ratio of soldiers to total urban population which, although based on demographic estimates, indicates a trend throughout the period in question for an increasing military population in Rome.[1] During the reign of Augustus the ratio of soldiers to civilians can be estimated to have been around 1:125–100, while from the reign of Severus the ratio was around 1:45–25. It can be inferred from these ratios that the city of Rome was becoming increasingly militarized. In contrast to the provincial soldiery, the city troops were literally on the emperor's doorstep and were ideally placed to voice their displeasure to him in person. Maintaining the loyalty of the soldiers in Rome was therefore a key concern for the emperor.

The aim of this chapter is to explore the role of the Rome garrison within the political system of the Principate. The emperor's personal security was entrusted to a number of different units and this could potentially lead to conflict between them. I will examine the identities that these units created and the extent to which these conflicting identities provoked rivalry and occasionally even violence. The emperor delegated command of the separate military formations within the city to prefects, the most important of whom were the Praetorian prefects. The role of the Praetorian prefects will be explored in terms of their military abilities, responsibilities and the influence which they exercised over the soldiers. Finally, the means by which the emperor and potential usurpers were able to win and maintain the support of the troops in Rome will be examined.

CONFLICTING IDENTITIES?

The presence of different military units in close proximity to each other undoubtedly created tensions between their members.[2] Even sharing the same camp, as the urban cohorts and the Praetorian Guard were accustomed to do until the third century, did not necessarily promote a good relationship between the two units.[3] On the assassination of Caligula in AD 41 the Guard elevated Claudius, yet the urban cohorts supported the Senate and accepted the watchword from the consuls.[4] This division between the two units has been seen as a deliberate political act, in that the urban cohorts were asserting their political will by lending their support to the Senate. However, the fact that the urban cohorts shifted their allegiance to Claudius when it became clear that he had the support of the Guard suggests that they were no match for the latter and therefore deserted the Senate to prevent their own annihilation. An alternative factor may have influenced the division between the Guard and urban cohorts, namely a conflict of unit identities which resulted in an underlying tension and rivalry.

The Praetorian Guard expressed their identity in a number of ways. They took the scorpion of Tiberius as their symbol, which indicates the importance of the concentration of the soldiers in one camp to the unit as a whole. The scorpion symbol was unique to the Guard and appears on funerary sculpture as well as on metropolitan art.[5] Their self-importance was probably also bolstered by their appearance on the imperial coinage. This elite identity was also expressed in their marital behaviour. A study based on funerary epitaphs has demonstrated that the Guard had unusually low rates of 'married' servicemen when compared to the rest of the military units across the empire, as low as 5 per cent in the first century AD.[6] Although it can be suggested that this represents a particular subculture prevalent within the Guard that favoured commemoration by comrades as opposed to kin, it is interesting to note that the closest modern analogy is the low marriage rates within the US Marine Corps, which also prides itself on a reputation as an elite unit.

Praetorian marriage rates only began to approach those of the legions in the third century, which is an indication of the fundamental change that had taken place with the Severan influx of Danubian troops into Rome. Dio records the horror felt by the populace upon the arrival of terrifying and uncouth soldiers who accompanied Severus and proceeded to fill the city.[7] It was felt that they were immune even to the pleas of the Vestal Virgins on account of their barbarian blood.[8] The new composition of the Guard had a profound impact on the social fabric of Rome itself. The relationship between the emperor and the Guard was also altered by the recruitment change. Danubian recruits to the Guard maintained their provincial identity.

2

Four soldiers spread across three different Praetorian cohorts who came from the same village in Thrace jointly erected a dedication and, in another case, twenty men from eight different cohorts who all originated from the area around Philippopolis set up their own dedication.[9] The preservation of a local identity is significant in that it suggests that provincial communities which produced recruits for the Guard now had individuals in Rome who could raise their concerns with the emperor.[10]

As well as voicing the concerns of their provincial communities, the third-century Guard could also represent the provincial armies from which they came. Funerary monuments erected by Praetorians in this period offer some support to the notion that, even in death, these soldiers were affirming their mutual identity with the troops on the Danube. A specific type of funerary sculpture, the 'ring buckle' gravestone, was erected by soldiers in Pannonia, Rome and other locations where *Illyriciani* were stationed.[11] Presumably this style was spread by the movement of soldiers from Pannonia to Rome and elsewhere in the empire, including Britain. Danubian troops in Rome were ideally placed to voice the concerns of their comrades in the provinces. The Guard complained to Ulpian about the harsh discipline that Dio had imposed on soldiers in Pannonia and demanded that he be handed over to them.[12] As a result, Dio was forced to spend his consulship outside of Rome to avoid the anger of the soldiers. It is possible in this case that the Praetorians were responding to a communication from their comrades in Pannonia requesting their intervention against Dio. However, the links between the third-century Guard and the troops in Pannonia must not be over exaggerated. The petition from the villagers of Scaptopara, discussed below, was directed in part against the depredations of the military. Identity is often expressed in a situational context and third-century recruits could express themselves either as members of provincial communities, representatives of the provincial armies or members of the Praetorian Guard depending on their exact circumstances.

The *equites singulares Augusti,* or imperial horse guard, also possessed a dual identity as both soldiers from the provincial armies and members of an elite military formation in Rome. The unit title itself proclaimed their attachment to the emperor. A letter from Vindolanda was sent to a surveyor at the fort by Ascanius, who describes himself as a *comes Augusti.*[13] The friendly tone of the letter and the Batavian origin of the recipient suggest that Ascanius was a member of the *equites singulares Augusti* and this indicates that the unit regarded themselves as *comites Augusti*. The close attachment of the *equites singulares Augusti* to the emperor may have resulted from their origin as Trajan's personal guard, as the archaeological context of Ascanius' letter corresponds to the early stages of the unit's existence. It is possible that the affirmation of their close association with the emperor provoked a sense of rivalry with the Guard.[14] The *equites singulares Augusti* also displayed their unit identity through their religious dedications, the uniformity of which was unique among the units in Rome. The vast majority of the altars erected by veterans at the *Castra Priora* were dedicated to the same group of eighteen deities.[15] The mixture of Roman and Germanic religious influences indicates the assimilation of gods worshipped by the early recruits with Roman deities to form a coherent group. This religious identity endured in individuals after they returned to the provincial armies. The deities attested at the *Castra Priora* are echoed in a series of altars from Scotland that were erected by Marcus Cocceius Firmus, a centurion of II Augusta, who was presumably promoted from the *equites singulares Augusti*.[16] The homogeneous nature of the religious dedications of the soldiers, veterans and promoted former members of the *equites singulares Augusti* acted as a means of affirming their shared identity and signified the elite status of their unit.

The close proximity of the various units in Rome and the means by which they displayed their unit identities can only have promoted tensions between the soldiers. In his study of the experiences of British soldiers on the Western Front in 1914-18, Holmes found numerous instances of confrontations between soldiers from different regiments.[17] In some instances, violence between soldiers took on a ritualized form with traditional insults about the quality and history of a particular unit, the actual meaning of which had long been forgotten, used to provoke an aggressive response. Unit identity replaced national allegiances, as English soldiers serving in Irish regiments would fight alongside their comrades against their own countrymen. It is therefore not surprising to find confrontations between the different units in Rome.

The clearest example of infighting among the units in Rome concerns the downfall of the politician Cleander in AD 190.[18] A grain riot was directed against Cleander, who was suspected of hoarding grain. He sent troops to disperse the demonstrators and the imperial cavalry scattered and killed some of the populace. At this point, the demonstrators were reinforced by soldiers, presumably from the urban cohorts, and forced their way to Commodus' estate where the emperor ordered the execution of Cleander as a means of appeasing their anger. Unfortunately, it is not clear whether the cavalry sent by Cleander were from the Guard or the *equites singulares Augusti*. Nevertheless, it is clear that the demonstrators had the support of some of the soldiers who were willing to fight against other units within the city. It has been demonstrated that there were a number of conflicts between the Guard and the populace of Rome in the period AD 190–238 in which the urban cohorts played an ambiguous role and which culminated in Praetorians attempting to set fire to sections of the city.[19] Such tensions escalated after

Severus' reform of the Guard, when the soldiers had far less in common with either the urban cohorts or the city population as a whole. However, relations between the Guard and the populace were probably never particularly warm. Pertinax ordered the soldiers to stop insulting civilians and prohibited them from carrying axes or striking passers-by.[20] Epictetus records that soldiers in civilian dress provoked civilians into making remarks against the emperor and then dragged them away to prison.[21]

Given the inevitable tensions between the different military units in Rome, it is perhaps surprising that the emperor allowed the soldiers to express their unit identities in such strong ways. A possible explanation is that strong military identities and rivalry between different formations fostered a conscientious approach to their duties and limited the possibility of the units combining in a military coup. Unit pride played a significant role in ensuring that the soldiers carried out their role diligently. Otho is alleged to have delayed launching his bid for power out of consideration for the cohort on duty at the palace.[22] The same cohort had been on duty when Caligula had been murdered and had deserted Nero shortly before his death. In order not to add further ill repute to the cohort in question, Otho waited until they had been relieved by another cohort before commencing his coup. It can therefore be suggested that conflict between the different Rome units was not generally politically motivated but rather was a natural result of competing unit identities.

THE PRAETORIAN PREFECTS

The distinct identities of the units in Rome were reinforced by their separate command structures. The emperor delegated command of the city units to specific individuals. Thus, the *vigiles* were commanded by the *praefectus vigilum*, the urban cohorts by the *praefectus urbi* and the Praetorians by the *praefecti praetorio*. It was the latter prefecture alone that was held, under normal circumstances, by two individuals and that acquired the greatest importance in the imperial administration. The presence of a Praetorian prefect beside the emperor became a symbol of imperial power, as is demonstrated by Avidius Cassius' appointment of a prefect immediately after the outbreak of his revolt.[23] The collegial nature of the office contributed to its importance, by allowing more work to be delegated to a pair of prefects than a single individual alone. Given the importance of the Praetorian prefecture throughout the period in question, the criteria that the emperor used in selecting candidates for this role are worthy of consideration. Did the type of individuals who served as Praetorian prefects change as the nature of the Principate evolved? The level of influence that the prefects possessed over the Guard also deserves further investigation, given that this influence could be used to incite the soldiers against the emperor. The Praetorian prefecture should be analysed as an integral part of the military garrison at Rome, rather than being studied in isolation as an administrative post.

Any analysis of the backgrounds of the Praetorian prefects is hindered by the lack of evidence for the individual characters, qualities and previous posts of the vast majority of their number.[24] A few prominent characters therefore assume a greater importance and scandalous prefects tend to predominate in the historical record. Perhaps the best known holder of the office, Sejanus, was completely atypical of the prefects as a body of men. As has been adroitly noted, his background and family connections ensured that he was a formidable figure in imperial court politics, even without the Praetorian prefecture.[25] Sejanus' extraordinary prominence was a result of a number of factors, not all of which were directly related to his tenure of the prefecture, notably his own ambition, Tiberius' willingness to delegate responsibility to him, and the trust that Tiberius placed in him, which may, in part, have been a result of Sejanus' good fortune in saving the emperor's life during a rock fall.[26] Sejanus' prominence was particularly accelerated by Tiberius' desire to escape from the pressures of public life, which gave Sejanus enormous power in Rome itself by allowing him the opportunity to exploit the power vacuum within the city. It can be seen that Sejanus was a product of a particular set of circumstances and was not representative of the holders of the prefecture as a whole.

The Praetorian prefecture was an equestrian post, although a number of prefects were related to senatorial families. A few prefects had backgrounds in the lower echelons of Roman society. Nymphidius Sabinus was the son of a freedwoman, although he claimed to be the illegitimate son of Caligula.[27] Plotius Firmus had begun his career as an ordinary soldier.[28] Bassaeus Rufus was believed to be of uncouth rustic origin and, in two cases, imperial freedmen were appointed.[29] In certain circumstances, *primipilares* were elevated to the prefecture, presumably by a combination of hard work and talent, although personal contact with the emperor could boost the chances of further promotion. Casperius Aelianus may have become acquainted with Vespasian and his sons during the Flavian bid for power. Marcius Turbo had probably known Hadrian since he was a centurion in the same legion in which Hadrian served as tribune. Likewise, Sulpicius Similis had served Trajan personally as a centurion, and Plautianus was a childhood friend of Severus. It is perfectly explicable for the emperor to select men with whom he was familiar to command the Guard. The loyalty of the prefects must have been of prime importance given the potential that the office held for revolt.

The personal preferences of an emperor dictated the type of individual he would choose as Praetorian prefect. A letter from Domitian to Laberius

6

Maximus, which probably records his promotion to the prefecture, indicates that his personal qualities of *fides* and *pietas* were reasons behind his elevation.[30] Pliny touchingly records the distress felt by Trajan when an unnamed friend asked to be relieved from his duties as Praetorian prefect.[31] The emperor escorted his friend to the seashore and watched with a heavy heart as he sailed away. Although this may have been a rhetorical device, Pliny emphasizes the novelty of an emperor choosing a prefect not from those who put themselves forward for the task but from those who shied away from it. The predilections of individual emperors for certain qualities in their prefects preclude generalizations about the type of individuals selected for the role.

It is possible to note that some emperors held particular qualities in high regard when appointing their prefects. Macrinus, for example, appointed two prefects who had both previously served as *princeps peregrinorum*.[32] The emperor himself had previously shared the prefecture with Oclatinius Adventus, who had also commanded the *frumentarii*.[33] Macrinus' preference for former commanders of the *frumentarii* as prefects can be explained by his admiration of their skills as spies. He used the *frumentarii* to gather intelligence regarding the seduction of a serving girl by two soldiers and to satisfy his boundless curiosity.[34] His admiration for the qualities of his former colleague, whom he adlected into the Senate, and to whom he awarded a consulship and the post of *praefectus urbi*, may well have influenced him to appoint men with similar experience to command the Guard.

The Severan emperors appear to have had a slight preference for eminent jurists and lawyers as prefects, probably on account of their wise counsel and skill at legal affairs.[35] This reflects the changing role of the office of Praetorian prefect and its increasing judicial role.[36] It has been suggested that the civil expertise of these individuals was balanced by being paired with experienced military men, for example Opellius Macrinus with Oclatinius Adventus, in effect a separation of powers.[37] It should be acknowledged that it is far from clear that this was a deliberate policy and the number of eminent lawyers who held the prefecture was probably insufficient for this system to have existed. The tenure of Ulpian as sole prefect may not represent the triumph of the civil aspects of the Praetorian prefecture, but rather the appointment of a trusted individual to an influential position. Ulpian's murder at the hands of the Praetorians demonstrates that, in this period at least, legal ability was no substitute for building a rapport with the soldiers.[38]

According to Dio, in his speech of Maecenas, the Praetorian prefects had command over all the troops in Italy. While not a true representation of the state of affairs in the early first century, this statement may indicate the responsibilities of the prefect when Dio was writing in the early third century, particularly with regard to the deployment of II Parthica in Italy by

Severus, which was commanded by a legionary prefect. Given the military aspect of the prefecture, it is worth considering how much previous military experience prefects had and whether the emperor utilized their abilities as military commanders. The majority of equestrians who held the office would probably have had some military experience as a tribune or prefect of an auxiliary unit. However, it is unclear how long these posts were held and the extent to which they prepared an individual for more wide ranging commands is unknown. *Primipilares* who rose to the prefecture obviously had significant experience in commanding soldiers. Some of the prefects had commanded the fleet at Ravenna or Misenum.[39] Others had previously commanded the *vigiles* or the *frumentarii*.[40] Prior military experience in Rome would make the individual familiar with the security system in the city.

Another post that appears to have been significant when selecting prefects was the prefecture of Egypt. Until AD 70, this represented the pinnacle of the equestrian career path and three Praetorian prefects are known to have been promoted to Egypt.[41] After this date, the Praetorian prefecture took precedence and fourteen prefects of Egypt are known to have been promoted to command the Guard between AD 70 and 235.[42] The Egyptian prefecture entailed the command of both the legionary and auxiliary units in the province. Although large-scale military operations were rare, the Egyptian prefect could demonstrate competence in upholding law and order and maintaining control of soldiers over a large geographical area, abilities that would stand him in good stead for commanding the Guard.[43] The post also offered experience in administrative and legal affairs, which would be of use in gaining further promotion.

Personal soldierly qualities were emphasized by some of the prefects. Sejanus claimed to be a humble soldier and sentry protecting the emperor and Marcius Turbo resolved to die on his feet.[44] Although the majority of the Praetorian prefects had some military experience, it is unclear how relevant this would have been in commanding the Guard. The military abilities of some of the prefects may be indicated by their use as commanders in combat operations. The earliest use of a Praetorian prefect as a military commander was in AD 69, when Otho sent Licinius Proculus to command his army against Vitellius. In this case, Tacitus states that the prefect was inexperienced in war and selected in desperate times for his indefatigable energy on behalf of the emperor.[45] Under Domitian, Cornelius Fuscus was defeated and killed in Dacia. He had previous command experience from fighting for the Flavian cause in AD 69.[46] Although not in a command capacity, Trajan sent his prefect Claudius Livianus to negotiate with Decebalus.[47]

The use of Praetorian prefects in a military context reached an apogee under Marcus Aurelius. Three of his prefects commanded armies, which is probably a reflection of the high frequency of combat operations that took place during his reign. Furius Victorinus accompanied Lucius Verus to the East in AD 162.[48] Victorinus and his army were destroyed during the Macromannic Wars, perhaps as a result of the plague rather than enemy action.[49] Macrinius Vindex was defeated and killed in battle against the Marcomanni.[50] Bassaeus Rufus was present as part of the emperor's military *consilium* in AD 169.[51] The emperor sent Tarrutenius Paternus with a large force to deal with the Scythians in AD 178.[52] Later, Didius Julianus sent one of his prefects, Tullius Crispinus, into the field against Severus, although he failed and was executed by the latter.[53] These examples demonstrate that emperors occasionally called on their Praetorian prefects to take on more extensive military commands. However, it is not clear whether these commands were delegated to the individuals concerned because of the rank they held or the qualities and capabilities that they possessed, for which they were originally promoted. The commands of Licinius Proculus and Tullius Crispinus, in particular, appear to have been the result of desperation at a time of civil conflict. In a similar way, the pressure for able commanders created by the Marcomannic Wars forced Marcus Aurelius to seek suitable individuals wherever he could find them.

The extent to which the prefects had influence over the soldiers is an important question, as the stronger the influence, the greater the potential for revolt against the emperor. In this context, Titus' assumption of the Praetorian prefecture during his father's reign is significant, as he used it to safeguard his succession by guaranteeing the support of the soldiers and allowing him to use them to eliminate potential rivals.[54] In certain circumstances, individual prefects do appear to have had a significant level of influence over their men, mainly due to the force of their own personalities. The downfall of Sejanus was enforced by the *vigiles*, as the loyalty of the Praetorians was in doubt, although Tiberius later rewarded the Guard with a donative of a thousand denarii each for staying loyal to him.[55] Tacitus states that by concentrating the Praetorians within one camp, the prefect was able to exert himself in gathering support from them.[56]

A particularly interesting example of the influence of a prefect over the soldiers is the career of Casperius Aelianus, who was prefect under Domitian and again under Nerva.[57] It is not clear why Aelianus lost his first prefecture, but there is no reason to suggest that there was any other cause than retirement. The Praetorians were greatly distressed at the assassination of Domitian and the return of a popular former prefect with extensive military experience may have been offered as a compromise by the new emperor. Indeed, Aurelius Victor records that the Senate came to an arrangement with the soldiers in order to appease them.[58] The appointment of Aelianus to the prefecture was a catastrophic mistake. The Praetorians revolted and demanded vengeance against those whom they believed had been involved in Domitian's murder. Nerva was forced to hand over the prefect, Petronius Secundus, and the chamberlain, Parthenius, for execution and was made to publicly thank the soldiers for their intervention.[59] Order was only restored after a three-month interval when Aelianus and the other unnamed ringleaders were summoned to Germany by Trajan and executed.[60]

Aelianus' motives in fomenting the Praetorian revolt are unclear. It has been suggested that he was acting on behalf of Trajan by destabilizing Nerva's regime and pressuring him to adopt a successor.[61] He was therefore eliminated by the new emperor as a potential embarrassment when he had served his purpose. The reality may have been somewhat different. Aelianus' obedient response to Trajan's summons does not represent his collusion in a wider conspiracy but rather his belief that he had acted correctly. If Suetonius is to be believed, the soldiers were in a mutinous state of mind prior to his appointment. As Praetorian prefect, he may have felt that it was his duty to avenge the fallen emperor and therefore had nothing to fear from Trajan, who had himself displayed considerable loyalty to Domitian.[62]

The examples discussed above indicate that certain prefects were able to exert a significant level of influence over the Praetorians. However, these individuals represent a minority when compared to the body of prefects as a whole. The vast majority remained loyal to the emperor. Even when prefects were involved in political intrigues, it did not necessarily follow that the Guard were also implicated. On the contrary, prefects were usually involved in conspiracies because of their status as important figures within the imperial administration rather than because of their relationship with the Praetorian Guard. It is noteworthy that the assassination of Commodus, which involved the prefect Laetus, was carried out during a festival when the soldiers were unarmed.[63] Evidently, Laetus could not provide military support for the conspiracy by winning over the Guard. We may also note that the assassination of Domitian was accomplished without Praetorian support, despite the involvement of the prefects.

Otherwise influential prefects such as Sejanus and Perennis were destroyed without any intervention from the soldiers to protect them.[64] Nymphidius Sabinus won over some elements of the Guard in attempting to secure the sole prefecture by generous promises of future reward.[65] Yet when he tried to gather the soldiers' support for his bid for supreme power, the Praetorians showed their reluctance to desert the emperor and killed Sabinus when he appeared in the camp.[66] The Severan prefect, Aulus Plautianus, gathered a support base from the Guard. According to Herodian, many of the officers were devoted to him and he had purposefully treated a particular tribune with great affection in order to groom him as an assassin against both Severus and Caracalla.[67] Dio records that Plautianus' bodyguards were so eager in carrying out their duties that they once prevented Severus' escort from entering the presence of the prefect.[68] However, his personal popularity did not lead the soldiers to prevent or avenge his execution. In reality, prefects could rarely compete with the affection which the soldiers had for the reigning emperor.

The opportunity for building a relationship for the soldiers was limited by the time each prefect had in office. Gavius Maximus, for example, had considerable time to familiarize himself with the soldiers during his twenty-year term of office under Antoninus Pius.[69] Commodus, on the other hand, changed his prefects with extraordinary frequency; in one case the post was held for just six hours.[70] In such circumstances, it is highly unlikely that the soldiers would have been concerned with building any sort of relationship with an individual who could be demoted imminently.

On a day to day basis, it is uncertain how much contact the prefects had with the Praetorians. Indeed, even in times of crisis such contact could be severely limited. During the downfall of Messalina, the prefects were bypassed and command of the Guard was handed to Narcissus who issued orders directly to the centurions and tribunes.[71] Sole prefects had a better opportunity to accrue power and influence over both the soldiers and the emperor. Afranius Burrus was awarded the prefecture as a result of the machinations of Agrippina, who argued that a single prefect would be better for military discipline.[72] Streamlining the Praetorian command structure in this way was potentially hazardous and a pair of prefects discouraged treasonous ambitions.[73] The collegiality of the Praetorian prefecture weakened the influence that either prefect could have over the troops and it was only in exceptional circumstances that a prefect was able to even come close to winning the political support of the soldiers against the emperor. It is unlikely that the post of Praetorian prefect would have been permitted to continue to exist if it continuously proved to be a focus for opposition against the emperor.[74]

MAINTAINING THE LOYALTY OF THE ROME COHORTS

In contrast to the rest of the imperial soldiery, the troops based in Rome would have had frequent contact with the emperor, both directly and indirectly. His appearance was familiar to them from personal experience rather than simply from his image on coins and images. Even the most unmilitary of emperors had to consider the way in which he presented himself to the soldiers in Rome. The close proximity of the Guard in particular ensured that they had the potential to play a significant role in imperial politics within the city. For this reason, the emperor had to take various steps to win and maintain the support of the soldiers in Rome. This was embodied most directly by the issuing of the watchword on a daily basis by the emperor to the Praetorians who protected him. The watchword chosen was, at times of crisis, often imbued with political meaning.[75]

The relationship between the emperor and the city troops was strengthened by financial incentives. Indeed, the images on the coins themselves could be used to display this relationship. *Adlocutio* scenes showing the emperor addressing members of the Praetorian cohorts were used under Caligula and Nero.[76] Hadrian issued a coin that showed him with a group of soldiers and the legend COH PRAET S C, which formed part of his wider coin series issued to the provincial armies.[77] Under Commodus a series of coins from around AD 189–91 displayed FIDEI PRAETORIANORVM, which may be linked to the downfall of Cleander and the fighting that broke out among the various military units in the city.[78]

Claudius issued a series of coins bearing the legends IMPER RECEPT and PRAETOR RECEPT commemorating the support that the Praetorian Guard had given him at his accession.[79] After the murder of Caligula, Claudius was discovered hiding in the palace by a Praetorian, who hurried him to the camp where he was acclaimed emperor by the soldiers. Certain members of the Senate, with the support of the urban cohorts, were discussing a return to a republican form of government.[80] The support of the Praetorians gave power to Claudius and provided protection against his enemies. The images shown on these coins include the Praetorian camp and a Praetorian greeting Claudius and, while showing his gratitude to the Praetorians, demonstrated to other audiences, such as the senatorial order, that Claudius had the backing of the soldiers. These coins are unique and their topical political significance indicates that Claudius himself had sanctioned their design. He owed his elevation to the Praetorians and this series of coins demonstrates his immediate reliance upon their support.

Donatives acted as a means of ensuring the loyalty of the troops, particularly at potentially dangerous times like the accession of a new emperor. The Praetorians were in a prime location to accept rich rewards from emperors in Rome. In his will, Augustus bequeathed 1000 sesterces to each soldier of the Praetorian cohorts, 500 to the urban cohorts and 300 to each legionary, which Tiberius doubled and then repeated in his own will.[81] Claudius awarded 15,000 sesterces to each member of the Guard on his accession and distributed a further 100 sesterces on the anniversary of his elevation.[82] In making a payment to the troops at the beginning of his reign, Claudius set a precedent that was followed by subsequent emperors. Pliny praises the fact that Trajan paid the Praetorians only half of their donative.

In the light of their severe disciplinary problems prior to his accession he may have been tempted to award them nothing, but was probably dissuaded by the way in which the giving of a donative at the start of a new reign had become deeply ingrained within the relationship between the emperor and the Guard.[83] Failure to give a donative to the troops could potentially lead to the loss of their support. Galba refused to award a donative promised earlier by Nymphidius Sabinus by claiming: 'I levy my soldiers, I don't buy them.'[84] Didius Julianus simply did not have the financial capital to pay the lavish donative he had promised the Praetorians.[85] It is unsurprising that both of these emperors were murdered by the Guard.[86]

The size of donatives rose steeply during the second century AD. Marcus Aurelius and Lucius Verus paid 20,000 sesterces on their joint accession and it has been suggested that this amount was also paid out by Hadrian and Antoninus Pius.[87] Pertinax offered 12,000 sesterces to the Guard, although he claimed to have been willing to give 20,000 sesterces.[88] The connection of Praetorian support with financial incentives was made most obvious during the so-called 'auction of empire'. After the murder of Pertinax, it is alleged that the Praetorians sold the empire to the highest bidder between two competing candidates, Didius Julianus and Sulpicianus, in the Praetorian camp. The former won with a bid of 25,000 sesterces.[89] Herodian claimed that this set an ugly precedent in encouraging the soldiers to place their greed for money above loyalty to individual emperors; in fact, even Julianus' winning bid was not outrageously high when compared to previous donatives.[90] But it was not just the size of the donative that convinced the Praetorians to support Julianus. Sulpicianus was father-in-law to Pertinax and they feared that he would exact revenge for the latter's murder. Furthermore, Julianus promised to restore the memory of Commodus and give them the same level of freedom that they had enjoyed under his rule (in contrast to the strictness of Pertinax's reign). Finally, Julianus claimed that his donative could be paid immediately out of the financial reserves he kept at his residence.[91]

However, there are inconsistencies in the surviving accounts of this event that cast doubt on its historical validity.[92] Cassius Dio and Herodian are the only surviving authors who describe the so-called 'auction' and their accounts are not consistent. Cassius Dio claims that the soldiers were inclined to accept Sulpicianus' offer of 20,000 sesterces because he was already in the camp, he was urban prefect and was the first to offer this amount. It was only when Julianus offered an extra 5000 sesterces that the Praetorians switched their support.[93] Herodian, on the other hand, states that Sulpicianus reached the camp after Julianus, but the soldiers were averse to even consider him as a candidate because of his relationship to Pertinax.[94] The notion of an 'auction of empire' probably came from Severan propaganda. Indeed, it plays a role in Herodian's version of Severus' speech to his Danubian troops:

> And now, as you know, this great empire which stretches over land and sea, has been shamefully purchased by a man who is hated by the people and no longer trusted by the soldiers of the city, whom he has deceived.[95]

Severus also mentioned it during the harangue he delivered to the Praetorians prior to their dismissal, as well as their failure to protect Pertinax.[96] The complete disbandment of the Guard demonstrated that the new emperor would not accept disloyalty. Severus could not trust soldiers whose allegiance could be so easily bought. Furthermore, it allowed him to reward his Danubian troops by transferring them directly into the Guard.

The size of donatives dropped drastically under the Severan emperors. Severus awarded 10,000 sesterces on the tenth anniversary of his accession and Caracalla issued the same amount after the murder of Geta.[97] This substantial decrease in the cost of donatives may be explained by the change in the composition of the Guard under Severus. As the Severan troops seem to have been aware of the sums awarded by previous emperors, it cannot be claimed that he was able to exploit their ignorance by awarding a smaller donative.[98] By filling the Guard with his legionaries, Severus ensured that they were under obligation to him for their new status and therefore he did not need to rely on maintaining their support by financial incentives alone. These men were staunch supporters of the Severan regime and were unlikely to be seduced by a rival bid for power. The fact that Severus authorized the first military pay rise in over a century may have also decreased the need for lavish donatives.

As well as through the distribution of money, the close proximity of the emperor to the soldiers protecting him on a daily basis allowed him to build up a personal relationship with some of them. Augustus stayed at a villa belonging to a former member of his bodyguard whom he also invited to dinner.[99] Caracalla personally mixed great bowls of wine to share with the soldiers and kept senators waiting while he conversed with them.[100] The relationship between the emperor and the soldiers who attended him was undoubtedly boosted by patronage on a personal level. In AD 46, when awarding Roman citizenship to the *Anauni* and neighbouring tribes, Claudius explicitly stated that he had been influenced in this decision by the fact that some of their men had served in the Guard and a few even reached the centurionate.[101] In AD 238 the villagers of Scaptopara in Thrace petitioned Gordian through a member of the Guard for relief from the exactions of soldiers and travellers passing through their village.[102] These isolated examples offer a glimpse of the potential influence that members of the Guard were able to exert by exploiting their close contact with the emperor. It is conceivable that the majority of such favours bestowed by the emperor upon the soldiers protecting him were on a personal level and never made it into the epigraphic record, an example of which is the intervention of Otho in a boundary dispute involving a Praetorian discussed below.

The appearance of the emperor before the soldiers emphasized both his own status as commander-in-chief and his concern for their welfare. After giving his maiden speech to the Senate and awarding a donative to the soldiers, Nero personally led the drill of the Guard with a shield in his hand.[103] In AD 168 Marcus Aurelius delivered a speech to the soldiers in the Praetorian camp that explained the implications of certain privileges that he had awarded to their veterans.[104] Aurelius specifically identified himself with the soldiers by referring to '*veterani nostri*'. By personally delivering this information to the troops, the emperor emphasized that these benefits came from him. In a similar way, Praetorians were addressed by the emperor in the first person in their *diplomata* as opposed to the third person used in those awarded to other troops.[105] In times of political crisis, emperors also appeared before the troops as a means of winning their protection and support. Claudius addressed the troops after Messalina's betrayal became apparent.[106] Caracalla fled to the Praetorian camp after killing Geta, presumably in order to relay his version of events to them before they were exposed to adverse propaganda regarding the death of his brother.[107] The appearance of the emperor before the soldiers during times of political crisis demonstrated their significance as a factor for keeping him in power. It also indicates a need for the emperor to brief them personally to ensure that they were fully aware of the implications and nature of the situation and to exploit any emotional ties which the soldiers may have had towards him.

The accession of Otho offers a clear example of the means by which an ambitious individual could seduce the loyalties of the Guard away from the emperor. Otho built up such a strong personal relationship with the Praetorians that some of their number, overcome with grief, committed suicide on his funeral pyre.[108] This relationship began by the means of outright bribery. When Galba visited his home for dinner, Otho was in the habit of giving money to each soldier in the escort.[109] He also placed some of the Praetorians under personal obligation to him, in one case by settling a boundary dispute between a soldier and his neighbour.[110] Otho's generous behaviour was in stark contrast to that of Galba, who refused to issue a donative.[111]

There could also have been more practical reasons for the loyalty of some of the Praetorians to Otho. According to Suetonius, Galba had instigated a purge of former supporters of Nymphidius Sabinus among the ranks of the Praetorians by discharging those whom he suspected of disloyalty.[112] These circumstances prompted some of the Guard to switch allegiance to Otho in the hope of preserving their status. Indeed, Otho's rise to power can be seen as the result of a fundamental breakdown in military discipline among the Guard under Galba. The centurions and tribunes lost control over their men and were unable to prevent them from elevating Otho. The soldiers took precautions to prevent their officers from gaining access to the new emperor in case they were tempted to assassinate him.[113] The ill-discipline of the troops was given ample expression during their nocturnal riot through the palace, in the course of which a number of tribunes and a prefect were wounded.[114] Although Otho appeased the troops with a donative of 5000 sesterces per man, the centurions and tribunes stripped off their uniforms and demanded to be released from their dangerous duties. Despite the return of a semblance of order after Otho's intervention, the soldiers still acted on their own initiative in carrying out unsanctioned surveillance operations on senior individuals suspected of planning a coup against Otho.

This breakdown in military discipline may have been prompted by a crisis of identity among the soldiers of the Praetorian cohorts caused by the death of Nero. The emotional attachment of the troops in Rome towards members of the Julio-Claudian dynasty was demonstrated by their emotive response to Messalina's betrayal of Claudius and their unwillingness to attack Agrippina.[115] It can be suggested that the termination of the dynasty and the failure of Galba to fill the vacuum left by Nero in issuing donatives and rewards led to the soldiers' lack of confidence in their officers. The extraordinary degree of loyalty that some Praetorians felt towards Otho was probably a reaction to his assumption of the patronal role formerly held by Nero. Feelings of guilt regarding their desertion of Nero may also have contributed to their high level of allegiance to Otho and the suicides that occurred upon his death.[116]

Ironically, the disbandment of the Guard by Vitellius, who replaced them with his own men, probably solved the crisis within the Guard. It is worth quoting the speech that Tacitus claims Antonius Primus delivered to the former Praetorians before the battle of Cremona:

Then he spoke with greater sharpness to the Praetorian Guards. 'As for you,' he said 'you are finished as soldiers unless you beat the enemy. What other emperor and what other camp is there to which you can transfer? There, among the foe, are the standards and equipment which are really yours, and for the beaten the sentence is death. Dishonour you have drunk to the dregs.[117]

Rather than simply shifting their allegiance to the new emperor, the former Praetorians were forced to support his rival contender for the throne, in order to regain their former status and self-respect. Vespasian carried out a specific policy of enlisting these redundant Othonian Praetorians and it has been suggested that he deliberately depicted himself as the avenger of Otho, both to recruit soldiers and to give his cause an air of legitimacy.[118] Vespasian, by virtue of his sons, was able to provide a new dynasty for the soldiers to support. By their involvement in combat at Cremona and during the capture of Rome, the Othonian Praetorians were able to cement their position as supporters of the Flavian regime.

The potential of the Praetorian cohorts to provide military support for an usurpation explains the monopoly that the emperor held for the distribution of benefits and awards to them. Tiberius angrily rebuked a senator who proposed that veterans of the Guard should be allocated seats among the equestrian section at the theatre.[119] It is alleged that one of the reasons that Hadrian compelled Servianus to commit suicide was the fact that he made a point of rising from his seat to meet the soldiers.[120] Potential attempts to tamper with the loyalty of the Praetorians could not be tolerated by the emperor and it is not surprising that usurpers from outside of Rome attempted to win their support. In AD 69, Fabius Valens sent letters to the city troops in the name of the army in Germany asking for their support. Earlier correspondence between soldiers in Germany and the Praetorians had requested the immediate removal of Galba.[121] Similarly, Severus sent letters to the Guard requesting their support and demanding that the assassins of Pertinax be kept under guard.[122]

CONCLUSION

The deployment of soldiers in Rome was a necessary evil to protect the emperor from personal attack. The increasing number of troops within the city reflects the insecurity felt by certain emperors, which could only be overcome by strengthening the formations close at hand. The inevitable rivalry between the different city units led to occasional outbreaks of violence but also limited the possibility of a military coup. The administrative burden created by the city troops was delegated to trusted individuals as prefects. However, the emperor maintained his supreme command over the soldiers. By personally issuing the watchword he asserted his authority on a daily basis. The emperor's monopoly over the pay, benefits and privileges awarded to the soldiers limited their exposure to malign influences and acted as a means of maintaining their support for his rule.

Yet the support of the soldiery in Rome was not sufficient to keep an emperor in power. Durry noted that although the Praetorian Guard was able to create new emperors, only the legions elevated the founders of dynasties.[123] On certain occasions, notably the accessions of Claudius, Otho and Didius Julianus, the soldiers of the Guard were able to put forward their own nominees, but they could not rival a contender who had the support of soldiers outside of Rome. Claudius remained in power by virtue of his membership of the Julio-Claudian dynasty. Both Otho and Didius Julianus were removed by legions acting on behalf of their own candidates. Before the reform of Severus, the Guard could not compete with the legions in terms of combat experience and prowess and, even after Severus, was too small to fight effectively against a provincial army. The political influence of the soldiers in Rome was a result of their close proximity to the centre of imperial power, which meant that they were on hand to intervene in times of crisis. As the closest military presence around the emperor, the importance of the soldiers in Rome was as his basic means of defence and, potentially, his most immediate threat.

Chapter 2

Discipline and Morale

On joining the Roman army, the recruit became part of a wider military community with its own ideals, rituals and codes of behaviour. The severance of the recruit from his home community caused by his adhesion to the army is highlighted by Aelius Aristides:

> You travelled to all your subject lands and searched for those from there who would perform this service. And when you found them, at the same time you severed their ties with their own country and gave them your city in return, so that in future they were ashamed to declare their former origins.[1]

A similar view is expressed by Livy, who labels the army camp as the soldier's *patria altera*.[2] Recruits from the settlements around forts, probably the illegitimate children of serving soldiers, named their *origo* as *castris*, highlighting the importance of the camp as a home.[3] The complex process of joining the army also emphasized the transition from the civilian to the military world.[4] Membership of the military community brought with it personal status and financial security, which many recruits would have been unlikely to achieve as civilians. The homogeneity in clothing worn by soldiers, which appears to have been established by the third century, contributed to their collective identity, although it probably evolved by emulation rather than by imperial command.[5] The soldierly identity was sufficiently important for some veterans to remain in close proximity to their former unit.[6]

However, the integrity of the military community as a single entity was endangered by the deployment of the army. Strategic threats demanded that the majority of the soldiers were deployed along the frontiers of the empire, often clustered in distinct 'army groups', for example on the Rhine and Danube.[7] The permanent stationing of units in specific localities, which became the norm by the second century, meant that they attained regional characteristics, which threatened the unity of the army as a whole. During the second battle of Cremona in AD 69, the legionaries of III Gallica turned to face the rising sun in accordance with Syrian religious tradition. The Vitellians mistook this as a sign that Flavian reinforcement were approaching.[8] This mistaken inference demonstrates the vast gulf that separated soldiers serving in different parts of the empire. A side effect of the acculturation of regional characteristics by the troops was a growing tension between imperial objectives and local priorities. This is illustrated by the anger of the German soldiers who accompanied Severus Alexander to the east when barbarian attacks across the Rhine threatened their families.[9]

Within the context of a divided army, discipline and morale acted as a means of imposing uniformity across the various regional military groups. In this chapter, I will examine the enforcement of discipline within the context of the management of the army. The emperor portrayed himself as the upholder of military discipline, yet expediency forced him to delegate military command to his subordinates. I argue that it was these individuals who were forced to impose discipline upon the troops and that this exposed them to personal danger. This will be followed by a discussion of the recent polarization of *disciplina* and *virtus* as two conflicting motivating factors in the behaviour of the soldiers, particularly in combat. My contribution to this ongoing debate will emphasize the role of the emperor as the personification of martial *virtus*. I will then analyse the various factors which maintained morale, particularly those which concerned the identity of the individual as both a member of a unit and of the military community as a whole. Potentially, morale was threatened by casualties and mortalities suffered during military campaigns. I will examine the methods used to circumvent the corrosive impact of these on the military community. Finally, it will be seen that the breakdown of discipline and morale resulted in mutinies, which represented the collapse of the authority of senior officers and a possible threat to the emperor.

EMPERORS, COMMANDERS AND DISCIPLINE

Many of the problems associated with the management of the Roman army can be explained by a fundamental incompatibility between the different discourses on military discipline. The ideal, as represented by Dio of Prusa, saw soldiers as the shepherds who, in concert with the emperor, protected the flock of the empire.[10] Likewise Ulpian, in his etymology of the word *miles*, includes the suggestions that the term originated from *malum*, the evil that the soldiers provide a bulwark against, or *malitia*, the rigours that they undertook on behalf of the State.[11] This ideal discourse was probably propagated by the emperor himself in order to reinforce his reputation as an able commander who had the troops under his command.[12] It is perhaps not surprising that many emperors claimed to have reformed military discipline, often in contrast to the laxity of their predecessors.[13] Fronto contrasted the measures energetically implemented by Lucius Verus with what he perceived as the decline in military standards under Hadrian.[14] The emperor's claim of disciplinary reform emphasized his status as commander-in-chief and reassured the elite classes that the army would be kept under control.

How did the emperor propagate his own concept of military discipline? For most emperors, military campaigns were infrequent and personal contact with the provincial armies was rare. Hadrian was a prolific visitor of provincial armies, but his concern may have been a result of the heavy losses and resultant damage to morale which the army suffered during his reign.[15] Not every provincial visit by an emperor was successful. Suetonius' account of Caligula's visit to the troops in Germany 'exaggerates severe military discipline to the point of parody', including the attempted decimation of the men he held responsible for the mutinies of AD 14, which was hastily aborted when the soldiers began to arm themselves.[16] Emperors also used their behaviour towards the troops in Rome to emphasize the virtue of *disciplina*. Pertinax tried to curb the behaviour of the Praetorians by forbidding them from striking civilians or carrying axes.[17] Septimius Severus disbanded the Guard completely, in part because of their undisciplined behaviour.[18] It is tempting to see the Praetorian Guard as a microcosm of the wider army, with the emperor using his treatment of the former to influence the behaviour of the latter and create a personal reputation as a strict disciplinarian.

A direct means of disseminating the importance of military discipline was the official cult of *Disciplina*, which first appeared on coins issued in AD 134–8 during the later years of the reign of Hadrian.[19] As well as the bronze coinage, *Disciplina* also featured on gold aurei suggesting that this design was aimed at officers as well as ordinary soldiers. The designs on these coins are very similar and show Hadrian in military dress advancing to the right followed by three or four soldiers who carry legionary eagles or standards. The variant spelling of *discipulina* is found on an uncommon type and is also used on some of the inscriptions from Britain.[20] Antoninus Pius issued sesterces with the legend DISCIPLINA AVG predominantly at the beginning of his reign.[21] After AD 145 this is shortened slightly to DISCIPLIN AVG.[22] The variant spelling of *discipulina* did not feature on the coinage issued by Antoninus Pius and, as far as we know, *disciplina* was not used again on the imperial coinage after his death.

The epigraphic evidence for the cult of *Disciplina* differs from the narrow date range suggested by the imperial coinage. Fifteen inscriptions refer to this cult, all of which come from military sites and, where the archaeological context is clear, are associated with headquarters buildings, indicating that they had official sanction.[23] These inscriptions were set up by both auxiliary and legionary units, but their geographical range is extremely limited, as they originate only from northern Britain and Africa. Eight inscriptions of this kind come from Britain and the remainder from Africa. The complete absence of epigraphic evidence for *Disciplina* from elsewhere in the empire suggests that this is not due to a lack of archaeological preservation, but rather that the cult was only present in the military camps of Britain and Africa. It is clear that the majority of the inscriptions to *Disciplina*, which are datable, can be assigned to the reigns of Severus or his sons. The earliest epigraphic evidence for the military veneration of *Disciplina* is from Chesters under Hadrian and the latest is from Gemellae under Valerian and Gallienus. The resurgence of inscriptions dedicated to *Disciplina* during the Severan period can be explained as a localized trend conveyed by the movement of individuals eager to demonstrate their loyalty to the new regime, in particular through the transfer of centurions from Britain to Africa.[24]

It is noteworthy that the official propagation of *Disciplina* through the imperial coinage was so short-lived. The close emotional attachment of the soldiers to the military standards may have been of greater importance to them, than the abstract virtue advertised on the coinage. Under Marcus Aurelius, military coin types such as FIDES and CONCORDIA EXERCITVVM were used more commonly than under his immediate predecessors, and the portrayal of Faustina as MATRI CASTRORVM also appeared.[25] These coin types perhaps received a more favourable reception from the soldiers because they appealed specifically to them. The disappearance of *Disciplina* from the imperial coinage suggests that it was not effective in imposing a code of behaviour on the troops.[26]

The emperor delegated command of the provincial armies to his governors and army commanders. The emperor issued *mandata* to all imperial *legati* and proconsuls, which gave them instructions for their time in post. The letters between Pliny and Trajan indicate that the *mandata* contained details on military recruitment and deployment.[27] Yet the instructions were not definitive, as Pliny's letters make clear.[28] It has been adroitly noted that Pliny's letters contain not a single example of spontaneous correspondence from the emperor.[29] There were other means by which the emperor could convey his ideas on military discipline to his provincial subordinates. Augustus compiled a collection of *exempla* which was circulated to his governors.[30] Presumably the material was selected to demonstrate and reinforce Augustus' own priorities and wishes. The *Digest* mentions a lost work on military discipline entitled *Disciplina Augusti*.[31] Both of these appear to have been solitary attempts to promulgate a disciplinary program.

From the evidence gathered above, it can be surmised that the senatorial and equestrian officials sent to command the troops were given considerable latitude in dealing with military discipline. Septimius Severus and Caracalla formally established that soldiers should be tried and punished wherever their crimes were committed, which enshrined in law a procedure that had probably long been in use.[32] When dealing with the case of a centurion who was embroiled in an affair with a tribune's wife, Trajan 'made a statement on military discipline, for he did not wish all cases of this kind to be referred to him'.[33] Furthermore, the legal framework of military discipline was vulnerable to the whims of individual emperors. The legal sources demonstrate that, when approached, emperors often sought to mitigate the punishments prescribed to soldiers for specific offences, especially in peacetime. This is particularly apparent in the writings concerning the treatment of deserters. Punishments for desertion ranged from execution to reinstatement in the army without pay for the time the soldier was absent (although even this could be restored with the intervention of the emperor).[34] The deserter's rank, pay, service record and any extenuating circumstances were taken into account when punishment was decided. The intervention of the emperor in the punishment of soldiers reinforced his reputation as their benefactor and strengthened his relationship with them.

The lack of clear guidance from the emperor placed the emphasis for maintaining military discipline squarely on the army commanders.[35] The reality of discipline in the army camps was usually very different from the ideal image propagated by the emperor. It was the task of the army commanders to reconcile the ideal with the reality of military discipline. The very real possibility of mutiny created the paradox that it was more expedient to punish a single soldier than it was to punish a group, despite the fact that the latter were potentially more dangerous.[36] In response to the vast gulf between the discourses on military discipline at the centre and periphery of the empire, some officers and commanders invoked the 'old discipline'. Whether such a golden age of orderly soldierly behaviour ever existed is debatable, but it clearly was an important, if nostalgic, concept in the minds of those dealing with the soldiers. Germanicus sought it in vain in the mutinous German legions and Tiberius bemoaned the dearth of it in army recruits.[37] During the mutiny of AD 14, the *praefectus castrorum* at Nauportus, Aufidienus Rufus, was attacked for attempting to reintroduce old disciplinary measures.[38] In reality, the soldiers of the Principate could not live up to the standards of an imagined past. The military tribune, Subrius Flavus, inspected the grave that had been dug for him prior to his execution for plotting against Nero. Noting that the grave was of insufficient size, he commented 'faulty discipline even here' to the burial party.[39]

The prominence given in the literary sources to strict disciplinarians like Domitius Corbulo, Pontius Laelianus and Ulpius Marcellus can be explained by the unusual severity of their command style.[40] According to Tacitus, most commanders, unlike Corbulo, did not punish soldiers for their first offence.[41] Under normal circumstances, they attempted to negotiate the fine line between *disciplina* and mutiny. During the siege of Jerusalem, Titus was dissuaded from executing a group of soldiers, who had been tricked by some Jewish fighters feigning surrender, by the appeals of their comrades.[42] The imposition of discipline that was deemed too severe could lead to the loss of military support and, ultimately, to extreme physical danger for the commander concerned. In AD 69, Trebellius Maximus lost the support of the soldiers in Britain and was forced to flee.[43] His successor, Vettius Bolanus, was also unable to enforce discipline. According to Tacitus, XX Valeria Victrix, which Agricola was sent to command, was so unruly as to frighten governors of consular rank.[44] During his later governorship of the province, Agricola dealt only with major offences and was content to let minor offences go unpunished if the offender was repentant. This sounds suspiciously like an apologetic for continuing problems with military discipline in the province. Indeed, during the same period a cohort of Usipi murdered their centurions and instructors in response to the discipline to which they were subjected.[45]

There are other indications that commanders struggled to instil discipline. The Pannonian legions complained to Ulpian about the harsh measures implemented by Dio.[46] They must have believed that Dio instigated these measures of his own accord, rather than on the initiative of the emperor. Around the same time, the governor of Mesopotamia was murdered by his soldiers. Finally, a papyrus from Dura-Europos consists of a letter from a high official to the unit commander concerning a group of soldiers who had deserted from the camp and were wandering around the region causing trouble.[47] The author, probably reacting to a petition from a civilian, demands that the unit commander force these men to return to their base and subject them to military discipline. This letter is a graphic example of the difficulties which army commanders faced in controlling their men.

According to Pliny, Domitian wanted the soldiers to be undisciplined in order to keep his subordinates busy and prevent them from rebelling: 'Thus our generals had less to fear from foreign foes than from their master's treachery, and more from the swords their own men held than from their enemies.'[48] We may surmise that Pliny had every reason to be prejudiced against Domitian, but the removal of the emperor from responsibility for the imposition of military discipline in the minds of the soldiers is evidenced by complaints about the measures imposed by their commanders. In AD 47, Curtius Rufus, governor of Upper Germany, made his soldiers work in a silver mine. In response, the troops asked the emperor to award triumphal ornaments to army commanders before they took up their post.[49] In this case, the soldiers believed that they had suffered in order to fulfil their commander's personal ambition and had no qualms about bringing this fact to the emperor's attention. The distancing of the emperor from the maintenance of military discipline was deliberate. By placing responsibility for this on his subordinates, the emperor ensured that the anger of the troops would be directed at them rather than him. In this way, the army commanders acted as a buffer, preserving the relationship between the emperor and his soldiers from harm inflicted by the actions of his subordinates.

VIRTUS AND DISCIPLINA

A recent study has concluded that the Roman army was torn by a conflict between *virtus* and *disciplina*.[50] In this analysis, *virtus* is seen as the spur for aggression initiated by the individual with *disciplina* as the institutionalized restraint on such behaviour. In other words, there was a conflict between the ambitious aggression of the individual motivated by the tantalizing prospect of decorations and promotion, and the synchronized unity of the army. However, it can be argued that this reconstruction is overly simplistic by positing two polarities which, in reality, were not mutually exclusive. The notion of *virtus* developed as a concept inextricably linked to martial prowess. A clear example of *virtus* as an impetus for unauthorized behaviour is the rivalry between two of Caesar's centurions, Titus Pullo and Lucius Vorenus, which culminated in their joint onslaught against the enemy.[51]

In contrast to the competitive political arena of the Republic, under the Principate *virtus* became the 'virtual monopoly of the emperor, his family, and of the trusted generals and Roman soldiers whom the emperor controlled'.[52] The emperor acquired a unique role as the paragon of *virtus*. This attribute was advertised on the imperial coinage with the legend VIRTUS AUGUSTI.[53] It is noteworthy that coins that bear this legend often show the emperor as a cavalryman charging into battle or trampling a fallen enemy, an image that has Republican precedents.[54] In this case, imperial *virtus* is directly linked to a martial context and with personal aggression in particular. The behaviour of the emperor as *commilito* further emphasized the value of personal military endeavour, whether in actual combat or merely the daily rigours of army life.[55] In this context, Caracalla's behaviour in seeking personal combat with enemy leaders is especially revealing.[56] To a certain extent, it can be argued that the tough soldierly image of the ideal emperor encouraged the troops to display personal martial qualities which were detrimental to modern perceptions of military discipline.

It is true that historical *exempla* emphasized the need to curb the aggressive behaviour of the individual and the most frequently recorded incidents of ill-discipline concern the control of soldiers in battle. The consul T. Manlius Torquatus executed his own son in 340 BC for engaging in single combat with the enemy contrary to his father's orders.[57] In a similar vein, Titus claimed that 'among the Romans even victory without orders is a disgrace'.[58] On a number of occasions Roman armies were out of control in battle, but whether this was because of a conflict between *virtus* and *disciplina* or simply reflects the inability of commanders to control troops during combat operations is unclear.[59] There are numerous attestations of soldiers engaging the enemy before they had been ordered to do so, which reflects a lack of discipline and command authority.[60] After combat, or simply while on the march, commanders often had trouble in preventing soldiers from plundering civilian settlements. In part, this was caused by the frustration of soldiers, which found an outlet in indiscriminate pillaging.[61] On the other hand, plundering could be a consequence of a commander's lack of control over his men, particularly during periods of civil war when loyalty to the State was subverted by allegiance to a particular imperial contender.[62]

Yet it can be suggested that *virtus* often played a significant role in military success.[63] The walls of the Antonia fortress in Jerusalem were successfully scaled by a miscellaneous group of soldiers who appear to have acted on their own initiative.[64] Aggressive behaviour had a positive impact on the group dynamics of the army as a whole, in encouraging and inspiring reticent troops to engage the enemy. The success of Pullo and Vorenus would have boosted the morale of the soldiers by demonstrating that the enemy could be beaten.[65] On occasion, even emperors engaged in thoroughly reckless combat activities by deliberately exposing themselves to danger, in order to enthuse the soldiers and motivate them to fight.[66]

Virtus could also be displayed through *labor*, the manual work that the soldier undertook in the absence of combat-related activity.[67] This was emphasized by emperors behaving as *commilitones*, in undertaking similar tasks as their men and demonstrating that manual labour was fit to be carried out by the commander-in-chief as well as the lowliest common soldier. The importance of keeping troops busy in order to prevent *otium*, or idleness, and discontent is clearly expressed in the literary sources.[68] Domitius Corbulo ordered his troops to construct a canal from the Meuse to the Rhine, after his aggressive military operations were halted by Claudius.[69] Building projects kept the soldiers fit and ready for combat, as well as minimizing the opportunities for ill-disciplined behaviour.[70] Soldiers also displayed their *virtus* through prowess in training scenarios.[71] The evolution in the application of *virtus* from martial bravery to toughness in *labor* reflected the need to provide peacetime soldiers with an outlet to display their manliness. It is no surprise that the same emperor who praised the soldiers at Lambaesis for their feats in training displayed his personal *virtus* by marching twenty miles in full military kit.[72]

MORALE

Morale can be defined as the individual soldier's emotional attachment to the army in which he serves. Cumulative military morale dictates the effectiveness of the army as a whole. It was advantageous to the emperor if the morale of his armies was high, as it decreased the potential for mutinies and revolts, as well as improving their performances in combat. The importance of maintaining military morale was recognized by Roman commanders, as is demonstrated by the inclusion of relevant techniques in the military handbooks written during the imperial period.[73]

The morale of a Roman soldier was intrinsically connected to his identity as a member of a unit. In contrast to Republican military practice, Augustus gave his legions a permanent footing. A consequence of this reform was that the legions gradually developed separate institutional identities.[74] The unique characters of individual legions gave their soldiers pride and helped bind the unit together.[75] Rivalry between different units acted as a spur for motivating the soldiers. Julius Caesar showed his preference for Legio X and, in doing so, encouraged the other legions to win his favour by emulating them.[76] Similarly, Titus' secure perimeter around Jerusalem was constructed with great speed owing to his deliberate provocation of inter-unit rivalry.[77] Honorary legionary titles were also used as a means of rewarding particular units.[78] Units as a whole could be punished for their collective behaviour. Legio XII Fulminata suffered two defeats within a decade, once under Lucius Caesennius Paetus, who surrendered to the Parthians, and later under Cestius Gallus in Jerusalem in AD 66. As a punishment for the first defeat, the legion was given an unfavourable posting to Cappadocia. By AD 70, it had regained a reputation for courage, motivated by a desire for revenge.[79] In extreme circumstances, a legion as a whole could suffer *damnatio memoriae*, not only as a result of poor performance in battle, but also as a means of punishing disloyalty.[80] Legio III Augusta was disbanded by Gordian for its role in suppressing his predecessors, although it was later reinstated under Valerian.[81]

While the rivalry for honours between different military units could be a useful tool for ensuring their continuing loyalty, it also meant that they had to be managed extremely carefully so as not to provoke jealousy between the different provincial armies. During the mutinies of AD 14, Tiberius was criticized for not personally dealing with the crisis in person rather than sending Germanicus and Drusus as his representatives.[82] However, had Tiberius visited one army rather than another, he would have indicated a personal preference for the legions concerned. This would have inflamed the anger of the soldiers who did not receive a visit from him and would only have made matters worse. By staying at Rome and delegating the task to others, Tiberius probably made the right decision.[83]

The soldiers' pride in their unit was physically embodied in the standards. As well as the legionary eagle, each cohort had its own standard, which was housed along with the portrait of the emperor and other important members of the imperial family.[84] Their religious significance was overstated by Tertullian, but their emotional importance to the soldiers cannot be underestimated.[85] In battle, the loss of a legionary eagle was regarded as a disgrace, and exposing it to the enemy was a means of encouraging the soldiers to pursue and protect it.[86] The importance of the standards was reinforced by the honour guard, which was deployed on a daily basis to protect them, and the storage of the soldiers' savings in the strong room beneath the shrine.[87] The standards featured prominently in the ceremonial life of the unit. The conception of the legion was celebrated on the *natalis aquilae* and the standards were decorated with garlands as the military interpretation of the civilian rose festivals. Retiring *primipili* formally laid down their vine stick beside the legionary eagle.[88] After the capture of the Temple in Jerusalem, sacrifices were made to the standards as part of a formal ceremony.[89]

As well as being symbolic of the unit as an entity and thus acting as a focus for displays of unit loyalty, the standards also represented military allegiance to the emperor, which was emphasized by the occurrence of real eagles as portents pertaining to both military success and future imperial rule.[90] The juxtaposition of the imperial portraits and military standards within the unit shrine was no coincidence. Indeed, the same location was used to display imperial proclamations of relevance to the troops.[91] From the very beginning of the Principate, emperors sought to associate themselves with the military standards. Augustus oversaw the return of standards captured by the Dalmatians.[92] More famously, he recovered the standards lost to the Parthians at Carrhae. This event became a fundamental element of Augustan propaganda and was celebrated in art, literature and on the imperial coinage.[93] Despite the diplomatic background to the return of the standards, it was portrayed as though it was the result of a military triumph.[94] The standards were deposited in the temple of Mars Ultor in the Forum of Augustus, as a symbol of the emperor's prowess as commander-in-chief and it was decreed that all future recovered standards would be kept in the same location.[95]

It is unsurprising that later emperors perceived the value of associating themselves with military standards. In AD 16, the recovery of some of Varus' lost standards 'under the leadership of Germanicus, under the auspices of Tiberius' was marked by the erection of an arch in Rome.[96] It is noteworthy that the emperor was directly linked to their recovery. Claudius later received an acclamation for the retrieval of the final Varian standard under his auspices.[97] Trajan recovered the standards lost during the defeat of Cornelius Fuscus under Domitian.[98] The retrieval of captured standards emphasized the role of the emperor as the avenger of previous military defeats. It also intrinsically linked him with both the first *princeps* and the main objects of soldierly devotion. During his harangue of mutineers in AD 14, Germanicus explicitly stated that some of their number had received their standards from the emperor, perhaps when their legion was first raised.[99] The clearest demonstration of the link between the standards and the person of the emperor comes from Ammianus Marcellinus, who describes how Silvanus wore a purple robe made from silk taken from a military standard during his attempt to seize power.[100] In this case, the usurper displayed the military support for his rule by wearing part of the physical embodiment of unit loyalty.

The unit expressed its solidarity most clearly through its ceremonial life. Ceremonies played an important role within the Roman army by bringing the soldiers together in a formal setting. The ceremonial life of the army was regulated through a structured framework imposed by the military religious calendar, as demonstrated by the *Feriale Duranum*. Under normal circumstances, formal occasions were therefore directly controlled by the emperor and could be utilized to disseminate specific themes about the ruling dynasty.[101] The formal nature of ceremonial parades emphasized the military hierarchy by displaying the senior officers to the troops. Formal parades were held during the siege of Jerusalem and the Dacian Wars and provided an opportunity to restore army morale.[102] Outside of military campaigns, similar ceremonial events must have taken place for the distribution of pay and oaths of allegiance, which reinforced the soldier's identity as a member of the unit. On a smaller scale, ceremonial activities took place on a daily basis in the form of the formal morning meetings at which orders were transmitted and a standard oath was recited.[103] Both occasions were utilized for ritual activities in the form of sacrifices, presided over by the senior officer present, which emphasized the army's hierarchical structure.[104]

Morale was maintained not only by inclusion in the military community, but also by the prospect of temporary release from it. Numerous requests for leave have been discovered at Vindolanda, suggesting that this was not a rare practice.[105] The granting of leave was dependent upon the military situation that the unit faced.[106] Excessive grants of leave were believed to undermine military discipline.[107] Otho attempted to regulate this system by providing funding for the bribes usually extorted by centurions when granting leave to their men.[108] As well as authorized absences from camp, soldiers could also hope for a relaxation of normal duties on account of official holidays. The *Feriale Duranum* reveals that soldiers could look forward to the relaxation of normal duties in order to celebrate festivals throughout the year, although the irregular placement of official holidays indicates that this was an unintended consequence of the creation of the military *Feriale*.[109] It is significant that many of these festivals were directly linked to members of the imperial family, who could therefore take credit for providing a respite from the rigours of army life.

'LEAVE NO MAN BEHIND': MAINTAINING MORALE IN THE FACE OF CASUALTIES AND DEATH

Death or severe injury in battle were constant possibilities in the lives of the troops. It is therefore not surprising that steps were taken to alleviate some of the concerns which these possible eventualities caused. Although these measures probably evolved in a piecemeal fashion rather than as the result of a systematic program, they acted as a means of maintaining the morale of the ordinary soldier with regard to the possibility of death or severe injury in service.

The prospect of heavy casualties during a campaign must have had a negative effect on military morale. Julius Caesar claimed to be extremely careful in risking the lives of his soldiers.[110] Imperial propaganda emphasized the caution which emperors exercised in risking their soldiers' lives. Augustus warned his subordinates never to engage in battle unless the chance of victory outweighed the risk of defeat.[111] During the siege of Jerusalem, Titus sought to protect his soldiers by ordering them not to place themselves in personal danger when attempting to prove their worth.[112] Fronto praised Lucius Verus for showing such concern in safeguarding his soldiers, to the extent that he would purchase peace rather than risk their lives for his own glory. Fronto contrasted his concern with Trajan who, he claimed, pursued personal glory without regard for the safety of his men.[113] Refraining from exposing the troops to unnecessary dangers would not only win the support of the soldiers, but also demonstrated military competence. Velleius Paterculus claimed that Tiberius' German campaigns caused no losses to his army.[114] Similarly, Claudius stated that the conquest of Britain was accomplished without any Roman fatalities.[115] These claims probably represent official propaganda rather than actual reality, but they indicate an awareness that soldiers should not be placed in unnecessary danger.[116]

30

In combat situations, casualties could hardly be avoided. Under the Principate, the medical service available to soldiers was of a high professional standard; although it is unclear as to how quickly the wounded could be evacuated from the battlefield to receive treatment.[117] During imperial campaigns, emperors showed personal concern for wounded soldiers.[118] This would undoubtedly have boosted their popularity among the rest of the army. Individuals whose injuries prevented them from continuing to serve in the army could receive a medical discharge, *causaria missio* rather than *honesta missio*.[119] This was awarded only after the individual concerned had been examined by a doctor and had his case investigated by a suitable judge.[120] Soldiers discharged on medical grounds were entitled to the privileges and benefits granted to veterans on a scale in proportion to their length of service.[121] This prevented the plight of invalided veterans from becoming a source of dissent among their former comrades. It also offered some comfort to soldiers participating in military campaigns, in the knowledge that they would not be abandoned by the army if they were wounded in combat.[122]

Another measure that would have reassured soldiers facing battle was the freedom allotted to them in the form and composition of their wills. This privilege was first awarded by Julius Caesar, revived by Titus and continued by his successors until it was formally enshrined in the *mandata* for provincial governors by Trajan: 'Therefore, let them make their wills in any way they wish, let them make them in any way they can, and let the bare wishes of the testator suffice to settle the distribution of their property.'[123] The informal nature of soldiers' wills is demonstrated by an incident from the siege of Jerusalem when a soldier trapped on a rooftop pledged to make his rescuer his heir. Unfortunately, the rescuer was crushed by his falling comrade.[124] The ease with which soldiers could compose their wills ensured that they could be certain that their heirs would benefit from their death, which would not be possible if they were forced to make a normal will while on campaign.

In death, the soldier could expect that, if possible, his remains would be buried. Onasander, in his treatise on generalship provides the rationale for the burial of the fallen:

> The general should take thought for the burial of the dead, offering as a pretext for the delay neither occasion nor time nor place nor fear, whether he happens to be victorious or defeated. Now this is both a holy act of reverence towards the dead and also a necessary example for the living. For if the dead are not buried, each soldier believes that no care will be taken of his own body, should he chance to fall, observing what happens before his own eyes, and thereby judging of the future, feeling that he, likewise, if he should die, would fail of burial, waxes indignant of the contemptuous neglect of burial.[125]

Onasander clearly links the burial of the fallen with the maintenance of the morale of the living. As well as thinking of his own fate, it can be assumed that the soldier would also wish to see his fallen comrades buried in an appropriate manner. Tacitus castigated L. Apronius for failing to bury his war dead during the Frisian revolt.[126] Similarly, there was revulsion at Vitellius' failure to bury the dead after the first battle at Cremona.[127] On the other hand, Germanicus' recovery and burial of the soldiers killed alongside Varus can be seen as an act of fraternal piety from the German legions to their former comrades. It was particularly important in the aftermath of the recent mutinies, as it emphasized the membership of the soldiers in a greater military community. It can be assumed to have also boosted the morale of the troops, by demonstrating the lengths to which their commander, a member of the imperial family, would go in order to bury their former comrades. Yet it is noteworthy that he did not have imperial sanction for his actions and Tiberius disapproved on the grounds that a campaigning army should not be exposed to the remnants of a previous disaster and that Germanicus should not have exposed himself to the dead in light of his religious authority.[128] It is possible that Tiberius was jealous of any military popularity that Germanicus won by burying the remains of Varus' army.

Unlike modern armed forces, the Roman army as an institution did not go to extreme lengths to recover its fallen soldiers, nor did it commemorate its dead in any monumental form.[129] In 43 BC, Cicero proposed that a public monument be constructed to house the remains of the Pansa's troops who had perished at the hands of Antony's men.[130] In this case, the motive behind the proposed monument was entirely political; namely to record the Roman citizens killed by Antony rather than to memorialize the fallen. There is no evidence to suggest that the memorial was ever constructed.[131] A similar politically motivated memorial was erected by the people of Nursia for their fellow citizens who perished at Mutina, which bore the inscription: 'Fallen for the cause of freedom'.[132] The memorial and accompanying inscription aroused the anger of Augustus, who fined the city heavily.

It was impossible for catastrophic military losses to be completely covered up, as is the case of the Bar Kokhba revolt when Hadrian omitted the traditional greeting on the health of the legions from his senatorial dispatches.[133] The lack of official commemorative monuments for soldiers killed on campaign prevented the number and severity of casualties from being widely known.[134] A permanent record of campaign fatalities immortalized the incompetence of the emperor in question. Perhaps for this reason, Germanicus covered the mass grave of the Varus' legions with a grassy mound without any form of monumental inscription.[135]

Modern concepts of the need to bring soldiers home, dead or alive, were absent from the Roman mindset. This is evident not only in the treatment of

the dead, but also in attitudes towards prisoners of war.[136] Horace worried
that Crassus' soldiers captured at Carrhae would marry Parthian women
and forget Rome, not that they would be mistreated.[137] Nor did he suggest
that they should be rescued. Likewise, Trajan refused to ransom the corpse
of his general Longinus or the lives of ten Roman prisoners.[138] In contrast
to modern sentiments, emotional investment was made in the recovery of
military standards from the enemy, rather than prisoners and fallen soldiers.
This was in the best interest of the emperor as it was easier for him to
arrange the recovery of standards by diplomatic or military means, than
it was to organize the rescue of captive or deceased soldiers. Augustus'
construction of the temple of Mars Ultor as the spiritual heart of imperial
military endeavour emphasized the retrieval of lost standards rather than the
fate of ordinary soldiers.

The only surviving military commemorative monument is the enigmatic
altar at Adamklissi. As well as the altar, the site also contains a mausoleum
and a circular *tropaeum* decorated with metopes displaying combat scenes
between Romans and barbarians.[139] The altar was inscribed with the names
of up to 3800 soldiers, both legionaries and auxiliaries, under the heading
'*fortissimi viri qui pro republica morte occubuerunt*'. The altar can be dated to
the reign of Domitian, but the site as a whole is instructive for how an emperor,
in this case Trajan, could utilize the memory of past defeats to emphasize his
own greatness and reinforce his relationship with the soldiers.[140]

The unique nature of the Adamklissi altar demands explanation. Why did
Domitian choose to erect such a monument recording the scale of military
losses on the Danube? His careful cultivation of his relationship with the
soldiers, including the first military pay rise in over a century, makes him
an unlikely candidate to have authorized such a monument. Lacking the
military reputation which his father and brother enjoyed and frustrated by
the revolt of Saturninus, it would be strange for Domitian to have highlighted
his military inadequacies in this manner. A more convincing explanation
for the erection of the altar is that it was constructed on the initiative of
the soldiers themselves. The precedent for such an act can be found in the
erection of the tumulus for Drusus in Mainz.[141] On that occasion, the troops
requested imperial authorization only when construction was underway. The
poor craftsmanship evident in the altar also supports the notion that it was
not constructed using the resources available to the emperor, but rather those
available to an army on campaign.[142]

The altar was later juxtaposed with a *tropaeum*, which can be securely
dated to the reign of Trajan. The dedication of the *tropaeum* to Mars Ultor
indicates that Trajan sought to portray himself as the avenger of the fallen
soldiers commemorated at Adamklissi.[143] In doing so, he identified himself

with the troops who had erected the altar by honouring their comrades, which could only have boosted the morale of his own soldiers and reinforced his reputation among the army. The construction of the *tropaeum* as a physical statement of Trajan's martial prowess contrasted sharply with the altar to fallen soldiers. The monuments at Adamklissi encourage comparison between the two emperors' military policies. In stark terms it demonstrated that Domitian buried his soldiers, but Trajan avenged them.[144]

MUTINIES: THE BREAKDOWN OF DISCIPLINE AND MORALE

A contemporary view on the psychology of mutinies is revealed by Tacitus:

> After that, there was no question of any man showing loyalty or remembering his previous oath, and the mutiny followed the classical pattern of all mutinies: the view of the majority was suddenly found to be the view of everybody.[145]

The absence of military loyalty in this situation posed a potential threat to the emperor's rule. Tacitus' view is echoed by Vegetius, who states that mutinies begin with a few discontented individuals and that a wise general should identify and segregate this minority.[146] He also suggests that soldiers should undergo vigorous and prolonged training exercises to minimize their opportunity for mutiny. The connection between *otium* and indiscipline was clearly recognized.[147] The Pannonian mutiny of AD 14 was preceded by a relaxation of duties after the death of Augustus, which provided an opportunity for disaffection to spread.[148]

Despite their relative scarcity in the literary sources it can be suggested, on account of the prevalence of advice on dealing with them, that the occurrence of mutinies was a constant problem in the management of the army, but not all of these posed a direct threat to the security of the emperor. Frontinus included a section in his work on subduing mutinous soldiers, using examples from the Republican era.[149] The legal sources detail the punishments prescribed for seditious behaviour. Attacking an officer or resisting punishment, including breaking a centurion's vine stick, was a capital offence, as was failing to protect him from attack.[150] Leading a mutiny also resulted in execution, although lesser forms of insubordination could be punished by demotion. Mass insubordination resulted in the dishonourable discharge of the culprits, which represented personal expulsion from the military community.[151] This had significant repercussions for the individuals concerned, as it involved the loss of all benefits and privileges normally awarded to veterans.[152] The shortage of references to mutiny within the historical record reflects the political need to safeguard the reputation of the emperor as a capable general who exercised complete control over his soldiers.

Certain methods for dealing with mutinies appear to have been used with some frequency and indicate that commanders were prepared for dealing with serious insubordination. At Placentia in 47 BC, Julius Caesar allegedly subdued a mutiny by addressing his men as *quirites* rather than soldiers.[153] This episode became a shining example of how to quell mutinous troops and was included as such in the work of Polyaenus.[154] Germanicus used a similar tactic during the German mutiny of AD 14.[155] Severus Alexander is also reputed to have used this method of shaming mutineers into obedience, although this could be explained as the use of a literary *topos* by the author of the *Historia Augusta* to demonstrate how the ideal emperor deals with mutinous soldiers.[156] Addressing the soldiers as citizens implied that their conduct had excluded them from the army community. The same notion could also be communicated in other ways, such as suspending normal military routine around the camp.[157] Germanicus' evacuation of Agrippina and Gaius from the camp was a direct insult against the soldiers' sense of identity, by implying that the general's family were no longer safe in their presence.[158]

A second method used to quell a mutiny was the deliberate exposure of the commander to physical harm. Germanicus threatened to stab himself rather than endure the mutinous German legions, only for a soldier to offer him a sharper sword.[159] During the mutiny against Flavius Tampianus, Antonius Primus vowed that 'he would die by the hand of the troops or by his own'.[160] In similar circumstances, Avidius Cassius emerged wearing only a loincloth and told the mutineers to kill him and thus add murder to their list of crimes.[161] The use of this ploy involved a high element of risk. Although it failed to work for Germanicus, both Antonius Primus and Avidius Cassius were successful in suppressing their mutinies. Exposing oneself to physical violence, either through suicide or murder, relied heavily on the strength of the relationship between the commander and his men. In the case of Cassius, his appearance emphasized his complete lack of fear and won the support of the men. Primus had already acquired the support of his soldiers, but reinforced his plea for calm by appealing to the legionary standards. These scenarios demonstrate that traditional methods were applied to the suppression of mutinies, either as *topoi* in the narrative constructions of contemporary writers or, if the historical authenticity of these events is accepted, by the military commanders themselves.

The suppression of mutinies often contained an element of purification. The role of purification in restoring armies to discipline has been noted in Greek warfare:

> Repentance, change of heart, rejection of anarchy, reassertion of the army's corporate identity as a disciplined unity: such was the message of this purification.[162]

It can be suggested that the involvement of Roman soldiers in the punishment of their comrades was a symbolic act of purification. Although it was increasingly seen as an archaic practice, decimation was still used, albeit infrequently, under the Principate.[163] In describing the mechanics of both decimation and the individual punishment of *fustuarium*, Polybius makes clear that the act was carried out by the victim's comrades.[164] After the Pannonian mutiny, some of the ringleaders were hunted down by the soldiers whom they had previously led.[165] At the conclusion of the Rhine mutiny, the troops again dealt with the instigators, although on this occasion there was, at least, a semblance of a trial. According to Tacitus, 'the soldiers revelled in the massacre as though it purged them of their offences'.[166] Likewise, after the drunken Praetorian rampage through Rome under Otho, it was the soldiers who demanded the execution of the ringleaders.[167] By purging the unit of unwanted elements, the process delineated the period of ill-discipline from the resumption of normal duties. The direct involvement of the soldiers strengthened the cohesion of the unit as a whole and may have served to expunge disgrace and shame for their behaviour.[168]

The causes of mutinies differed according to the immediate situation which the soldiers faced, but can usually be attributed to factors which had an impact on their daily lives, such as service conditions or the conduct of military campaigns.[169] The intensity of the incidents also varied, ranging from what can be seen as outbreaks of political violence, in which officers were attacked or killed, to military strikes, in which the soldiers simply stopped work. The latter posed little direct threat to the emperor himself unless he happened to be present at the scene of the mutiny or if the disturbance spread to other units.[170]

In AD 198, Septimius Severus besieged the city of Hatra in northern Mesopotamia. The first siege ended without success and, despite a high level of preparation, the second also failed owing to a mutiny among his expeditionary force. According to Cassius Dio, 'Europaean' troops refused to participate in the siege and the remaining Syrian troops were completely ineffective.[171] The mutineers were probably the western contingent of Severus' army.[172] Although the exact cause of the discontent is unclear, their length of combat service and perceived command incompetence in the management of the siege were probably to blame. Indeed, a Praetorian tribune was executed for criticizing Severus' handling of the operation.[173] The execution of the popular general Julius Laetus may also have contributed to the soldiers' sense of unease.[174] This incident can be seen as a military strike, in which the troops simply refused to participate further in the campaign.

On the other hand, the mutinies of AD 14 were far more violent and politically dangerous to the emperor than the mutiny at Hatra. Primarily, the danger was a result of the political uncertainty arising from the death of Augustus as to whether Tiberius would be able to smoothly assume power or if the Principate would slide back into the civil conflicts that had torn apart the Republic. These mutinies, at a crucial juncture in the political evolution of the Principate, were of sufficient concern from the perspective of the emperor for Tiberius to send Drusus and Germanicus to the scene of the mutinies and consider going himself.[175]

In fact, the mutineers' grievances were mainly concerned with service conditions rather than wider political events. They complained about prolonged lengths of service, low pay (which was further decreased by extortionate bribes to avoid arduous duties), poor quality land awarded on discharge and the brutality of centurions.[176] The mutineers in both Pannonia and Germany attacked centurions, officers and other senior figures. This catastrophic breakdown in discipline can also be attributed to the presence of soldiers recruited in special circumstances in both of the affected areas.[177] These men were presumably conscripted during the state of emergency that followed the Pannonian revolt and the Varian disaster, which also contributed to the delayed discharge of veterans.[178] It can be suggested that the unconventional origins of these men made them less adhesive to the military community and unwilling to endure service conditions. In taking advantage of the death of Augustus to voice their grievances, perhaps because they were more politically aware than their comrades on account of their time in Rome, they became the active nucleus that fomented the mutiny.

Mutinies embodied the soldiers' assertion of their political voice, by demonstrating their anger in the most unambiguous way.[179] Outbreaks of mutinous behaviour were more prevalent during periods of civil conflict, when loyalty to a particular imperial candidate overrode the normal command hierarchy. Shifting political loyalties decreased confidence in their officers, and soldiers mutinied to show their displeasure at strategic decisions.[180] The general atmosphere of ill-discipline during Galba's reign undermined his position. His refusal to deliver a promised donative to the soldiers created a fertile environment for Otho to gather support for his usurpation.[181] Indeed, Otho's elevation by the Praetorians can be seen as an act of mutiny because it was carried out by the soldiers themselves without any involvement from their officers, who faced hostility and violence from their men.[182]

The conduct of the Batavian cohorts in AD 69 had been of a mutinous nature long before they joined the revolt of their people. In particular, they showed outright hostility and committed acts of violence against the legionaries with whom they were encamped.[183] The self-image of the Batavians as an elite formation undoubtedly contributed to their antagonism towards soldiers from other units.[184] But their behaviour was also encouraged by the general air of ill-discipline during the civil wars. This was particularly prevalent on the Rhineland where Hordeonius Flaccus, legate of Upper Germany, was mistrusted by the soldiers for his adherence to the Flavian cause and was eventually murdered by his men and is evident in the swearing of allegiance by Roman troops to the *imperium Galliarum*.[185] A charismatic leader, in the form of Julius Civilis, was able to exploit the complaints, fears and animosities of the soldiers for his own ends. Like the outbreaks of AD 14, the mutinous behaviour of AD 69 became a threat to the position of the emperor for two main reasons. First, the discontent passed to other units or native communities and, second, because of the general political context where, in each case, the legitimacy of the ruling emperor could be called into question.

The propensity of mutinies to rapidly spread was particularly troubling, hence Vegetius' advice to quarantine suspected troublemakers.[186] Even mutinies of a highly localized nature had the potential to explode into mass insubordination which could threaten the emperor's survival. Tacitus' account of the mutinies of AD 14 suggests that the soldiers were seized by a collective madness or *furor* that spread between different units.[187] The connection between madness and mutiny allowed contemporary writers to rationalize what appeared to be inexplicable, namely the spontaneous outburst of aggressive behaviour by the soldiers against their officers. In reality, mutinies did not require a medical explanation as a temporary affliction, but rather represented the soldiers' affirmation of their latent physical and political power.

CONCLUSION

The Roman imperial army was far less disciplined than its twentieth and twenty-first-century counterparts. The emperor navigated a delicate balance between imposing military discipline and maintaining the support of the soldiers. To sustain his popularity among the elite classes in Rome, he had to appear to keep a tight control over the troops. On the other hand, from the viewpoint of the soldiers, an emperor who was a strict disciplinarian was an unattractive prospect. In part, he accomplished this awkward juxtaposition by abdicating responsibility for discipline to his subordinates, who faced the anger and displeasure of the troops and absorbed the ensuing mutinies and physical attacks. The army commanders therefore became a necessary buffer layer between the emperor and his soldiers.

On a more positive note, military morale was maintained by allowing the soldiers to assert their identity as individuals, as members of a unit and as an empire-wide community in both life and death. This sense of an integrated community combated the danger of the army fragmenting into regional groups. It can be suggested that one of the defining characteristics of this military community was its tradition of loyalty and obedience to the emperor. Martial values such as *virtus*, unit pride and comradeship permeated the rank and file, regardless of unit affiliation. The emperor played a crucial role in the creation and promulgation of military ideals. His personal behaviour as a *commilito* displayed mutual ideals and a shared identity with the soldiers.[188]

The subjugation of the late Republican armies under a single commander-in-chief dictated the need for alternative outlets for soldiers to demonstrate their prowess and aggression in the absence of warfare. The evolution of *virtus* to encompass *labor* was one such arena, as it encouraged the troops to occupy themselves in manual tasks. It was in the best interests of the emperor that the soldiers were kept busy in the absence of active campaigning. Although most mutinies were highly localized and of a non-political nature, there was always the potential that mutinous behaviour could spread to other military units, as it did in AD 14. Ill-disciplined troops threatened not only their commanders and local civilian population, but the position and personal safety of the emperor himself.

Chapter 3

The Legionary Centurionate

The architecture of the imperial army was designed to promote social mobility. It was entirely possible for a new recruit to entertain the ambition of rising steadily through the ranks to obtain entry to the centurionate, including the prestigious post of '*primus pilus*' or first centurion and subsequently enjoy access to some of the most prestigious administrative posts within the imperial administration. The legionary centurionate therefore occupied a particularly important space within the army, not only on account of the influence they hold over the rank and file, but also as a body of potentially talented men who could prove valuable as bulwarks of loyalty towards the emperor. This chapter will explore the role of centurions in managing the army and fostering loyalty towards the imperial regime. On account of limitations in the range of evidence, I will necessarily focus on legionary centurions, although my arguments can equally be applied to their auxiliary counterparts.

THE STATUS OF CENTURIONS

The variety of backgrounds from which men were attracted to join the centurionate demonstrates the prestige and value of membership. There were three main routes into the auxiliary centurionate.[1] Centurions could be appointed from the ranks of both the *auxilia* and the legions. The promotion of legionaries to positions within auxiliary units maintained the uniformity of training and discipline across the different branches of the Roman military. Civilians, probably the offspring of important provincial families, could also receive direct commissions into the auxiliary centurionate. Although a centurionate in an auxiliary unit was neither as lucrative nor as prestigious as a post in a legion, the auxiliary centurion was still an important figure both within the army and the surrounding civilian population.[2] Given that the *auxilia* made up at least half of the army, the influence of the auxiliary centurion over the soldiers under his command must have been comparable to his legionary counterpart.

Promotion into the legionary centurionate involved a substantial pay increase. After Augustus' military reforms, centurions in cohorts II–X received a salary of 13,500 sesterces. Centurions in the first cohort earned 27,000 sesterces and a *primus pilus* earned 54,000 sesterces. These salaries increased in line with later military pay rises.[3] Entry into the centurionate of the first cohort, the *primi ordines*, entailed a pay increase to the equivalent of thirty times the legionary salary. Membership of the *primi ordines* also guaranteed a far better standard of accommodation than that enjoyed by other centurions. The accommodation provided for the centurions of the first cohort in most legionary forts was double the size of the housing used by the other centurions and often included a courtyard.[4] Unlike the rank and file before the Severan period, it seems likely that centurions were able to legally marry.

Entry into the legionary centurions was also attractive to members of the equestrian order. The salaries of a *centurio legionis, primus ordo* and *primus pilus* corresponded directly to those of a *praefectus cohortis, tribunus militum* and *praefectus alae* respectively.[5] The most conspicuous difference between the careers offered by the legionary centurionate and equestrian military commands was one of lifestyle. A centurion could expect to be in constant employment until his retirement or death, while an equestrian officer received a series of postings with gaps of unemployment in between. As well as financial security, only the centurionate could offer access to the primipilate. Moreover, centurions acted as a reservoir of military experience and knowledge, in contrast to the temporary positions held by military tribunes and legionary commanders. Unlike these latter officers, who were usually deployed singly or in small numbers, centurions usually existed in large groups of up to fifty-nine in a single legion, which gave them a greater social cohesion as a body of men.[6]

The pinnacle of posts within the centurionate was occupied by the post of *primus pilus*, which could lead to more senior positions across the empire.[7] The retiring *primus pilus* also received a payment of around 600,000 sesterces.[8] Potential posts after the primipilate included tribunate in the Rome cohorts, camp prefectures and prefectures of the Egyptian legions.[9]

A centurion could even reach the prefecture of the Praetorian Guard.[10] An example of such an individual is the case of Arrius Varus, who began his career commanding a cohort under Corbulo in the East. Tacitus reports that Varus laid secret charges against Corbulo with Nero.[11] For this act, he was rewarded with a primipilate by the emperor. Varus was connected to Antonius Primus and, after the downfall of Vitellius, obtained the Praetorian prefecture.[12] His tenure was somewhat brief as he was transferred by Mucianus to the supervision of the grain supply.[13] Varus' later fate is unknown, although Tacitus hints darkly that his betrayal of Corbulo was to prove his downfall. It is possible that he was destroyed by the group of former Corbulonian officers who were involved in the Flavian rise to power.

Although Varus rose to prominence through civil war, centurions could also reach the Praetorian prefecture during times of peace. Perhaps the most famous of these men was Q. Marcius Turbo, who commanded the Guard under Hadrian. A gravestone from Aquincum in Pannonia, belonging to a legionary who served in II Adiutrix, records that he served under a centurion named Marcius Turbo.[14] If this is the same individual as the Praetorian prefect, it also reveals the occasion when Hadrian and Turbo first came into contact with each other. The future emperor is known to have served as a military tribune of II Adiutrix at Aquincum in AD 95–6. It seems likely that the centurion made a good impression on Hadrian and laid the foundation for his future promotion. Presumably, Turbo later obtained the post of *primus pilus*, perhaps with the help of the future emperor, which allowed him access to more senior positions. During Trajan's first Dacian war, he commanded the Misenum fleet. He later held special commands in Mauretania, Egypt and Dacia before reaching the Praetorian prefecture.

One of the Praetorian prefects serving at the end of Trajan's reign was Sulpicius Similis. He had also begun his career as a centurion, and an anecdote from Dio indicates that he came into contact with the emperor while still serving in that position. When Similis was summoned to the presence of the emperor ahead of the existing prefects, he reprimanded Trajan for talking with a centurion while the prefects were left waiting outside.[15] Similis must have been serving as a centurion in the Praetorian Guard at this point or in a legion involved in one of Trajan's wars. A fragmentary inscription records that he held the prefecture of Egypt before his command of the Guard.[16] The anecdote of Dio suggests that Similis was held in high regard by the emperor and this may have contributed to his advancement.

There are other examples of centurions reaching the Praetorian prefecture but unfortunately there is no way to discern whether their advancement was due to personal contact with the emperor. It may be the case that hard work and talent explain their rise to prominence. Gavius Maximus held the prefecture for twenty years under Antoninus Pius. He had served as *primus pilus* before progressing through various posts including the prefecture of the Misenum fleet prior to obtaining the command of the Guard.[17] Similarly, Rustius Rufinus who commanded the Guard under Severus had started his career serving as a centurion in a number of legions.[18] After holding the primipilate, he served as a tribune in the *vigiles*, urban and Praetorian cohorts. He also commanded the fleets at Misenum and Ravenna and served as a procurator in Syria. All of this experience ensured that Rufinus was well qualified to command the Praetorians. The fact that he was commissioned directly into the centurionate as an equestrian is of interest. During his time as a centurion he also commanded a century of the Praetorian Guard.

The loyalty of centurions to the imperial regime had ramifications beyond the walls of the army camp to the civilian settlements beyond. The centurion represented a symbol of imperial authority not only to soldiers but to the population as a whole. In certain areas, the centurion also represented imperial oppression. An intriguing tablet from Vindolanda records an appeal by a merchant to a senior figure, perhaps the governor, regarding an assault upon him by a centurion:

> ... he beat me all the more ... goods ... or pour them down the drain (?). As befits an honest man, I implore your majesty not to allow me, an innocent man, to have been beaten with rods and inasmuch as I was unable to complain to the prefect because he was detained by ill health, I have complained in vain (?) to the *beneficiarius* and the rest of the centurions of his unit. Accordingly (?), I implore your mercifulness not to allow me, a man from overseas and an innocent one, about whose good faith you may inquire, to have been bloodied by rods as if I had committed some crime.[19]

The presence of this petition at Vindolanda suggests that the complaint was made against one of the auxiliary centurions based at the fort. In military areas, centurions functioned as the visible face of Roman imperial power. The Icenian revolt in Britain was, in part, provoked by the ruthless depredations of centurions.[20] Commodus allowed the Dacians to hold only one public assembly each month, in the presence of a legionary centurion.[21] Juvenal, in a savage attack on the privileges of the military, states that a civilian's criminal case against a soldier would be judged by centurions within the confines of a military camp.[22] A study of the role of bandits during the imperial period has suggested that Cassius Dio used stories of brigands tricking and humiliating centurions as a social criticism against the incompetence of the military apparatus.[23] Given the authority that centurions held over the local population in certain circumstances, there may well have been a ready audience for such anecdotes.

Certain regions were placed directly under the control of a *centurio regionarius*. These individuals controlled the areas in question and were responsible for maintaining law and order, although their exact jurisdiction is unclear. They are attested in Britain at Bath, Carlisle and Ribchester.[24] Elsewhere in the empire they are recorded in Egypt, Galatia, Lugdunensis,

Moesia, Noricum and Pannonia. According to Pliny, Trajan authorized the transfer of a legionary centurion to Byzantium to assist the magistrates there with the crowds of travellers, including soldiers, who passed through the city.[25] It would be of great interest to learn the criteria used for the selection of these officers. Clearly, these tasks required men of proven loyalty and competence who could cope with the considerable administrative burden the post would entail.

Literacy appears to have been an important factor in the selection of candidates for this position. The commander of the garrison at Vindolanda was asked to supply the *centurio regionarius* at Carlisle with a recommendation regarding a candidate for an unknown position.[26] In Egypt, numerous papyri record petitions made to centurions regarding criminal offences. An analysis of the geographical spread of such petitions has demonstrated that the vast majority come from the Fayum region, a frontier area, which suggests that, in this locality at least, petitioners directed their complaints to military officers rather than the civil administration.[27] The centurions selected for this task must have been men of intelligence and initiative and their selection indicates the high esteem held for centurions within the imperial administration by using them for more important tasks than that of infantry leaders. Indeed, the role of the centurion as a figure of Roman imperial authority is also demonstrated by the use of legionary centurions as official envoys.[28]

There is a range of evidence demonstrating that some centurions were literate to a remarkably high degree. One of Martial's most avid readers was a centurion aiming for a primipilate.[29] Enthusiasm for contemporary literature was probably uncommon throughout the legionary centurionate as a whole.[30] It can be safely assumed that directly commissioned centurions would have been better educated than those who had advanced through the ranks. The familiar tone of a letter from a centurion to the prefect at Vindolanda suggests that both the correspondent and recipient were of equal social status and that the centurion had been directly commissioned.[31] A study of the sociolinguistics of the legionary centurionate has revealed a number of poetic inscriptions set up by centurions, some of which show evidence of bilingualism.[32] However, it is not clear whether these were composed or simply commissioned by a centurion. The level of literacy across the body of centurions probably varied enormously. The high level of bureaucracy throughout the army, which relied upon written records, also suggests that a degree of literacy was demanded of the officers for the system to work. It may also have opened the way to more important imperial positions after the primipilate.

On the other hand, centurions were promoted for other reasons than their administrative skill. An individual who displayed martial prowess or leadership skills could also hope for entry into the centurionate and therefore an element of illiteracy cannot be ruled out. As mentioned elsewhere in my fuller discussion of literacy within the imperial army, some soldiers completed their entire term of service without being able to write their name.[33] Illiterate centurions have left no record of their existence and it may be that they at least learnt the basic literacy skills required for their administrative duties. The increasing professionalization of the career structure open to *primipilares* would have motivated centurions to attain literary skills in order to further their own careers.

CENTURIONS WITHIN THE ARMY

The geographical origins of legionary centurions are worthy of consideration, particularly because a divergence between the origins of centurions and legionaries may have had an impact on the relationship between the two groups.[34] During the first century AD, there was a clear distinction between the centurions of the western and eastern legions, in particular between the Greek speaking east, Egypt and Africa and elsewhere in the empire.[35] Centurions from legions based in the western provinces who were involved in campaigns in the east invariably returned to their original legions on the cessation of hostilities. This separation was not completely on geographical grounds, as men from the Latin settlements in the east could enter the western legions. This arrangement presumably ensured uniformity between the origins of the soldiers and centurions in ensuring that they had similar backgrounds and linguistic abilities. From the reign of Trajan onwards, the transfer of centurions between legions in the east and west was facilitated and the geographical separation ceased to exist. This change was possibly caused by the need for experienced centurions in the military campaigns waged by Trajan and his later successors, which overrode the need to transfer centurions using geographical criteria in favour of utilizing the best men for the job.

From the early second century AD onwards, the centurionate across the empire became a remarkably heterogeneous body. This diversity was fostered by the variety of routes by which men entered the centurionate. Italians were present in small numbers in both the legions and the centurionate and there is no evidence to suggest that they were ever deliberately excluded from the army.[36] However, the better pay and privileges available to members of the Praetorian Guard presumably tempted most Italian recruits to seek a post in the Rome cohorts. If their career progressed satisfactorily, such men could then be transferred into the legionary centurionate. Equestrians commissioned as centurions came from a variety of Italian and provincial backgrounds. It is only to be expected that the majority of centurions who began their military careers in the ranks would share the provincial background of their men, particularly as recruitment became more localized. However, the prevalence of multiple centurionate careers ensured that, although a centurion may have shared a common background with the soldiers of the legion in which he was first promoted, he could be transferred through a number of legions in different provinces. There was no guarantee that a centurion would come from the same province or even the same geographical area as the men under his command.[37] This divergence may have affected the relationship between the centurion and the soldiers and forced the former to seek other means to win the support of his men.

Centurions were the primary enforcers of military discipline, which inevitably created an ambiguous relationship between them and their men. In the words of Tacitus, centurions were '… the traditional objects of military hatred and always the first victims of its fury'.[38] This is particularly evident in the extreme violence meted out to centurions by their men during the mutinies of AD 14. The Pannonian mutineers executed a centurion who bore the nickname '*cedo alteram*' or 'give me another' on account of his habit of calling for another stick when he had broken the first in beating a soldier.[39] Legionaries attempted to give every centurion sixty lashes, one for each of their number in a legion.[40] The anger of the soldiers does appear to have had some justification, as Germanicus was persuaded to instigate a review and dismiss those who had been too harsh.[41] However, the level of violence varied between individual centurions, and some of them were actually protected by their men. Julius Clemens was spared on account of his quick wits and was used as a spokesman by the mutineers.[42] Soldiers of two legions actually came to blows over whether to execute a particular centurion.[43]

The authority and leadership of the centurions extended onto the battlefield. Since the surviving evidence suggests that, at a tactical level, individual cohorts lacked an overall commander, it is likely that the centuries were commanded by their centurions as individual combat units.[44] The prevailing opinion of modern scholars is that centurions fought in the front rank during battle.[45] This assumption is made on the basis of the high mortality rate of centurions in combat which suggests that the centurions were present in the very forefront of the action. But there may be other reasons for the high mortality rate of centurions. An individual fighting in the front rank of the army was incapable of any command function, literally fighting for his life and unable to give orders. It has been argued persuasively that the *optio* was placed at the rear of a century to physically discourage soldiers from fleeing from battle.[46] If this was the case, it would make sense for the centurion to be closer to the front of the century to direct the fighting. However, in order for him to exercise control of the century, the centurion would need to separate himself from the fighting while remaining close enough to observe what was happening and make on the spot command decisions.

Assuming that cohorts were usually deployed in three ranks, centurions may have stood in the second rank and their high casualty rate can be explained by their consequent role in battle.[47] In this position, centurions were ideally placed to intervene should things start to go wrong, and could step into the front rank in order to hold the line together in moments of crisis. If a unit gave way and began to withdraw prematurely, centurions could stand their ground and face the enemy with whatever resistance they could gather.[48] Therefore it is plausible that high numbers of centurions were killed during moments of crisis on the battlefield, when they tried to physically hold the army together. It should also be noted that while the numbers of centurions killed are thought worthy of note by our sources, the actual numbers of soldiers who died are often not mentioned and therefore the emphasis on centurion fatalities may, in some instances, reflect differing cultural attitudes towards the commemoration of officers and soldiers.[49]

Given the reasonably frequent occurrences of displays of courage by centurions in the literary sources, it is worth examining them in more detail. The clearest evidence for the behaviour of centurions in battle comes from the writings attributed to Julius Caesar, with his clear preoccupation with the actual mechanics of combat. During a battle with the Nervii, he records that all the centurions of the fourth cohort of the twelfth legion had been killed and the majority of the remaining centurions were incapacitated. Among these catastrophic losses, Caesar highlights the fate of a *primus pilus*, Publius Sextius Baculus, who had endured so many wounds that he could no longer stand upright.[50] At a later date, Baculus rose from his sickbed and, despite being severely malnourished, took command of the camp defences against an enemy attack until, after sustaining severe wounds, he was dragged to safety.[51] The fact that Caesar took the trouble to record Baculus' actions in detail indicates that he personally held the centurion in high regard. During the Spanish war, two centurions from the fifth legion crossed a river in order to firm up the battle line. It appears that these individuals were acting on their own initiative, rather than under a direct order, as a response to the combat situation they observed. Both men died as a result of this action.[52]

While such interventions were probably part of the role of the centurion, some of their more reckless acts were motivated by material desires rather than to salvage a perilous situation. Caesar mentions centurions who had been advanced from the lower ranks on account of their personal valour.[53] During the civil war, a centurion was awarded 200,000 sesterces and promoted to the rank of *primus pilus* when he presented Caesar with his shield, pierced by 120 arrows.[54] The presence of a senior commander provided a valuable opportunity for a centurion to show his worth. At the Battle of Pharsalus, a former *primus pilus* promised Caesar that he would have reason to be grateful to him by the end of the day, before personally leading the attack.[55] In Judaea, an auxiliary centurion named Julianus personally intervened to hold back the Jewish rebels when the Roman battle line began to give way and eventually died a heroic death in front of Titus and his comrades.[56] A funerary epitaph for a *primus pilus* records that he received 75,000 sesterces and a promotion from Caracalla for his bravery in battle against the Carpi.[57] During the review of the German centurions in AD 14, each centurion stated the number of campaigns in which he had personally participated, his distinctions in battle and military decorations he had received.[58] This indicates the importance of prowess in battle for the centurionate as a whole as a means of obtaining rewards and promotions.[59]

THE RELATIONSHIP BETWEEN ARMY COMMANDERS AND CENTURIONS

Undoubtedly, the imperial military system permitted army commanders to distribute appointments as a form of patronage. Within a letter by the younger Pliny, he asked an army commander to provide positions for his friends:

> Your command of a great army gives you a plentiful source of benefits to confer, and secondly, your tenure has been long enough for you to have provided for your own friends. Turn to mine – they are not many.[60]

In another letter, Pliny records that he arranged for a commission to the centurionate for one of his fellow townsmen, and funded the necessary equipment and clothing.[61] Demonstrating that not all commanders viewed appointments as tools of patronage, the general Agricola allegedly refused to allow his choice of centurions to be swayed by petitions or personal recommendations, but rather selected the best available candidates.[62]

Two papyri from Egypt show that the prefect was responsible for commissions and promotions concerning auxiliary centurions. The first example records the centurions and decurions of two auxiliary units stationed in the province. One centurion was commissioned from civilian life and another was promoted from the legionary cavalry, both of which were authorized by the prefect.[63] In the second instance, a civilian named Sextus Sempronius Candidus was made a centurion by Sempronius Liberalis, the prefect of Egypt.[64] The similarity of their names suggests that the centurion may have had a family connection to the prefect. However, not every attempt was successful in obtaining the desired commission. The grammatician Marcus Valerius Probus grew tired of waiting for a posting as a centurion and devoted his life to academic study instead.[65]

The potential appointment of centurions by army commanders presents a paradox. This mechanism arguably allowed commanders to build a body of loyal men under their patronage who could have significant influence over the troops. It is important to note occasions when emperors exercised their power to purge the centurionate.[66] Vespasian discharged a young man who had gained a commission to alleviate his financial distress but was personally unsuited to military service.[67] Hadrian is alleged to have allowed only individuals of good repute to be appointed as centurions.[68] There is clear evidence of the targeted movement of centurions during times of political unrest, presumably as a result of emperors seeking to deploy competent officers of proven loyalty into specific legions.[69] Beyond these examples, challenging communication speeds and an unenviable bureaucratic burden suggest that it was impractical for emperors to personally make all appointments to the centurionate. Nevertheless, it is certainly possible that such appointments were perceived to be at the discretion of the emperor, thus securing the loyalty of the individual through perception in a manner which would have been impossible to achieve in reality.

LOYALTY, REWARDS AND PROMOTIONS

The *primus pilus* L. Maximius Gaetulicius, erected an altar in fulfilment of a vow he made as a youthful recruit aiming for the primipilate fifty-seven years earlier.[70] A similar career aspiration is emphasized in an inscription erected by a centurion in Africa:

> I wanted to hold slaughtered Dacians. I held them.
> I wanted to sit on a chair of peace. I sat on it.
> I wanted to take part in famous triumphs. It was done.
> I wanted the full benefits of the chief centurionate. I have had them.
> I wanted to see naked nymphs. I saw them.[71]

The centurion could hope to distinguish himself by winning military decorations which were, like many other privileges of military life, believed to come from the emperor himself.[72] In this way they acted as an incentive for the centurion to remain loyal to his emperor as well as to prove his valour in combat. The decorations awarded to centurions usually consisted of *armillae*, *phalerae* and *torques* with the addition of a *corona aurea, muralis* or *vallaris*. With the exception of the *primi ordines*, all eligible centurions, whether in the Rome cohorts or the legions, received similar types of awards with slight variations in individual cases.[73] In addition, *primi ordines* could expect a *hasta pura*. The differentiation between the decorations awarded to the *primi ordines* and those given to the other centurions emphasized the seniority enjoyed by the officers of the first cohort.

One particular decoration was awarded only to centurions and, even then, only in a very small number of cases. Four centurions are recorded as having received the privilege of *albata decursio* and, in each case, it is stated that it was received from the emperor himself. The rarity of this award is demonstrated by the fact that these inscriptions make up only 1.4 per cent of all known inscriptions dealing with military honours.[74] The four cases on record can be dated to the first or early second century AD. The earliest example belongs to L. Antonius Naso. He was awarded this honour early in his career while he held a centurionate in XIII Gemina.[75] His next post was as prefect of *civitas Colapianorum*, which was perhaps held concurrently with the primipilate of XIII Gemina. He then served as a tribune in I Italica and the *vigiles*, urban and praetorian cohorts. While in the latter post, Naso was decorated by the emperor Nero, presumably for his assistance during the Pisonian conspiracy. He also received a second primipilate. On returning to the Guard, Naso was cashiered by Galba.[76] His career revived under Vespasian when he was appointed as procurator of Pontus and Bithynia. The exact circumstances of the award of *albata decursio* to Naso are unknown but it is possible that it contributed to his first primipilate and later posts. The second holder of the honour of *albata decursio* also received a primipilate as his next post.[77] This unnamed individual was rewarded for his role in the invasion and annexation of Commagene in AD 72/3. A possible link between this award and combat service is also suggested by the career of Cn. Julius Rufus, who was given the honour of *albata decursio* by Trajan for his role in the Parthian war while serving as *primus pilus* of I Italica.[78] Rufus had previously been decorated for his actions during Domitian's *bellum Germanicum et Sarmaticum*.[79] An inscription recovered recently from Ankara records a centurion of IV Scythica, M. Julius Rufus, who received this honour from Domitian, although the exact circumstances are not specified.[80]

The rarity of the award suggests that it was extremely prestigious; it is clear that it could be awarded to all centurions irrespective of seniority. The name suggests that centurions honoured in this way were permitted to wear a white uniform while on parade. This would have drawn attention to the individual concerned by giving him a unique appearance on formal occasions and probably aided the further progression of his career. Vitellius and his senior officers wore white on their entry into Rome and it could be suggested that the effect of such attire was highlighted by the contrast with the uniforms worn by the ordinary soldiers.[81]

It is possible only to speculate on the exact criteria required for this honour. In two cases the connection with wartime service is explicit and two of the centurions had been decorated previously. With the exception of Julius Rufus, who finished his career as *princeps prior* of the second cohort, all of the holders of this award held or progressed to the primipilate. While it cannot be proven definitively in two of the cases in question, it seems plausible that it was awarded for a specific act in combat, perhaps killing a particularly prestigious adversary, for example. Although surviving attestations of this award are extremely rare, in the four cases on record it is stated that the award came from the emperor and it therefore contributed to the relationship between him and his centurions.

CONCLUSION

It is widely recognized that, in most circumstances, the legionary centurionate provided the professional backbone of the imperial army. For the emperor, centurions functioned as the primary tools of maintaining order over the troops, both in enforcing discipline but also in inculcating loyalty for the imperial regime. Entry to the centurionate offered social and career advancement, underpinned by the acquisition of status and financial benefits. It was therefore not unreasonable for a new recruit to anticipate that decades of diligent service would result in appointment as a centurion and potential acquisition of more senior roles across the empire as a result. Outside of periods of political instability, gradual career progression through the ranks and centurionate offered the best opportunity for advancement. As such, loyalty to the imperial regime was often the best option for securing and enjoying the lucrative benefits associated with the centurionate.

Chapter 4

Commanding the Emperor's Army

It is but rarely that men of eminence have failed to employ great men to aid them in directing their fortune, as the two Scipios employed the two Laelii, whom in all things they treated as equal to themselves, or as the deified Augustus employed Marcus Agrippa, and after him Statilius Taurus. In the case of these men, their lack of lineage was no obstacle to their elevation to successive consulships, triumphs and numerous priesthoods. For great tasks require great helpers, and it is important to the State that those who are necessary to her service should be given prominence in rank, and that their usefulness should be fortified by official authority.[1]

In this passage, Velleius is alluding to Sejanus' status under Tiberius. But he could also be justifying his own position. In AD 6, after serving on the Rhine with Tiberius as *praefectus equitum*, he was elected quaestor and, in the aftermath of the Pannonian revolt of the same year, was selected by Augustus to lead hastily gathered reinforcements to the conflict. After holding his quaestorship, Velleius returned to Tiberius as *legatus Augusti*.[2] Velleius' literary writing has often been dismissed as a work of cringing flattery. Yet his innate adoration and optimism towards the Principate reflects the positive attitude of many concerning a regime that had restored political stability after the disastrous civil wars of the late Republic and Triumviral era, and which appeared to offer advancement on the basis of talent rather than ancestry. Indeed, it has been argued that the success of the Augustan regime was due to its ability to win the support of men of relatively humble background, like Velleius, by offering them access to high political office.[3]

The sheer size of the empire forced the emperor to rely on trusted subordinates to personally command his troops. Auxiliary units were commanded by equestrian officers, who also held five of the six tribunates in a legion. The remaining tribunate was filled by a senatorial officer. Senators also held the legionary and provincial commands, with the exception of the equestrian prefects of Egypt and Mesopotamia. However, these army commanders posed a significant threat to the emperor. After all, the Principate itself had been founded by a seizure of power conducted by a military leader, a precedent which could not easily be forgotten.

In this chapter, I will explore the paradox between the need to find competent individuals to hold military commands and the danger which subversive army commanders represented to the emperor. The criteria that the emperor employed to select his officers from the senatorial and equestrian orders have long been the subject of scholarly debate. I will consider the historiography of this debate to examine whether there was a rapid career path open to men who displayed a talent for military command. This will lead to a study of upper class attitudes towards military service. Did senators and equestrians seek to gain or avoid army commands? How did the change in honours and rewards for military service under the empire impact on the willingness of the upper classes to serve in the army? These questions are inextricably linked to the scope for independent command afforded by the emperor to his subordinates. How much operational freedom was granted to army commanders and what limitations were imposed upon them? To give a clearer illustration of these issues, I will examine the career of Agricola to demonstrate that the conventional interpretation of his actions as governor of Britain can be overturned to reveal the tension created by the opposing demands of personal *virtus* and the restrictions imposed by the emperor on his immediate subordinates.

Roman political life was facilitated by the workings of patronage. A major military command potentially provided a large number of posts that could be dispensed by the general concerned. But this could allow an army commander to gather support within the army against the emperor. In order to understand the potential threat created by the distribution of army posts, I will analyse the most notorious group possibly created by such means, the so-called 'Corbulonian group', composed of officers who had served under Domitius Corbulo in the East and who, it is argued, were instrumental in the Flavian seizure of power. In conclusion, I will argue that the overriding factor that influenced the emperor's selection of his army commanders was his own personal and political security. The actions and trial of Piso, illuminated by the *Senatus Consultum de Cn. Pisone Patre*, will serve as an illustration of the contemporary official view of the dangers posed by a renegade army commander.

SPECIALIZED PATTERNS OF PROMOTION?

It seems obvious that, for the empire to survive, the emperor had to find competent commanders to lead his soldiers. It is not immediately clear how the emperor found suitable candidates for military commands. Yet it has been argued that, not only was there a permanent body of suitably qualified men, but that these individuals enjoyed a rapid and specialized career path in order to make them available for senior posts. This theory, established by Sir Ronald Syme and Eric Birley, has been the subject of much debate.[4]

In the context of the age at which senators obtained the consulship, Syme found that:

> an exceptional and favoured category can be established, the *viri militares* who, with only the command of a legion and a praetorian province intervening, proceed in a straight run to the consulate, which they seem to reach at thirty-seven or thirty-eight.[5]

Eric Birley used similar criteria to delineate one of the three groups into which he divided senators on the basis of their relationship with the emperor. The group in which he placed the *viri militares* were 'selected with special reference to their capacity for generalship, and that they were required to offer themselves for military service before even they were qualified by age for entering the Senate'.[6] In this reconstruction, candidates were selected in their late teens for accelerated career progression towards the consulship, in order to make them available for consular commands as soon as possible. Birley also suggested that, as the number of posts expanded but the number of candidates remained the same, members of this group spent an increasingly disproportionate amount of time away from Rome and so this particular career path proved less attractive to members of established senatorial families.

The theory that there ever existed a homogenous group of *viri militares* is extremely problematic. Roman authors used the term to apply to a wide range of men with differing army ranks and experience. It certainly was not limited to senatorial officers. A comprehensive study of consular legates from the Flavians to Severus Alexander rejected the existence of a special career path. Out of seventy-three individuals, who held one or more consular legateships and whose pre-consular career path is known, only nine followed the career path specified by Syme.[7] It also demonstrated that early consulships were usually held by men from established senatorial families, who were generally excluded from senior military commands.[8] Doubts also arise on practical grounds. By selecting his future generals while they were still in their teens, the emperor ran the risk that his candidates would be killed by disease or tainted as a security risk before they had been of use to him. In AD 16, Tiberius argued against electing officials five years in advance and earmarking praetorships for legionary commanders on these grounds.[9] It is also unclear as to what criteria could be applied to detect promising military talent at such an early age. Furthermore, from the emperor's perspective, a homogenous group of competent military commanders would pose a significant threat to his own security.

The general concept of specialization in senatorial and equestrian career paths has been challenged, with particular emphasis on the latter. A study of the prefects of Egypt was undertaken as a 'test case'. This analysis demonstrated that the prefects rarely had extensive legal or military experience. Although they often had experience in the financial field, this would have been of limited use for the complexities of the Egyptian taxation system.[10] In other words, candidates for the prefecture were not selected on the basis of previous relevant experience. Rather, the emperor sought to promote men on the basis of 'general experience and moral excellence'.[11]

Undoubtedly, individuals could be promoted on the basis of military competence, particularly when such talents were especially in demand. Some commanders attained a formidable reputation, such as Sex. Julius Severus, whom Dio designates as Hadrian's best general.[12] The reigns of Marcus Aurelius and Commodus saw a number of new men promoted from equestrian status on the basis of their military potential.[13] The ravages of the Antonine Plague and the Marcomannic Wars inevitably reduced the number of potential candidates for important commands. It is therefore unsurprising that able commanders were drawn from wherever they could be found. An equestrian officer, Valerius Maximianus, attracted the attention of the emperor when he killed an enemy chief with his own hands. After a series of equestrian military posts, he was adlected into the Senate and proceeded to hold an unparalleled six legionary commands. His promotion into the senatorial order came as he reached the senior procuratorial level, which would have moved him away from active military command. His adlection was therefore designed to keep him available for active service.[14] The advancement of talented equestrians under Marcus Aurelius and Commodus did not represent the emergence of a deliberate programme of rapid advancement for able soldiers, but rather a series of *ad hoc* responses to an unprecedented decrease in available commanders caused by unusual circumstances.

The notion of a select group of *viri militares* who enjoyed an accelerated career towards the consulate is no longer tenable. Nor, in the absence of further epigraphic discoveries of relevance, can the existence of a special military caste be sustained. Prosopographical analysis is prone to identifying groups or patterns that have no significant basis in reality. Inscriptions can tell us which posts an individual held and in what order, but rarely why they received them. Even the most spectacular career need not be explained by any specific talent but rather by the favour of the emperor.[15] It stands to reason that the most trusted counsellors would be kept by the emperor's side in

Rome rather than dispatched to the provinces. Prior to his accession, Nerva had been influential with Nero and all of the Flavian emperors, but appears never to have held a provincial command. Furthermore, overt specialization was unusual in the higher levels of the imperial administration. For example, even men of predominantly military experience were promoted to the highest financial office, the secretary *a rationibus*.[16] Army commanders did not necessarily require extensive training before they took to the field.[17] There were military handbooks available under the Principate to advise them on their duties.[18] Officers could also rely on the experience and talents of their centurions, who formed the professional backbone of the army. The senators and equestrians who commanded the army were not, in general, professional soldiers but non-specialists, a point which begs the question: how enthusiastic were the upper classes at the prospect of army service?

THE ATTITUDE OF THE UPPER CLASSES TO MILITARY SERVICE

The coming of the Principate saw a profound shift in what it meant to command soldiers. The Augustan regime radically transformed the military chain of command:

> You begin with one man, whose authority is all pervasive and who oversees everything, nations, cities, legions and the generals themselves, and you end with one man who commands four or two men – for we have omitted everything in between – and when just as the spinning of thread always proceeds from a larger to a smaller number of strands, so in this way one is ever ranked after another up to the end.[19]

In this context, the entire army hierarchy was under the emperor's complete control, from the highest general to the lowest soldier. The emperor's domination over military affairs curtailed the opportunities for members of the upper classes to demonstrate their own martial competence.

Yet the ideology and values of military service remained of importance in Roman society even under the Principate, albeit under new parameters.[20] Statius makes two allusions to the prestige of conscientious military service, particularly within family traditions. In one poem he exhorts a teenage military tribune, Crispinus, to follow in his father's footsteps. The father in question was Vettius Bolanus, governor of Britain, and Statius imagines a native showing Crispinus various fortifications and arms dedicated on account of victories by his father.[21] Elsewhere, Statius has a young boy being encouraged by his warlike grandfather to remember the 'triumphs of the house' in the hope that he will accomplish worthy feats.[22] The bellicose grandfather can be identified as C. Hosidius Geta, who was awarded *ornamenta triumphalia* for his role in the invasion of Britain.[23]

Similarly, Cassius Longinus, a prominent jurist, conducted his military duties in Syria while governor with exceptional diligence, particularly with regards to discipline and training, on account of his family traditions.[24] Under Tiberius, M. Furius Camillus was eager to engage Tacfarinas as a means of restoring his family's martial reputation and establishing that he lived up to the deeds of his ancestors.[25] More graphically, an inscription erected by a proconsul of Africa revels in the exploits of his son: 'What great courage is revealed! The sword is red from killing the enemy and worn away with the slaughter; the spear by which the fierce barbarians were pierced and fell completes the trophy.'[26] The preoccupation with familial standards of behaviour, which was prevalent in the Roman upper classes during both the Republic and Principate, encouraged a conscientious attitude towards military command.

Enthusiasm for martial affairs is also evident in individual responses to military titles. Marcus Holconius Rufus, *Augusti sacerdos* at Pompeii, received the title of *tribunus militum a populo* from Augustus, which elevated him to the equestrian order. Although the rank does not appear to have involved service in the army, Holconius Rufus embraced the ideology of military command by erecting a statue of himself dressed in a cuirass, *paludamentum* and grasping a spear.[27] Interestingly, the face of the statue appears to be recut from a head of Caligula and the statue's pose is similar to imperial portraits. The distribution of honorary titles, presumably as a means of maintaining the loyalty of prominent individuals in Italian towns, indicates the value which individuals attached to military office holding.[28]

For actual army commanders, an important generalship conferred prestige even in the absence of warfare. Syria represented the climax of a significant number of consular careers.[29] The lure of this attractive post was allegedly used as a means of extricating Agricola from his British governorship. Tacitus explicitly states that the Syrian command was 'always reserved for men of seniority'.[30] The importance of the Syrian command can be attributed to the significant army presence in the province (four legions in the first century AD) and its proximity to Parthia, which bestowed considerable military responsibility on the office holder. It can be presumed that the distance from Rome and the immediacy of the Parthian threat allowed the governor of Syria significant latitude in dealing with emergencies of a military nature.

Republican standards of military behaviour continued to a certain extent under the Principate, particularly in the way that senators described military service in terms of their own personal autonomy. It is striking that

Tacitus' description of the activities of British governors almost completely excludes the involvement of the emperor. Tacitus' governors act like their Republican counterparts rather than imperial subordinates. A similar sense of independence is expressed in the funerary inscription of Tiberius Plautius Silvanus concerning his Moesian legateship:

> ... in this post he brought over more than 100,000 of the people who live across the Danube to pay tribute to Rome, along with their wives and children, leaders and kings. He suppressed an uprising among the Sarmatians, although he had sent a large part of his army to an expedition in Armenia; he compelled kings who had previously been unknown or hostile to the Roman people to worship the Roman military standards on the river bank which he was protecting. He sent back to the kings of the Bastarnae and the Rhoxolani ... their sons who had been captured or taken from the enemy. From some of them he took hostages and in this way strengthened and extended the peaceful security of his province. And the king of the Scythians was driven by siege from Chersonesus, which is beyond the Borysthenes. He was the first to help the corn supply in Rome by sending from his province a large amount of wheat ...[31]

The emperor plays no part in Silvanus' account of his activities in Moesia. Rather, he chose to describe his achievements as a result of his own decisions. He had no qualms in mentioning emperors elsewhere in his inscription, citing his quaestorship under Tiberius and his position as a *comes* of Claudius during the invasion of Britain. But Nero, the emperor under whom he held the Moesian command, is conspicuous by his absence. An extract from a speech by Vespasian is included, as a means of explaining his belated award of *ornamenta triumphalia*. Nero's omission can be seen as a personal *damnatio memoriae*, provoked by the deprivation of triumphal honours for his Moesian actions, for which he had to wait for Vespasian's intervention. Silvanus' evident bitterness at the delayed reward for his Moesian exploits demonstrates that the rewards and official recognition for military service were still of importance, even in the reduced forms available under the Principate.[32]

Epigraphic evidence, such as Silvanus' epitaph, demonstrates the pride that certain members of the upper classes took in their military service. The funerary inscription of Julius Quadratus Bassus reveals his outstanding army career, which included the governorships of Judaea and Dacia, as well as his involvement in the Dacian wars as *comes* of Trajan.[33] Quadratus Bassus died while governing Dacia and was carried to Asia by a full military escort under the command of a *primipilaris*. Hadrian paid for his memorial out of his personal treasury, which indicates the value that the emperor placed on his service. The highly visible nature of his repatriation undoubtedly advertised the potential rewards available to the upper classes for conscientious military service.

I have argued elsewhere that the position of commanders as the main instigators of military discipline made them a 'lightning rod' for soldiers' anger and discontent.[34] During civil wars and mutinies, officers were extremely vulnerable to physical attack by their men. The gulf between members of the upper classes and the soldiery is demonstrated by the case of Musonius Rufus, who was sent as an envoy to the Flavian troops marching on Rome and attempted to remonstrate with them by lecturing on the fallacy of war.[35] He hastily abandoned his speech when cautioned that he was in immediate physical danger. For upper class individuals, contact with ordinary soldiers was not without an element of risk.[36] Tacitus, whose wife's grandmother was murdered by rampaging troops and whose father-in-law had extensive military experience, described the soldiers as a *vulgus* or mob, and depicted the breakdown of conventional soldierly behaviour by citing acts of animalistic savagery.[37] Like Tacitus, Cassius Dio had reason to fear the troops, on the basis of threats to his personal safety made by the Praetorian Guard.[38] In this context, it is likely that there was a certain level of dislike within the upper classes towards soldiers. This is evident in the lack of attention paid to the soldiers by classical authors, who generally place a far greater emphasis on events in Rome to the detriment of the provinces and frontier areas.[39] When soldiers do appear in their narratives, it is usually as dangerous or boorish caricatures. This marginalization is intriguing, but it is unclear whether it reflects elite antipathy towards the army or simply the interests and prejudices of the authors.[40]

A possible indication of reluctance among the senatorial and equestrian classes towards military service may be found in the appearance of wives accompanying them to their provincial postings. This innovation was a product of the Principate, as it was extremely unusual for women to accompany their husbands on official business under the Republic. Augustus tried to regulate the practice by authorizing only occasional winter conjugal visits.[41] But such controls were probably relaxed for members of the imperial family, due to their longer provincial commands and the potential dynastic importance of their offspring. It is likely that the practice spread to other senior ranks under Tiberius, perhaps as a reaction to the prolonged postings which he was prone to allocate.[42]

In AD 21, the presence of governors' wives in the provinces was debated within the Senate. Aulus Caecina proposed that governors should be prohibited from taking their wives to their postings, by arguing that women exerted a negative influence and caused trouble within both the camp and province.[43] Marcus Valerius Messallinus replied to Caecina's speech by suggesting that the generally peaceful conditions in the provinces encouraged this practice. Drusus also spoke against Caecina, by citing the precedent of Livia's presence alongside Augustus in the provinces. Although Caecina's proposal was defeated, a *senatus consultum* passed three years later made provincial governors culpable for their wives' misdemeanours.[44] Nevertheless, the presence of wives and families alongside army officers became relatively widespread. The relaxation of restrictions on the presence of women in the army camps of the Principate can be explained as a measure aimed at making prolonged service in the provinces more palatable for the senatorial and equestrian classes. An additional benefit of this practice from the emperor's perspective was that it gave the officers concerned greater emotional investment in controlling their soldiers. An officer with a wife and family in the camp could not flee rapidly if mutiny broke out, as Germanicus demonstrated in AD 14.[45]

Under the emperor's dominance, the avenue to military glory was greatly restricted. In AD 8/9, Marcus Aemilius Lepidus should have received a triumph for his victories in Pannonia but, because he fought under the auspices of Augustus, had to make do with the *ornamenta triumphalia*.[46] In his *Res Gestae*, Augustus made no distinction between his own victories and those won by legates acting under his auspices.[47] Even the younger Pliny confessed that the prestige of generals could be dimmed in the face of the emperor.[48]

Augustus' rise to power did not result in an immediate restriction of military honours, but rather a gradual phasing out of the most prestigious honours available to non-members of the imperial family. According to Suetonius, Augustus lavished full triumphs on over thirty of his generals during the early part of his reign.[49] The last triumph was awarded in 19 BC to Cornelius Balbus for his actions in Africa. After this date, full triumphs were restricted to emperors and members of the imperial family. Instead, generals were awarded *ornamenta triumphalia*, which consisted of the regalia of the full triumph without the parade.[50] Other military honours were also gradually restricted. The *spolia opima* was denied to M. Licinius Crassus, who had personally killed an enemy king, because he fought under the auspices of Augustus.[51] Crassus was awarded a triumph, but the acclamation of imperator was given to the emperor instead. The last acclamation as *imperator* outside of the imperial family was granted to Junius Blaesus in AD 23 for completing the campaign against Tacfarinas.[52] The last *ovatio*, a lesser triumph, was awarded to Aulus Plautius in AD 47, as a reward for his services in the British campaign.[53]

How were the Julio-Claudian emperors able to impose such revolutionary changes in the military honours system without enduring widespread criticism from the upper classes? First, it was a gradual process created by the paradoxical need to reward supporters of the new regime while minimizing the political risk of having generals hold the title of *imperator* or parade through Rome at the head of a victorious army. The imperial family established precedents for the new system of honours. Agrippa declined to hold triumphs in 19 and 14 BC, while two years later Tiberius was permitted only triumphal honours rather than the full triumph voted to him by the Senate.[54] Balbus' triumph was recorded on the *Fasti Capitolini*. Conveniently, it took up 'the final centimetres of the bottom of the fourth pilaster, leaving no space for any further celebration to be recorded'.[55] This was a quite literal display of the fact that there would be no more triumphs outside of the imperial family.

Another factor that facilitated the reform of military honours was the change in composition of the senatorial and equestrian orders between Republic and Principate. As Tacitus noted, the upper classes had been severely depleted by the civil wars and proscriptions, leaving a core of loyal supporters of the new regime who found 'a cheerful acceptance of slavery the smoothest road to wealth and office'.[56] Beneath Tacitus' elegant turn of phrase is a demographic truth: that the majority of the older senatorial families withered away under the Principate. It is tempting to surmise that this facilitated the restriction of military awards, by reducing the number of families whose ancestors held full triumphs or the title of *imperator*.[57] The triumphal honours given under the Principate still possessed an innate social value as indicators of prestige and imperial esteem. Honorary triumphal statues immortalized the martial exploits of the generals concerned.[58] The upper classes were more alarmed that the worth of these awards would be devalued by being given to unworthy individuals, than that they were a less prestigious version of a Republican institution. Pliny mentions the awarding of triumphal statues under Domitian to 'many who had never stood in the battle line, never seen a camp, never heard a trumpet except on stage'.[59] The limited honours for military command were sought-after and remained a focus for competitive military activity.[60]

Contemporary concepts of *virtus* evolved in response to the new political circumstances of the Principate. *Virtus* could now be won, not by conquest, but by loyal and competent service under the emperor. Commanders demonstrated their *virtus* through their soldiers' competence in training and *labor*, as did the troops themselves.[61] Under Nero, commanders of the German armies engaged in competitive construction projects in the hope of reward.[62] In his speech at Lambaesis in AD 128, Hadrian emphasized the transmission of *virtus* from the commander to his soldiers: 'The outstanding manhood (*insignis virtus*) of noble Catullinus, my legate, shows itself in that under this man you are such men.'[63] Throughout his speech, Hadrian was careful to describe Catullinus as *meus legatus*, to show that Catullinus' competence ultimately flowed from the emperor himself. In this way, the relationship between Hadrian, Catullinus and the soldiers at Lambaesis conformed to the chain of command illuminated by Aelius Aristides, with a downward distribution of martial prestige and *virtus*.

Emperors sought to provide alternative outlets away from actual military activities. This attempt to redefine *virtus* is particularly visible during the reign of Domitian. After the events of AD 69 and the revolt of Saturninus, Domitian was not unaware of the danger from the unbridled ambitions of his army commanders. Similarly, his lack of personal military attributes (in contrast to his father and brother) probably motivated him to exploit prowess in hunting as a viable alternative to combat for displaying *virtus*. A bronze equestrian statue from Misenum showed Domitian in cuirass and military cloak about to kill a crouching lion.[64] Elsewhere, Domitian displayed his hunting skills during public displays at his Alban estate. According to Dio, his hatred of Acilius Glabrio was aggravated by the latter's efficient killing of a large lion at the same location, which dented his own prestige.[65]

It is highly unlikely that this imperial virtue failed to filter down to the emperor's legates and commanding officers. Hunting was a congenial activity in which to indulge during an otherwise unremarkable posting. Hunting shared many attributes with military command, not least the skilful management of a body of men in pursuit of a cunning adversary. Dio of Prusa commended hunting as a 'field for the practice of every military activity', particularly through extreme physical exertion.[66] The epigraphic record contains numerous instances of officers involved in hunts. An altar from Weardale was erected to Silvanus Invictus by a cavalry prefect, in thanks for the capture of a boar of remarkable size which his predecessors had been unable to locate.[67] A centurion at Cologne set up two dedications to Diana on account of capturing fifty bears in six months, a phenomenal undertaking in any era.[68] The Vindolanda tablets also contain references to hunting. In one letter, the commander requests that his counterpart in another unit send him hunting nets, and elsewhere mentions '*venatores mei*'.[69] Imperial encouragement of hunting by military officers may have sometimes been of a more direct nature. An inscription from Lower Moesia records a hunt for bears and bison undertaken by an auxiliary tribune. The hunt was ordered by the emperor, Antoninus Pius, and organized by the provincial governor. As well as his own unit, the tribune was given vexillations from two legions and the Moesian fleet to accomplish his task. In this case, the military chain of command and a large amount of manpower were utilized for the purposes of a hunt, probably to obtain animals for the games held in Rome in AD 148.[70] It is a particularly graphic illustration of the importance of hunting, and its affinity with *virtus*, in the imperial army.

As I have described elsewhere, the vast size of the empire imposed severe restrictions on the movement of information.[71] This had drastic implications for the level of autonomy given to provincial governors. The absence of any centralized military bureaucracy at Rome suggests that the governors were well equipped to handle intelligence gathering and collation in the provinces.[72] Recourse to the emperor would have been impossible in cases where an immediate response was required. Emperors issued their provincial governors, *legati* and other appointees with *mandata* which covered matters of an administrative, legal and military nature. The exact contents are difficult to reconstruct as the extant evidence is confined to a few scattered references.[73] It is reasonable to assume that, in some cases, the *mandata* contained instructions of specific relevance to the military situation in a certain province or geographical area.[74] Indeed, the military contents of the *mandata* may have consisted of 'rules of engagement' to be followed by the commander concerned. Certain scenarios could be predicted in advance with some confidence and instructions could be provided in advance on details such as the forces to be mobilized, dispositions to be adopted and the level of support to be expected from other governors, should a particular scenario be realized. A possible example of the utilization of such instructions can be found in the response to the Frisian refusal to pay tribute. According to Tacitus' account, the governor of Lower Germany, Lucius Apronius, attacked the tribe on his own initiative using reinforcements from Upper Germany.[75] If imperial sanction had not been obtained directly for the operation, it can be assumed that the governors of the German provinces were following a procedure laid down in their respective *mandata*.

Obviously not all possible military scenarios could be predicted in advance. When the Roman candidate for the Armenian throne was killed in AD 51, the governor of Syria decided not to react but nevertheless sent a delegation to Pharasmanes 'for fear of condoning the crime or receiving contrary orders from Claudius'.[76] In other cases, commanders probably temporarily overstepped their instructions in order to deal with an emerging crisis. When Corbulo launched a campaign against the Chauci, Claudius sent a letter to him ordering that he withdraw behind the Rhine. The imperial dispatch suggests that Corbulo had written to the emperor for permission to exceed the instructions he had previously received.[77] The emperor wrote to his subordinates with detailed information for specific circumstances. Thus, Tiberius sent Vitellius a directive on how to resume diplomatic contacts with Artabanus.[78] Alternatively, a commander could write to the emperor to request his instructions over a specific issue. In AD 72, the governor of Syria informed Vespasian that the king of Commagene was conspiring with the Persians and requested imperial sanction for an invasion.[79]

Slow communication speeds across the empire gave the *legati* a degree of autonomy in responding to military crises. But they could not disregard the emperor's wishes and, while awaiting the emperor's orders, often had to predict his decision and respond accordingly. This inevitably provoked hesitation in pursuing a military course of action. When news broke of Tiberius' death, L. Vitellius withdrew from a campaign against the Nabataeans because he had not been empowered to wage war by the new ruler.[80] Corbulo refused to accept Caesennius Paetus' invitation to invade Armenia because he had not received direct authorization from the emperor.[81] Clearly Corbulo had learnt from his mistake under Claudius. The adverse impact on military efficiency from restraining the activities of army commanders was far outweighed by the need to prevent disastrous losses and maintain the martial prestige of the emperor.

It has been argued that the bloodshed of the civil wars decreased elite enthusiasm for military commands.[82] This argument is mainly based on the relative scarcity of literary references to army life. But this approach may be too schematic. For example, the almost total lack of references to the Dacian wars within Pliny's correspondence, even in letters to officers actively engaged in combat operations, could be viewed as evidence for a contemporary lack of interest in military affairs.[83] But these letters were literary constructs and were carefully edited for publication. In another context, the *Panegyricus* in praise of Trajan, Pliny was eager to praise the martial exploits of the new ruler. Handbooks written during the period in question demonstrate a continuing interest in military themes.[84]

There is another factor that has a bearing on upper class attitudes to warfare, namely the demographic shift in the composition of the upper classes, particularly during the Triumviral period. Men gained access to military and political offices who previously had little hope of attaining them.[85] Lucius Munatius Plancus was a *novus homo* who triumphed over the Raeti in 43 BC, was twice hailed as imperator and founded colonies at Lugdunum and Rauria.[86] He defected from the Antonian camp shortly before Actium and went on to become a staunch adherent of Augustus. Work began on his funerary monument at Gaeta, which echoes Augustus' mausoleum, around 20 BC. The monument is decorated with a continuous frieze that depicts military equipment and decorations, which serve to reinforce the martial emphasis of the inscription. The mausoleum may even have been topped by a victory trophy.[87] Plancus' monument displays personal pride in his army service and argues forcefully against a reluctance to engage in military affairs. Men whose access to high office had been facilitated by the upheavals of the civil wars were proud of their engagement in Rome's martial tradition.

The monopoly of the emperor over military affairs inevitably had an impact on the behaviour of his subordinates. Certain emperors were extremely suspicious of their army commanders. Domitian is a prime example of this, not least in his behaviour towards Agricola.[88] Pliny claims that Domitian's legates were paralysed by their fear of both the emperor and the soldiers.[89] This paralysis can be perceived in the almost total lack of tactical innovation in the imperial army up until the reforms of the later empire. The stagnation in tactical development is evident in Rome's failure to deal adequately with the rise of the Sasanian dynasty in the former Parthian empire.[90] Rome's military apparatus had failed to evolve and adapt to changing strategic circumstances, a weakness from which its enemies did not suffer. Only with the reforms of Diocletian and Constantine, which reorganized the old legionary-based army, did Rome respond adequately to the threats that the empire faced. Some of the blame for this failure to adapt can be placed on the army commanders' unwillingness to innovate, caused by their desire to avoid arousing the emperors' suspicions. Domitian executed Sallustius Lucullus, governor of Britain, because he developed a new cavalry lance, which he named after himself.[91] We cannot know whether the emperor was angered by the development of a new weapon or the fact that the governor assumed responsibility for it, but it is clear that such incidents cannot have encouraged a proactive approach to military command. It can be argued that military initiative and innovation were stifled by the non-specialist approach to army appointments, imperial interference and fear of incurring the emperor's wrath.

Like all aspects of the army, the emperor had to manage the ambitions and activities of his generals. In praising Antoninus Pius for the successful conclusion of a campaign in Britain, Fronto claimed that:

> ... although he had committed the conduct of the campaign to others, while sitting at home himself in the Palace at Rome, yet like the helmsman at the tiller of a ship of war, the glory of the whole navigation and voyage belonged to him.[92]

Fronto's metaphor of the emperor as a helmsman, directing the course of military campaigns from afar, is apt. It was in the emperor's interests to tightly control the activities of his army commanders for both practical and security reasons. There was always the possibility that ill-advised actions could draw Rome into a wider conflict. Poorly planned campaigns may also result in severe manpower shortages, which adversely affected the security of the empire as a whole, as in the disastrous loss of Varus' legions in Germany.[93]

Augustus compared the undertaking of massive risk in the hope of reward with fishing using a golden hook, in that the possible gain could never equal the potential loss. He urged that no campaign or battle should ever be fought unless the chance of victory outweighed the possibility of defeat.[94] The emperor also needed to ensure that none of his army officers would use their commands as a platform for a coup.[95]

AGRICOLA: A GOVERNOR IN CONFLICT

The career of Julius Agricola is unusual for a number of reasons. First, for the wealth of information we have on his activities in Britain from the account written by his son-in-law Tacitus. Second, his gubernatorial tenure was longer than any other British governor on record and indeed many others from the rest of the empire. Finally, he is the only individual known to have served his military tribunate, legionary command and governorship in the same province. Agricola's career was transformed by Tacitus into a grand narrative about the successes of a great general who is nevertheless retired into obscurity at the whim of a jealous emperor and forced to see his territorial gains relinquished. Beneath the biographical detail is an ever-present political moral, that good men can do great things even under tyrannical rulers.[96] I suggest that an alternative reading of the *Agricola* is preferable to the conventional interpretation. In this reconstruction Agricola emerges as a governor torn between his desire for personal martial *virtus* and the restrictions placed upon him by the emperor.

It is not unusual for modern scholars to view Agricola as a 'British specialist *par excellence*'.[97] But this claim can be refuted for a number of reasons. His long tenure in Britain was due to the fact that it straddled the reigns of three emperors: Vespasian, Titus and Domitian. The delay in his recall can be attributed to political events elsewhere in the empire and it is not unlikely that the deaths of both Vespasian and Titus significantly extended his tenure. Agricola's unique status as the only individual on record to have served as tribune, legionary legate and governor in the same province is intriguing. Yet it does not necessarily indicate a particular geographical specialization on his part. There would surely be other examples from across the empire if this were the case. The practice of serving as legionary commander in the same legion or provincial army as the tribunate was not particularly unusual.[98] Such coincidences inevitably happened, even if a system of completely random appointments was in operation. Similarly, there are a number of instances of governors commanding provinces in which they had previously served as legionary legates or tribunes.[99] Only in Agricola's case are all three posts held in the same province. However, the concept of specialization is not required to explain this. He was given his legionary command because the unsavoury reputation and undisciplined behaviour of that particular legion discouraged more suitable candidates.[100] Agricola probably saw a chance to win the attention of the new Flavian regime by accepting a post that no one else wanted.

Agricola's posts outside of Britain were of a decidedly unmilitary nature. He served as quaestor in Asia and governor of Aquitania, which had no military presence whatsoever.[101] Indeed, it is not inconceivable that Agricola was appointed as governor of Britain on the basis of his administrative experience, in order to supervise the civic reconstruction of the province in the aftermath of the warfare over the past twenty years.[102] Tacitus is careful to note that Agricola's campaigns began after the Ordovices attacked a cavalry *ala*; perhaps recounting Agricola's official explanation for his military endeavours.[103]

Agricola pursued an aggressive policy of conquest during his governorship. But there is reason to doubt Tacitus' emphasis on his father-in-law's military abilities. Recent archaeological research demonstrates that the major northern advances in the first century AD were probably made during the governorship of Petillius Cerialis. Dendrochronological dates for timbers from the fort at Carlisle prove that it was built under Cerialis, and excavations in Scotland hint at an earlier occupation before Agricola's governorship.[104] Petillius Cerialis, the son-in-law of Vespasian, is a more suitable candidate for advancing into Scotland, particularly in light of his previous unimpressive performance during the Boudiccan revolt.[105]

Even Agricola's great battle at Mons Graupius can be significantly downgraded from the importance attached to it in much modern scholarship. It is suspicious that the existence of the battle is based only on Tacitus' account.[106] Pliny and Suetonius, both of whom can be assumed to have read the *Agricola*, are silent on the matter. Xiphilinus' epitome of Cassius Dio emphasizes Agricola's circumnavigation of Britain (which was embarrassingly first accomplished by a group of deserters) rather than his martial achievements.[107] The ominous silence concerning the battle in other ancient sources suggests that it was little more than a skirmish. Indeed, the fact that Agricola only deployed his auxiliary forces in the battle supports this hypothesis.[108]

Although he was rewarded with triumphal honours, it is also clear that Agricola incurred the displeasure of Domitian. Tacitus attributes this to the emperor's jealousy of his successes. Although it may be the case that Domitian was angered by any governor whose success detracted from his own victories in Germany, it is entirely possible that Agricola took advantage of the rapid turnover of Flavian emperors during his governorship to pursue military glory for his own ends. A useful analogy can be drawn with a letter from M. Caelius Rufus to Cicero, who was himself no stranger to attempting to gain military glory on the slightest of pretexts:

> If we could only get the balance right so that a war came along of just the right size for the strength of your forces and we achieved what was needed for glory and a triumph without facing a really dangerous and serious clash – that would be the dream ticket.[109]

Mons Graupius was just such an engagement, in terms of both its size and importance. In the mind of an ambitious governor it could easily be transformed from a minor skirmish to a battle of epic proportions.

The bizarre events surrounding Agricola's departure from Britain suggest that he was perceived as a threat to the emperor. An imperial freedman was dispatched with a letter promising the governorship of Syria as the crowning achievement of his career. The letter was only to be delivered if Agricola had not yet left the province. Finding that Agricola was on his way across the Channel, the freedman returned to Rome with the letter.[110] If this episode has not been inordinately exaggerated by Tacitus, it suggests that Domitian was eager to extract Agricola from the province as quickly and as quietly as possible. On his return to Rome, he was snubbed by the emperor and received no further imperial appointments. It could be argued that Domitian is unlikely to have let a potential threat against him survive. On the other hand, Agricola's retirement came before the later purges. Furthermore, the Flavian dynasty had a habit of quietly retiring potentially dangerous generals, such as Antonius Primus and Verginius Rufus, rather than taking offensive action against them. This policy evidently later changed under Domitian, and it is noteworthy that the next recorded governor of Britain was executed.[111]

Tacitus' role in the formulation of Agricola's recorded exploits should not be overlooked. As a member of the senatorial order, he was also subject to the same competitive drive to demonstrate personal excellence. Tacitus appears not to have acquired any significant military experience, but his father-in-law's exploits undoubtedly made up for this deficit. Tacitus' affection for Agricola is evident in the text and his account may also have served as an apologetic for Agricola's conduct. Tacitus stresses Agricola's martial excellence, even excusing his civilian governorship of Aquitania as fulfilling the soldier's need for civil judicial experience.[112] Much of Tacitus' account has the flavour of the after-dinner musings of an old general, not least Agricola's naïve assertion that he could have conquered Ireland with a single legion and accompanying auxiliary units.[113] I have argued above that members of the senatorial and equestrian order were torn between the conflicting needs of exhibiting personal *virtus* and obeying imperial demands. I suggest that Agricola's behaviour, and Tacitus' account, is a graphic demonstration of this tension.

PATRONAGE

The persona that commanders presented to their men was extremely ambiguous.[114] On the one hand, they acted as *commilitones*, exerting themselves to display a shared identity with the soldiers by participating in the rigours of army life.[115] Effeminate or unmanly officers were scorned by the rank and file.[116] Yet the soldiers appreciated both the distinguished ancestry and aristocratic prestige of their officers.[117] Dio claimed soldiers despised commanders who lacked elite status.[118] Pride in serving under aristocratic commanders is evident even on soldiers' tombstones, where care is taken to identify the status of individual generals.[119] In this way, the army hierarchy echoed the structure of wider society.

The workings of patronage, which permeated every level of Roman society, played a significant role in military appointments. In a letter to Trajan, Pliny requested further military advancement for Nymphidius Lupus after his command of a cohort lapsed. Pliny states that he had known the latter's father, a *primipilaris*, since his military tribunate, and thus felt responsible for his offspring. In closing his letter, Pliny claims: 'Any promotion which you confer on my friend's son, sir, will give me also an occasion for personal rejoicing.'[120] A variety of individuals, usually of close proximity to the emperor, are described as obtaining military appointments for their favoured candidates. Vespasian was granted his legionary command by Narcissus.[121] Didius Julianus received his military appointment through the *suffragium* of Marcus Aurelius' mother, Domitia Lucilla, in whose household he had been raised.[122] Pertinax gained his military tribunate through the influence of Marcus Aurelius' son-in-law, Claudius Pompeianus.[123] Septimius Severus was granted his Danubian command by Aemilius Laetus, the Praetorian Prefect.[124] Even a Vestal Virgin, Campia Severina, was instrumental in obtaining a number of military appointments.[125]

Pliny's correspondence provides the vast majority of the extant evidence for the distribution of military tribunates by legates, rather than directly by the emperor.[126] In a highly revealing letter, he thanks Pompeius Falco for a military tribunate that he has conferred on a young friend of Pliny's. But it is only in this letter that Pliny provides Falco with the name and background of the new tribune.[127] Falco must have given the tribunate to Pliny's candidate without knowing anything of his background or qualities. A similar process is probably described in a letter to Suetonius, in which Pliny agrees to transfer the tribunate that he obtained for him from Neratius Marcellus to a relative: 'Your name is not yet entered on the lists, so it is easy for me to substitute that of Silvanus.'[128] The ease with which Pliny was able to transfer the tribunate suggests that Marcellus did not know the intended recipient. The only other evidence for the direct distribution of tribunates by imperial legates is a letter from the governor of Britannia Inferior dated to AD 222, which promised a tribunate, items of military dress and a salary of 25,000 sesterces to a Gallic friend as soon as a vacancy became available.[129]

The qualities emphasized in Pliny's letters for appointments and promotions are predominantly of a social nature, in terms of family background, moral outlook and general education. Indeed, the qualities he describes are indistinguishable from those sought for in a prospective aristocratic bridegroom.[130] Admirable social qualities were of value when appointing subordinate officers with whom one would have to socialize for long periods. Tacitus contrasted Agricola's productive tribunate with his colleagues who spent their time idly enjoying themselves and disappearing on leave.[131] A letter from Vindolanda was probably written by the commanding officer to a senator close to Neratius Marcellus, the provincial governor. The author requests that the recipient, Crispinus, provide him with 'friends that, thanks to you, I may be able to enjoy a pleasant period of military service'.[132] The author may be seeking further contact with those closest to the governor or agreeable candidates for posts at Vindolanda so that the commander could enjoy his posting in a companionable environment. Even the emperor was not above basing his appointments on social qualities. After spending two days drinking with them, Tiberius appointed Pomponius Flaccus as legate of Syria and L. Calpurnius Piso as urban prefect.[133]

An unrestrained distribution of military posts posed a threat to the security of the emperor, in that an important commander could build his own army faction. The emperor must have had a level of oversight concerning the allocation of appointments. Senior commands were probably only given by the emperor himself, although his trusted advisors could probably influence his decisions. Legionary commands also appear to have been distributed by the emperor, rather than his imperial legates. There are only four clear instances of legionary legates serving under close kinsmen, and two of these (Annius Vinicianus under Corbulo and Titus under Vespasian) were the result of unusual military commands.[134] The monopoly of the emperor over legionary command appointments was presumably designed to create a buffer layer of men who owed their posts to the emperor directly beneath the provincial governors. Tensions between legionary legates and governors are evident in Britain in AD 69, when the legates deposed the governor Trebellius

Maximus and ruled the province until his successor arrived.[135] On the other
hand, the distribution of tribunates by army commanders was relatively safe
as they were balanced by the directly appointed legionary legates. It is also
highly unlikely that any army commander would have had the opportunity
to select all of the tribunes in each of the legions under his personal control.

Some emperors took a personal interest in the appointments made by their
subordinates, perhaps by scrutinizing the lists of candidates mentioned by
Pliny in his letter to Suetonius. According to Macrobius, a man who had been
removed from his cavalry prefecture requested that Augustus still grant him
his salary so as not to face humiliation. The emperor advised the unfortunate
individual to tell everyone that he had received his pay and promised not to
deny it.[136] Vespasian withdrew a commission when the recipient delivered a
speech of thanks while drenched in perfume, claiming that he would have
preferred the candidate to smell of garlic.[137] In times of crisis, particularly
after a change of ruler, direct imperial control over military appointments
may have been imposed over a wider range of offices to ensure the security of
the new regime. Anecdotal evidence concerning the beginning of Vespasian's
reign shows this process in action. Dio records that Domitian and Mucianus
appointed such a large number of consuls, governors and prefects in rapid
succession that Vespasian wrote to thank his youngest son for allowing him
to remain as emperor.[138] In a similar vein, Suetonius preserves an anecdote
that, after Domitian made twenty appointments in a single day, Vespasian
expressed surprise that his successor had not also been appointed.[139]

The main threat from the prevalence of patronage in a military context was
that a general could gather support for a seizure of power by appointing his
supporters to crucial posts. Certainly, senior commanders were in a position
to dispense patronage to potential supporters. Fronto wrote to Avidius Cassius
concerning Junius Maximus, the tribune who travelled to Rome with news
of the conclusion of the Parthian War and lost no opportunity to boast of his
commander's exploits. He urged Cassius to reward his tribune: 'He deserves
your love and to profit by your patronage. Whatever you do to enhance the
honour of your eulogist will redound to your own glory.'[140]

It has been argued that Domitius Corbulo's prolonged tenure in the East
gave him ample opportunity to extend his *clientela* among the soldiers
and officers of the Eastern army and, more controversially, that this group
continued to act in unison after his death and facilitated the Flavian seizure
of power.[141] Corbulo's senatorial *legati* included Aurelius Fulvus, Marius
Celsus, Rutilius Gallicus and Vettius Bolanus; all of whom prospered under
the Flavian regime. His non-senatorial officers included Arrius Varus and
Tiberius Julius Alexander, both of whom were instrumental in bringing
Vespasian to power.[142] As well as the career patterns of former Corbulonian

officers, further evidence for Corbulo's importance to the Flavian regime can be found in the marriage of his daughter, Domitia Longina, to Domitian.

Despite the prosopographical evidence, the existence of any organized group of Corbulonian loyalists is extremely problematic. Corbulo represents the essence of a loyal general in his relationship with Nero and there is no firm evidence to suggest that he was ever involved in treasonous activities. This point is emphasized by Tiridates' remark to Nero, that in Corbulo the emperor had a good slave.[143] On the other hand, Corbulo had a formidable reputation as a strict disciplinarian who imposed a harsh regime over his army. The failure of the Eastern legions to revolt against Nero after Corbulo's death sheds doubt on his popularity among the rank and file. Although Corbulo's army group was broken up after his death, none of his officers were punished for their service under his command. Even if Corbulo left behind no subversive political agenda, it has been argued that his demise created a power vacuum that Vespasian filled by absorbing his *clientela*.[144] But it seems more likely that officers who had witnessed the downfall of their commanding officer, but decided not to act on his behalf, would seek to ingratiate themselves with the emperor rather than risk his wrath by giving their loyalty to another general. And even the most rapacious thirst for vengeance would have been quenched by Nero's death. The accession of Vespasian could play no logical part in any act of revenge on Corbulo's behalf.

The existence of the Corbulonian group owes much to the prosopographical method and its propensity to find connections and groups where none existed in reality.[145] In some cases, the inclusion of an individual within the Corbulonian group rests on a suspiciously circular argument. For example, Licinius Mucianus, who played an integral role in the Flavian usurpation, is included in the group on the sole basis of a reference by the elder Pliny to the fact that both Mucianus and Corbulo found the source of the Euphrates.[146] The importance allotted to former Corbulonian officers is due to their prominence in the surviving historical record, particularly in Tacitus' writings.

An examination of legionary legates shows that only three others are known to have served elsewhere in the empire during Corbulo's tenure in the East: Cornelius Pusio, Petillius Cerialis and Caesius Nasica.[147] Pusio became consul in AD 70 but is otherwise unknown. Cerialis was married to Vespasian's daughter and prospered under the new regime. Nasica has left no further record, but may have been Cerialis' elder brother.[148] His lack of further advancement probably indicates a premature death. This suggests that Corbulo's legates are unusual for the information we have on them and that their advancement under the Flavian regime is not necessarily surprising when compared to their contemporaries.

The marriage between Domitian and Corbulo's daughter seems significant in hindsight because he became emperor. But the marriage itself probably took place in AD 70, when Titus was the heir apparent and equipped with a strong soldierly reputation.[149] Domitian, on the other hand, was Titus' younger brother with no martial reputation. The concept that Domitian and Domitia were tasked with producing a grandson of Corbulo and Vespasian who would rule the empire is sheer fantasy.[150] If a dynastic marriage was intended to appease Corbulo's former officers, Titus would have been a far more advantageous bridegroom than his decidedly unimpressive younger brother. The significance of the marriage may, in fact, have been as part of Vespasian's policy of rewarding generals whose achievements had been neglected under Nero, as in the case of Tiberius Plautius Silvanus described above.[151] The marriage of Corbulo's daughter to a member of the new ruling house was intended to demonstrate that the general's reputation had been rehabilitated. Of course, such a move would have pleased individuals who had been close to Corbulo, but it is unlikely to have had any wider political motive.

Although the existence of a Corbulonian group equipped with a vendetta against Nero and a political agenda which continued under the next dynasty can be quashed, there remains the extraordinary adhesion of Corbulo's former officers to the Flavian cause. But there is no need to seek a political motive in this. As I have shown above, army postings encouraged and exploited social ties. Indeed, the whole system of military appointments and promotions existed within a nexus of patronal connections and obligations. It is therefore not surprising that in times of crisis men would seek the support of capable individuals whom they knew and trusted from previous experience. Rather than seeing Corbulo's prolonged command in the East as the opportunity to build up a vast military *clientela*, we should view it as fertile ground for a wealth of social relationships to form between his officers, which would re-emerge during the dangerous events of AD 69.

POLITICAL SECURITY AS A SIGNIFICANT FACTOR IN IMPERIAL APPOINTMENTS

The emperor relied upon his senatorial and equestrian officers to micromanage the army in person. But the sheer size of the empire and the concentration of the army in specific frontier areas tempted generals with the possibility of creating their own personal fiefdoms. Under Tiberius, Gaetulicus, the governor of Upper Germany, ventured to inform the emperor that he would retain his post indefinitely and view any replacement as an indication of his impending doom.[152] Tiberius appears to have had considerable trouble in filling his provincial commands and complained to the Senate that capable individuals refused the posts he offered them, including the Syrian command. Yet he kept Aelius Lamia and L. Arruntius, governors of Syria and Tarraconensis respectively in Rome for a decade. His procrastination in this case is strange, but could be explained as a concession to eminent individuals who wanted to hold a prestigious post without having to actually carry out the duties associated with it.[153]

The constant dilemma facing the emperor was to find men fit for military command who would execute their duties competently, without using it as a platform for a coup: 'he was afraid that the most able men would be a threat to himself, while fools would cause a public disgrace'.[154] Forthright claims of military talent were dangerous under the Principate. Cornelius Gallus, the first prefect of Egypt, was disgraced for setting up statues of himself and incising inscriptions that claimed that he had advanced further south than any previous Roman army or Egyptian monarch.[155] Gaius Silius was destroyed by Tiberius for foolishly boasting publicly that the emperor held the Principate only because he alone had prevented his troops from joining the mutinies of AD 14.[156] In Tacitus' memorable phrase: 'Qualities in other directions could more easily be ignored, but good generalship should be the monopoly of the emperor.'[157]

A startling insight into the potential threat that imperial officials posed to the emperor is revealed in the *senatus consultum de Cn. Pisone Patre*. In particular, this remarkable document demonstrates that the discourse on the virtue of loyalty was embedded in imperial ideology. Piso represents the direct antithesis of what an army commander should be, in both his attitude and behaviour. He acted on his own authority and ignored instructions from the emperor as well as letters from Germanicus and, in doing so, provoked war between Armenia and Parthia, contrary to the wishes of Tiberius.[158] More significantly, Piso had attempted to stir up civil war. The *senatus consultum* attributes the ending of the periods of civil war and the restoration of peace to Augustus and Tiberius, a view shared by Velleius.[159] The coming of the Principate is seen as a restoration of peace and security, Piso's actions promise a return to the chaos and bloodshed of the late Republic.

Piso's crimes ultimately did not concern his behaviour towards Germanicus, which is afforded little attention in the *senatus consultum*, but his interference with the military hierarchy and his suspicious behaviour in winning the support of the soldiers. His behaviour in many ways resembled that of a senator during the late Republic, notably in his shameless self promotion and blatant encouragement of factionalism among the troops.[160] It is tempting to see in Tiberius' reign a crisis of identity among the men who held (or should have held) provincial commands. Just as the mutinies of AD 14 may have represented a crisis of identity among the soldiery concerning what it actually meant to be an imperial soldier in terms of both duties and privileges, so too may a similar crisis have affected the emperor's senior commanders. Some of them, like Gaetulicus and Piso, acted like Republican officials rather than imperial subordinates. The stagnation in imperial appointments evident during his reign could have been caused by the unwillingness of suitable candidates to accept provincial posts owing to concerns about gauging their level of autonomy and relationships with the soldiers. The aberrant behaviour of certain army commanders should be seen as part of the wider discourse on the duties of an army commander under the empire.

Arguably, the most important statement in the *senatus consultum de Cn. Pisone Patre* is also one of the most overlooked in scholarly examinations of the text. In thanking the soldiers for their continuing loyalty to the imperial family, it states:

> The Senate believes that it belongs to their concern and duty that, among those who command them at any time, the greatest authority with them should belong to those who have with most devoted loyalty honoured the name of the Caesars, which gives protection to this city and to the empire of the Roman people.[161]

In other words, command authority rested not on military ability or competence, but on loyalty to the Julio-Claudian house. It is worth reiterating that this section is addressed directly to the soldiers themselves and copies of the text were to be set up in the legionary winter camps. There can be no clearer illustration of the fact that the soldiers were empowered to disregard any commander who was disloyal to the emperor or his family. Imperial loyalty was thus a key factor in the appointment and ideology of army commanders.[162]

As well as the soldiers, the emperor could rely on the ambitions of his subordinates to promote loyalty among his army commanders. Tensions between equestrian and senatorial officials could result in letters of complaint to the emperor and even occasional acts of outright violence. Thus a procurator could achieve the recall of the governor of Britain for incompetence.[163] In AD 69, the procurator of Belgica informed Galba of Vitellius' revolt.[164] But this is not to suggest that equestrians were more loyal than senators. Conflicts inevitably arose from the competitive tensions between imperial officials in a system which promoted competition rather than co-operation.[165]

Protecting the emperor from internal threats was an ongoing process. In the aftermath of the revolt of Avidius Cassius, governors were prevented from serving in provinces from which they came, presumably to prevent them from exploiting family connections and *clientela* for nefarious purposes.[166] Patricians were usually excluded from senior military commands, to avoid any conflict with the prestige or supremacy of the emperor.[167] In times of particular worry, commands could be limited to men of undistinguished background or advanced age, such as the raft of 'safe' appointments made during the later years of Nero's reign.[168]

Throughout the Principate, military honours were increasingly awarded for acts of political loyalty. Most notably, after the suppression of the Pisonian conspiracy, Nero awarded triumphal honours to Cocceius Nerva, Petronius Turpilianus and Tigellinus for their part in the detection of the plot.[169] On a lesser scale, the unprecedented *dona* awarded to the prefect C. Julius Karus may be linked to the downfall of the British governor, Sallustius Lucullus.[170] Trajan was promoted with extraordinary speed from his legionary legateship to an ordinary consulship two years later for his route march from Spain to Germany to defeat the revolt of Saturninus. Although Trajan's troops did not have to fight, the speed with which they marched demonstrated his loyalty to the emperor, a fact which Pliny could not suppress.[171]

In his discourses on kingship, Dio of Prusa emphasized the importance of loyal friends for a king, both for his personal security and the efficiency of his administration.[172] It would be foolish to argue that loyalty alone was enough to obtain an important command for an individual. Imperial appointment policies were far more complicated and depended on a range of personal qualities, as well as the personal whim of the emperor. However, I suggest that loyalty was always a significant factor in military appointments throughout the Principate and that it attained a predominant importance under certain emperors, such as Nero in the later part of his reign and Domitian, who actively feared the possibility of military revolt.

CONCLUSION

Senators and equestrians may have sometimes feared the soldiers, but they did not necessarily fear military service. Despite the political and existential upheavals at the birth of the Principate, some things remained the same. Members of the upper classes could still take pride from their competent execution of military service. As under the Republic, individuals felt pressure to live up to familial expectations and reputation, even if their personal talents lay elsewhere. Men without distinguished ancestors could seek prestige through attaching themselves to a successful general. One of Augustus' greatest problems, and indeed one of his major successes, was how to restrict the military honours available to his army commanders while still allowing them the chance to win martial glory. The presence of the emperor irrevocably altered the level of autonomy afforded to army commanders. Even the greatest of their victories were only accomplished under his auspices. Augustus resolved this quandary by gradually restricting the rewards available for military command. Under his successor, problems remained concerning what it meant to command soldiers under the Principate. Tiberius' stagnation of provincial command appointments may be symptomatic of reluctance among the upper classes to undertake army posts. But these problems were resolved, perhaps in part by the highly public trial of Piso which iterated the official view on the acceptable behaviour of army commanders and publicized it throughout the provincial army camps. The relaxation of constraints affecting the presence of officers' families was also aimed at encouraging army service among the upper classes.

Relationships between officers were of an intrinsically social nature. Promotions were secured through patronage, based on personal qualities rather than military competence. It is not surprising that commanding officers sought genial subordinates for postings in distant lands, especially when they could rely on their centurions for experienced advice. Organized political groupings of army officers are unlikely to have existed in reality, except for temporary alliances during times of political turbulence, but friendships made during army service could re-surface later, as in the co-operation of former Corbulonian officers during the Flavian bid for power.

The lack of specialist military training is not surprising in light of the general absence of specialism within the imperial administration. Competence could be accrued through experience in post or by careful examination of contemporary military handbooks. Apart from periods of crisis, the emperor favoured other qualities in his subordinates. Most important from the emperor's viewpoint was loyalty. Emperors and generals came from the same social milieu, and the latter could replace the former with the help of military support. Augustus' policy of allowing at least limited honours to successful army commanders was prudent as very few army commanders actually proved disloyal.

Chapter 5

Political Awareness
in the Army

In his study of the army and land in the late Republic, Brunt suggested that two factors motivated Roman troops to intervene in politics, namely their own self-interest or their allegiance to a higher cause.[1] The latter presupposes that the soldiers had some knowledge of contemporary political events. The aim of this chapter is to examine the level of political awareness of soldiers based outside of Rome. I will first discuss the means by which political information could be conveyed both to and between soldiers, differentiating between formal and informal methods of communication and the level of control which the emperor was able to exert over these. The imperial coinage as a particularly effective method of disseminating political information will be examined, especially with regard to the possibility of selective targeting of political messages to specific military units. Demonstrations of loyalty by the soldiers to the emperor and imperial family reveal the relationship between the *princeps* and his troops and function as an indicator of political awareness. I will speculate on the political beliefs of the soldiers themselves and the specific traits they looked for in an emperor. The actual level of political awareness of the soldiers is best assessed by their reactions to events within the imperial family. In the final section of this chapter I will explore the reactions of the troops to the deaths of Drusus, Germanicus and Geta. This analysis will demonstrate that the involvement of the military in politics was influenced by their political awareness and the imperial propaganda to which they were exposed.

THE DISSEMINATION OF INFORMATION

The infrastructure of the Roman army promoted information flow.[2] Roads, forts, signal stations and messengers all acted to increase the speed of communication between military units. Undoubtedly, the primary aim of this infrastructure was for strategic purposes, to facilitate the rapid movement of reinforcements in times of emergency. But this network also encouraged the spread of other types of information including, it may be argued, news of a political nature.

The dissemination of information across the empire was accomplished by both formal and informal means. Although a usurper could appeal to the soldiers' financial greed and even their local loyalties, the emperor alone was able to formally distribute favourable political information to military units across the empire. The order that the *Senatus Consultum de Cn. Pisone Patre* be set up in the winter quarters of the legions reveals a means of disseminating political information to the troops.[3] A letter from Hadrian to Rammius, prefect of Egypt, regarding the legal privileges of serving soldiers' offspring was displayed in the *principia* at Nicopolis.[4] Both of the legions based in Egypt during this period used the camp and therefore the display of this document was aimed at communicating information to as many troops as possible. The actual method of displaying the text is unclear but the permanent relevance of the information and the imperial command that it be disseminated to the troops suggests that it may have been inscribed on bronze or stone. From a later period, a letter issued by Licinius in AD 311 regarding military tax privileges was published on bronze by imperial command.[5] In all of these cases, the information was of political importance to the soldiers. The wide dissemination of news regarding military legal privileges fostered support for the emperor among the troops.

The Roman military calendar was also a means of distributing political information to the soldiers. The *Feriale Duranum* records religious festivals celebrated by an auxiliary unit, cohors XX Palmyrenorum, based at Dura-Europos around AD 225–7.[6] Over half of the festivals recorded on the document are connected to the imperial cult. The lack of any mention of local cult deities suggests that this text was created in Rome and distributed to military units across the empire.[7] Several festivals celebrating various events in the life of the reigning emperor, Severus Alexander, are mentioned including the anniversaries of his first consulship, the awarding of imperial titles and his salutation as *imperator* by the soldiers. It is likely that an official military calendar was issued by each new emperor with the addition of various celebrations of important events in his own life. The inclusion of these curial dates demonstrated to the soldiers that the emperor was fit to rule by displaying the various honours and titles that he had received. Festivals dedicated to other members of the imperial family emphasized the importance of the imperial dynasty as a whole. By highlighting the dynastic connections of current and past emperors, the military calendar served to iterate the tradition of obedience which prevailed throughout the army.

The Roman imperial army was a fluid rather than a static entity. The movement of troops, on official and unofficial business, promoted the informal spread of information. Unofficial communication between military units is evident in the spread of mutinies and rebellions.[8] The transmission of discontent was likely to have been accomplished by a variety of different means, reflecting the numerous ways troops could come into contact with other military units. During the mutinies of AD 14, there is evidence of contact between the mutineers and other soldiers. In Pannonia, Vibulenus claimed that his brother had been sent from the legions in Germany to discuss their common interests.[9] While this claim was false, the fact that the troops believed it indicates that communication between legions on this level was feasible. Soldiers in Lower Germany prepared a delegation to incite mutiny among the legions in Upper Germany.[10] In AD 69, the soldiers of various provincial armies attempted to communicate with each other by letter, presumably for their own political ends.[11]

The events of AD 14 and 69 were highly unusual and are not indicative of the general state of affairs throughout the period in question. However, there is enough evidence to conclude that contact and interaction between soldiers of different units was by no means unusual. Unit strength reports, although rare, provide a valuable insight into the deployments of military formations. A report from Vindolanda shows that out of a garrison of 752 men and 6 centurions, only 296 soldiers and a single centurion were actually present in the fort when the document was created.[12] A papyrus showing the strength of a unit in Egypt from the early second century AD also records a large number of men away from the military base.[13] Around 27 per cent of the unit were scattered over a wide area of countryside. A military document from Caerleon which probably records the future deployment of legionaries suggests that the posting and movement of troops over a large area was by no means confined to auxiliary units.[14] Indeed, it has been suggested that the position of the main base of a Roman unit may not represent the actual location of the majority of the soldiers.[15] The movement of troops recorded in these documents are limited to the same province as the rest of the unit. However there were more wide ranging movements of military units as *vexillationes*, usually in times of impending military action.[16] At the time of the death of Nero, for example, a large number of troops from a variety of different provinces were gathered at Rome in preparation for a campaign against the Alani.[17] Detachments that had taken part in conflicts elsewhere would return to their provinces with news regarding the prosecution of the campaign. This became a particular issue with campaigns that turned into fiascos such as Caligula's aborted invasion of Britain and Trajan's Parthian campaign. The transfer of a whole legion from one province to another was not unknown, although it was likely to have been unpopular with the soldiers themselves who probably developed ties with the local population. A legion that had recently been transferred from Syria, III Gallica, gathered support for Vespasian among the Moesian legions.[18]

As well as the official deployment of troops, which prompted the movement and interaction of soldiers of different units and thus promoted the spread of information, there were unofficial means by which soldiers could gather information about political events. Courier duty was open to abuse as soldiers could avail themselves of the opportunity to visit friends and relatives. A particularly interesting Egyptian papyrus contains a letter from a soldier to his mother.[19] The soldier, Saturnilus, states that he aims to visit her when he is sent as a courier to the prefect in Alexandria. Saturnilus indicates that he has obtained his task by bribery and this suggests that the post of courier was a sought after opportunity within the army, perhaps because of the opportunities it provided for visiting friends and relatives. Periods of leave also allowed soldiers to travel and interact with individuals outside of their unit and even pursue political activities. Troops on leave in AD 69 joined the imposter posing as Nero.[20] Certain centurions on furlough visited Tiberius during his sojourn on Rhodes and were believed to have delivered messages of a political nature for him.[21] Undoubtedly, the majority of soldiers on leave probably did not engage in overtly political activities, but rather spent their time visiting friends and family.[22] Nevertheless, even in this setting they would have been exposed to news from outside of the military sphere.

As well as by personal contact, information was also transferred by letter. Literate soldiers corresponded with friends and relatives whereas illiterate soldiers were reliant on news relayed by their officers and literate comrades. Among the tablets from Vindolanda is evidence of contact by letter with London, Gaul and Rome.[23] A particularly interesting letter, concerning financial arrangements and conveying greetings to mutual friends, was sent to a soldier in the Batavian cohort at Vindolanda by an individual who was a *comes Augusti*.[24] It has been suggested that this individual was a member of Trajan's elite horse guard, the *Equites Singulares Augusti*, and therefore indicates the possibility of personal communication between soldiers in close contact with the emperor and their friends elsewhere, which could act as a conduit for political news from Rome.[25] Instances of brothers serving in different military units support the possibility of the exchange of information on an informal basis.[26] It is also clear that both personal and official letters were conveyed by troops travelling on official duties.[27]

The frequency of communication by letter was dependent upon the level of literacy within the army. Texts found at Vindolanda and elsewhere in the empire show that the army depended to a considerable extent upon a high level of bureaucracy and it is likely that centurions and decurions were literate.[28] Written propaganda had been directed at legionaries during the late Republic; but this could have been read to the majority of the troops by their literate comrades or sympathetic junior officers and therefore does not indicate a high level of literacy amongst the ordinary soldiers.[29] Literate soldiers probably stood a better chance of promotion.[30] A set of papyri letters written by a soldier, Gaius Julius Apollinaris, reveal how his career progressed as a result of his ability to read and write.[31] On arrival at his legion in Petra, he was appointed as a clerk and in a later letter contrasted the ease of his post with the hard labour of rock breaking assigned to other legionaries. Over a decade later, a man of the same name and legion was serving as a *frumentarius*. If this is the same individual, as appears likely, it demonstrates the possibilities of reasonably rapid promotion open to literate soldiers. On the other hand, some men served their entire term of service without becoming literate.[32] Evidence for literacy has been found for a large number of individuals from a variety of different backgrounds but it is difficult to ascertain how representative these individuals were of the army and society as a whole.

The speed of communication is a major factor that had an impact upon the flow of political information reaching the soldiers. The majority of military units were deployed at the periphery of the empire which increased the likelihood of delays in communication with Rome. The poor condition of some roads restricted movement at certain times of the year.[33] The depredations of bandits were a severe problem in certain parts of the empire and even military travellers were not immune to these attacks.[34] It has been calculated that the speed of a Roman courier was around fifty Roman miles per day.[35] There were undoubtedly times of emergency when couriers moved faster than this, such as Tiberius riding 200 miles in a single day and night to reach the deathbed of his brother, but these speeds and the resulting damage to horses would not have been sustainable in the long term. An analysis of communication speeds by sea, which focussed on the latest attestations of emperors after their deaths, has concluded that communications between Rome and Egypt often took several months and were subject to seasonal variations caused by unfavourable sailing conditions.[36] There would also have been a time delay between news reaching the provincial capital and it reaching other parts of the province. Slow communication speeds ensured that the information that reached military units was very often old news. An altar was erected for the well-being of Commodus at Dura-Europos on 17 March AD 193, when he had been dead for seventy-six days.[37] Soldiers would have been unaware of moments of crisis in Rome until after they had passed. While the deaths of members of the imperial family would perhaps

(*Above*) In establishing the Principate, Augustus transformed the relationship between political power and the army. (*Gilmanshin/Shutterstock.com*)

(*Below*) This arch in Saintes, France, was erected in honour of Germanicus. His death created an adverse reaction among some of the troops. (*David Jimenez Moure/Shutterstock.com*)

(*Above*) The Drusus Stone in Mainz, Germany, is reputed to be the remains of a memorial erected by Roman troops on the death of Drusus. (*Peer Marlow/Shutterstock.com*)

(*Below*) The Imperial Family, as displayed on the Ara Pacis in Rome, played an important role in the relationship between politics and the army. (*wjarek/Shutterstock.com*)

(*Above*) The First Jewish-Roman War provided a platform for the future emperor Vespasian and his son, Titus, to demonstrate their military credentials. (*gracenee/Shutterstock.com*)

(*Below*) Vespasian founded the Flavian dynasty, based on the support of his troops, and ended the chaotic period of civil war in AD 69. (*Nevio/Shutterstock.com*)

(*Above*) Demonstrating the economic impact of war in Rome, the Colosseum was funded by riches secured in Jerusalem. (*Viacheslav Lopatin/Shutterstock.com*)

(*Below left*) As an experienced general, the accession of Trajan stabilised the empire and restored the loyalty of the provincial armies. (*Conde/Shutterstock.com*)

(*Below right*) Centurions possessed a distinctive identity within the Roman army and society in general, as demonstrated by the tombstone of Marcus Caelius. (*Charlotte Erpenbeck/Shutterstock.com*)

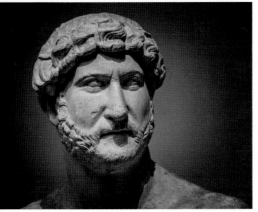

(*Above*) Hadrian dedicated a significant portion of his reign to travelling across the empire and winning the support of the provincial armies. (*Gilmanshin/Shutterstock.com*)

(*Right*) 'Reiter' tombstones depict victorious cavalrymen excelling in war, in some instances demonstrating the beheading of their enemies. (Hexham) (*Electric Egg/Shutterstock.com*)

A particular difficulty in maintaining the support of troops lay in their deployment at the perimeters of the empire in contrast to the concentration of political power in Rome. (*PJ_Photography/Shutterstock.com*)

(*Above*) In AD 128, Hadrian delivered an imperial speech to the troops at Lambaesis in Africa, providing an insight into how imperial oratory inspired soldiers. (*Cortyn/Shutterstock.com*)

(*Below*) The Column of Marcus Aurelius records the savagery and intensive combat of the Marcomannic Wars. (*Vladimir Korostyshevskiy/Shutterstock.com*)

(*Above*) Trajan's Column records the army on campaign during the Dacian Wars, including how Trajan interacted directly with his troops. (*Zoltan Tarlacz/ Shutterstock.com*)

(*Below*) Septimius Severus established the Severan dynasty and ordered his successors to 'enrich the soldiers'. (*Diego Fiore/Shutterstock.com*)

(*Above*) Writing tablets recovered from Vindolanda provide unparalleled insight into the operations of a military base and the social relationships of officers. (*Jaime Pharr/Shutterstock.com*)

(*Below*) The Feriale Duranum, discovered at Dura-Europos in Syria, provides an overview of the religious observances within the Roman military calendar. (*Simone Migliaro/Shutterstock.com*)

have caused oaths and religious formulae to be changed, other events would not have appeared as important with the passage of time.

MILITARY THEMES ON THE COINAGE

The extent to which the imperial coinage was used to relay political messages is controversial. Jones argued that it is impossible to know whether the various audiences of these coins understood the messages conveyed upon them. The relative lack of references to coins in the literary sources prevents us from obtaining a clear picture of how the various images and legends displayed upon them were received.[38] While conceding that coins could be used as vehicles for propaganda, he argued that the notion of coins as a means of its dissemination has been over exaggerated by modern scholars.[39] Sutherland argued in response that the topicality and clear commemorative relevance of some of the coins suggested that they did indeed have an 'intentional propaganda value'.[40] With varying literacy levels across the empire, it is unclear as to how many people were able to understand the legends on the coins. Sutherland suggested that only a basic grasp of Latin was needed to understand them and that the use of familiar imagery and symbolism would have assisted in transmitting this information. To sum up, he maintained that the coinage of the imperial period represents both the manipulation of public opinion and the mindset of the imperial administration.[41]

In more recent discussions there has been a reluctance to describe the messages conveyed on the coinage as propaganda, probably because of the negative modern connotations which the term has acquired. Instead, modern scholars have tended to focus on coinage as a means of communication between the imperial administration in Rome and their subjects elsewhere.[42] Indeed, a comparison has been made between the modern use of brands as a marketing tool and the use of images and legends on Roman coinage.[43] Both aim to use the constant repetition of a relatively simple image on everyday items to construct a positive opinion of both the product and the entity which created it. A recent survey of Roman imperial coinage identified the predominance of the personification of imperial virtues as a reverse type.[44] This suggests that it was an effective means of communication and was well understood by the intended audiences. The use of these simple images along with their association with the bust of the emperor on the obverse side served to reinforce the public perception of imperial virtues, while the titulature demonstrated the suitability of the emperor to rule, if the audience could understand its significance. The bust of the emperor had particular relevance for soldiers as it emphasized that their money came from him.[45]

The extent to which the emperor exercised personal control over the images displayed on the coinage is unknown. This has led to the suggestion that the designs were, in fact, chosen by the *triumviri monetales* or perhaps the emperor's servants and, in doing so, they probably chose images which would please the emperor.[46] The intended audience was therefore the emperor himself. The question of who actually chose a specific image for the coinage is unclear, but the political relevance of certain coins would seem to indicate that whoever did so had a firm grasp of the political situation. Radical new designs must have had imperial approval if they indicated a shift in policy, for example the coins issued under Claudius which indicated his reliance upon the Praetorian Guard.[47]

Much of the debate regarding the validity of the imperial coinage as historical evidence has focussed upon how individuals from different levels of society interpreted the messages displayed on them. There are two coin types that we may assume were specifically aimed at the soldiers and that they understood, namely the clasped hands type which was particularly prominent during the first century AD, and the legionary type coins. The soldiers probably understood the clasped hands motif as a symbol of friendship and co-operation. Early in AD 69, the legions in Syria sent a model of clasped hands to the Praetorians in Rome,[48] while the German legions received a similar object from the Lingones as a token of friendship.[49] It can therefore be presumed with some certainty that the soldiers were able to understand the implications of this motif when it appeared on the coinage.[50] The handshake or *dextrarum iunctio* represents friendship and equality and is common in both Greek and Roman art.[51] When the emperor is shown shaking hands with a subordinate, he is usually physically larger to indicate his higher status.

Coins bearing the clasped hands motif on their reverse first appeared during the turbulent period of AD 68–9. Galba was the first emperor who can be proven to have used this design, in his case with the legend FIDES MILITVM.[52] This was followed by a series of coins displaying clasped hands on both sides. The obverse side carries the legend FIDES EXERCITVVM while the reverse shows either FIDES or CONCORDIA PRAETORIANORVM.[53] This design is unusual for a number of reasons. The absence of an imperial bust or any indication of those by whom they were issued prevents them from being clearly identified. The fact that the coins refer to both the legions and the Praetorians is also of note, given that coins usually appeal to them individually. It has been argued that these coins were minted at Colonia Agrippensis, just before Vitellius' rebellion became apparent.[54] According to this theory, their purpose was to reassure the troops and perhaps the local populace, that their actions had the backing of the Praetorian Guard in Rome. Although Tacitus stated that morale was high among Vitellius' legions, these coins may have been issued to reinforce it and inspire confidence in eventual victory.[55] It could be argued that coins targeted at Vitellius' troops would surely show his image in order to present him as emperor. However, an explicit statement regarding the origin of these coins was unnecessary if it was perfectly clear that the coins were being distributed to the soldiers by Vitellius, perhaps as part of a military ceremony.

An alternative hypothesis claims that these coins were, in fact, targeted at the Praetorian Guard.[56] Fabius Valens, the Vitellian commander, was active in attempting to subvert their loyalty.[57] Given that the Praetorians were known to be staunchly loyal to Otho, it could be suggested that these coins appeal to mutual interests and comradely spirit rather than the identities and characteristics of their leaders. The identity of Vitellius as the issuing authority behind this coin series may be confirmed by the fact that he later used some of the same designs on his official issues.[58] It has also been argued that the coins were issued to flatter Vitellius by suggesting that he had the support of the Praetorians.[59] This fails to explain why the link between the legions and the Praetorians was made so explicit on these coins or why Vitellius himself is not mentioned. It is clear that these coins promote unity between the Praetorian Guard in Rome and the army units elsewhere, which is not unbelievable given that the legions in Upper Germany had asked the Praetorians to find a replacement for Galba after their refusal to swear allegiance to him in January AD 69.[60]

The clasped hands motif was used by Vespasian, although the design varied slightly by also using an image that showed two soldiers clasping hands.[61] Titus appears not to have used the design on coins with a specifically military audience. However, a sestertius from late in his reign shows Titus and Domitian shaking hands overlooked by *Pietas*, indicating their unity and friendship.[62] A sestertius of Domitian shows the emperor shaking hands with a soldier over an altar with standards in the background.[63]

Under Nerva the clasped hands motif was unusually prominent. The clasped hands design with the legend CONCORDIA EXERCITVVM was used more widely than at any other time.[64] This probably reflects the inherent instability of his reign and the rumours of discontent amongst various army units, in particular the Syrian legions, which abounded at this time.[65] It is noteworthy that Trajan appears to have used the motif only once at the beginning of his reign, when his support among the different provincial armies was not certain. The sestertius minted under Trajan shows the emperor shaking hands with a group of soldiers over an altar and is probably based on the similar coin issued by Domitian.[66]

After the first century AD, the design was rarely used, though it did appear at times when the loyalty of particular army units was in question. Marcus

Aurelius issued coins bearing CONCORD EXERC in AD 175, the same year as the failed revolt of Avidius Cassius.[67] Commodus issued a series of coins in AD 186 carrying the legend CONC MIL, some of which showed the emperor surrounded by soldiers, two of whom are clasping their hands together directly in front of his body.[68] The centrality of Commodus in this design is perhaps meant to suggest that the concord between the soldiers emanates from the emperor himself.[69] These were probably linked to the so-called *bellum desertorum*, when the bandit Maternus recruited a mob of deserters which caused unrest in Germany and Gaul.[70] This coin aims to inspire confidence in the soldiers and the emperor by emphasizing their unity, despite the activities of Maternus and his deserters. Clodius Albinus later produced coins displaying clasped hands with a legionary eagle and also the eagle with the standards bearing the legend FIDES LEGION during his attempt to seize power.[71] These were minted in AD 197 immediately before his defeat at Lugdunum. Indeed, the good condition of these coins indicates that they were minted immediately before the battle and were buried after the defeat without entering circulation.[72]

The legionary type coins were first produced by Marcus Antonius before Actium, with a basic design consisting of a legionary eagle between two standards with the name of the legion underneath.[73] The same type was used by later individuals to appeal to particular legions. Clodius Macer used the motif on coins for his two legions, III Augusta and I Macriana, in AD 68.[74] The coins were minted in Carthage and the ratio between the two legionary types is comparative to the number of soldiers in each legion.[75] In AD 193, Septimius Severus issued a series honouring a total of fifteen different legions.[76] These were based on the Rhine and Danube and, with the exception of XIII Gemina, all fought for Severus at either Issus or Lugdunum. The coins were aimed at legions that were loyal to Severus and were probably an attempt to gather their support. The eastern legions under Pescennius Niger and those in Britain and Spain under Clodius Albinus are ignored. The *exercitus* type coins minted under Hadrian are similar to the legionary issues in that they were targeted towards particular groups of soldiers. They depict different army groups on their reverses such as EXERCITVS SYRIACVS and represent the armies which Hadrian visited on his travels.[77] They usually show Hadrian on horseback addressing the soldiers, and would undoubtedly have reminded the troops of their association with the emperor.[78]

Military loyalty persevered after discharge from service, as a number of provincial coins minted under Augustus at Augusta Emerita (Mérida) in Spain bear the design of the legion from which the veterans had been discharged.[79] Veterans provided a link between the army and local people, as well as a possible source of reinforcements should a military crisis develop. Veteran settlements were originally of a strongly paramilitary nature.[80] The high concentration of former military men allowed them to function as bastions of conservative loyalty to the emperor as well as unofficial watch points. The colony at Aosta was set up in 25 BC for 3000 veterans of the Praetorian Guard and the town plan was similar to that of a military camp.[81] The settlers would have been able to keep a discreet watch on the recently secured Alpine routes. It can be assumed that veterans felt goodwill towards their benefactor, the emperor.[82] Keeping the veterans within the information loop was of prime importance in maintaining their role as a focus of imperial loyalty.

Various other coins have military connotations although we cannot be certain at whom they were aimed. There are a number of different coin types which, although not specifically aimed at soldiers, displayed and enhanced the image of the emperor as a successful military leader. It is likely that the repetition of this imagery reinforced the confidence of the troops in the emperor as commander-in-chief. Qualities with military applications, such as *virtus* and *providentia*, account for around 25 per cent of imperial virtues on denarii issued AD 69–238.[83] The ceremonial aspect of military life was extremely important in promoting both unit solidarity and loyalty towards the empire and certain aspects are represented on the coinage.[84] The ADLOCVTIO type design showing the emperor addressing the troops is fairly common.[85] It is also a recurring motif on Trajan's Column.[86] This particular design emphasizes the command of the emperor over his soldiers by contrasting his articulate gestures with the pacific nature of the listening soldiers.[87] The PROFECTIO type coins show the emperor on horseback with his soldiers.[88] The use of this imagery has been linked to victory in symbolizing the return of the conquering commander.[89] The ADVENTVS design is of a similar nature by portraying the emperor on horseback, often accompanied by soldiers.[90] This idealistic image displays the emperor perhaps embarking on a military campaign. Both PROFECTIO and ADVENTVS coins link the procession of the emperor with victory by suggesting his involvement in military operations.

The successful completion of campaigns were events worthy of commemoration on the coinage. For example, the image of the emperor as victorious general is reflected in coins issued by Vespasian and Caracalla, stating IVDAEA CAPTA and VICT PARTHICA respectively, which show the emperor in military dress with kneeling captives.[91] Military victories by an emperor had a broader political relevance in that they demonstrated his competence to rule the empire and therefore his success could discourage potential usurpers.

It is therefore plausible to argue that there were a number of different coin types which were likely to have had real meaning for soldiers. It must be considered, however, whether coins were specifically distributed to the troops for political reasons. It seems reasonably clear that the clasped hands and legionary type coins were primarily designed with the soldiers in mind. An analysis of the military coin supply has revealed that from the Flavian period onwards the level of coinage in circulation was more than adequate to support payments to the soldiers with only limited input from a centralized mint in Rome.[92] In other words, for the most part the income from provincial taxes was sufficient to meet expenditure on military pay.

An investigation of coin finds from the *canabae legionis* at Nijmegen has yielded remarkable results. The study demonstrates that, despite the fact that coin circulation was reasonably self-sufficient, there were large influxes of new silver coinage in certain years, namely AD 69, 70, 73, 80, 90 and 97. These influxes of silver coinage are not reflected in the bronze coins found on the site.[93] The majority of these influxes were probably caused by donatives, in particular those of AD 69, 70, 80 and 97. The influx of silver coinage in AD 90 may well be due to a donative issued after the revolt of Saturninus. The predominant reverse type of *aes* coinage found at Nijmegen which was issued in AD 90 is that on the theme of VIRTVS, emphasizing the courage and bravery of the legions who did not join Saturninus (which included X Gemina based at Nijmegen).[94]

A comparison with the coins found on both military and civil sites from the first and second century reveals that large differences occur between them both in terms of reverse coin type and quantity.[95] This suggests that the coin types represented in a site assemblage are not representative of the proportions which were originally minted and therefore indicates that the coinage with a topical theme was to a large extent targeted at certain audiences at specific times. This is illustrated by a comparison with the coin types issued in Upper Germany, Italy and Britain in AD 71.[96] The reverse coin types predominating in Upper Germany in this year carry the legends VICTORIA, SECVRITAS and ROMA indicating the cessation of the power struggle between rival army commanders. Those issued in Italy tend to focus on PAX, ROMA and CONCORDIA celebrating the end of a civil war which had seen combat in Rome itself. The province of Britain had played little part in the civil war and was the scene of Petilius Cerialis' campaign against the northern tribes. Coins issued in Britain show the legionary eagle and Victory. This suggests that at certain times, coins were introduced into circulation, in this case through the pay of the soldiers, and raises intriguing possibilities regarding the supply of coinage to the troops for political purposes.

The Roman soldier would have come into contact with a large number of different types of coin during his service in the army in the form of his pay, donatives and possibly as a discharge bonus. For the most part these coins probably came from among those already in circulation which had been harvested as taxes. Donatives, on the other hand, were of an explicitly political nature and as such it could be expected that they were freshly minted, especially on the accession of a new emperor. Coins with a topical theme, such as the clasped hands motif, may have been distributed at times of crisis with the possible intention of conveying a simple message to the troops. Many, if not the majority, of coins which came into the hands of soldiers were old. This would have limited the effect of the imagery and message conveyed on the coinage for political reasons. However, the possibility remains that at certain times new coins were distributed to the soldiers using imagery with a topical significance which they understood.

DEMONSTRATIONS OF ARMY LOYALTY

It is striking that, apart from the deaths of prominent members of the imperial family, there is little evidence for the reaction of the soldiers to other political events. It could be expected that in the wake of plots, real or imaginary, against the emperor, the legions would stress their loyalty by setting up inscriptions. Prominent individuals in the provinces did just that, often setting up inscriptions in fulfilment of vows given for the safety of the emperor and his family.[97] We might speculate that army commanders would be keen to demonstrate the loyalty of the soldiers under their command, if only to avoid being suspected of disloyalty. The lack of these demonstrations of loyalty as a response to political events in Rome demands explanation. It could be argued that the dearth of such evidence is simply a result of the lack of relevant epigraphic material. The inscriptions could have been worn away or destroyed over time. As will be discussed below, some of the inscriptions professing loyalty to Caracalla in AD 213 were re-used as building stone when their political context was no longer relevant. However, the survival of a number of these inscriptions suggests that other similar inscriptions should also have survived. The expense and time consumed in creating an inscription also indicates that they were unlikely to have been completely destroyed, although later damage cannot be ruled out. There may be other explanations for the lack of these inscriptions apart from their destruction.

While army commanders were likely to have known of events in Rome from their own personal contacts, it is not certain that the troops themselves would have been aware. It is possible that the erection of such inscriptions was outside the remit of the provincial governors and the emperor is unlikely to have wanted plots against him to be broadcast so publicly within the army camps. Inscriptions demonstrating military loyalty to the emperor may have been of a religious nature, in particular using the term *pro salute*. Inscriptions of this sort were often set up by soldiers requesting that the emperor be kept safe from harm. The *optiones* of III Augusta set up such an inscription to express their gratitude to the emperors for various rewards.[98] A cavalry decurion erected an altar to the *Genius* of Dura in fulfilment of a vow for the safety of Commodus.[99] In Upper Germany, these inscriptions may be linked to specific events, such as conspiracies, and link the survival of the emperor with the need for military loyalty and divine support.[100]

As has been noted above, the vows made for the welfare of the emperor on 3 January each year were an obvious way for the soldiers to demonstrate their loyalty to him. The *Feriale Duranum* states that a series of animal sacrifices should be made to the appropriate deities in fulfilment of the vows made the previous year.[101] A series of twenty-three altars dedicated to Jupiter Optimus Maximus have been recovered from the fort at Maryport in Cumbria.[102] They were erected by at least three auxiliary units under the command of either a tribune or prefect. Some of these officers made numerous dedications although their unit is mentioned only on their first.[103] It is clear that these altars were set up in fulfilment of a vow.[104] The most likely occasion for their dedication is the ceremony on 3 January when the soldiers gave thanks for the safety of the emperor and made new vows. The weathering patterns on the altars indicates that they were placed outside in rows for a long period of time with some form of barrier shielding their rear sides from the elements.[105]

An interesting parallel can be found in a series of eighty-five altars discovered at Sirmium, near Belgrade.[106] These were found *in situ* arranged in long rows within an open courtyard and were erected by *beneficiarii*. All are dedicated to Jupiter Optimus Maximus, with an attendant deity in a few cases. Other large groups of altars dedicated by *beneficiarii* have been found in Germany at Osterburken and Stockstadt, although these are dedicated to a greater range of deities. An altar from Carlisle was set up by a tribune of XX Valeria Victrix to Jupiter Optimus Maximus, Minerva, Mars Pater and Victory.[107] All of these deities are among those to be honoured annually on 3 January according to the *Feriale Duranum*. The large number of altars found at Maryport is extremely unusual given that they were erected by auxiliary officers rather than *beneficiarii*. It is clear that every military unit in the empire did not erect an altar on an annual basis or far more altars would still be in existence. The majority of military units must simply have made the animal sacrifices as stated on the military calendar. The probable arrangement of the altars at Maryport was an extremely powerful visual symbol of military loyalty to the emperor.

The clear identification of the commanding officer on each altar suggests that they were the work of ambitious men who were striving to demonstrate their loyalty, perhaps in the hope of further promotion. Some of the officers went on to have extremely successful careers. M. Maenius Agrippa, who is named on four altars, became prefect of the British fleet and procurator of Britain while his son was able to enter the Senate.[108] It is possible that some of the individual altars found at other military sites were set up under similar circumstances. Military expressions of loyalty to the emperor may not have been as clear as some of those set up by provincials, but were perhaps more commonplace than is immediately apparent.

It was in the best interests of the emperor to prevent news of any plots against him from reaching the army as it would only make him look weak and vulnerable. At times of critical weakness, between the death of an emperor and the accession of his successor, it appears that information was strictly controlled to prevent a usurper from taking advantage of the situation. The house where Augustus lay dying was surrounded by armed guards preventing any news of his condition from entering public circulation. His death was announced simultaneously as Tiberius was proclaimed his successor.[109] The speed with which Nerva succeeded Domitian, on the same day as his assassination, also indicates a need to control information.[110] The news of Nerva's accession would have been announced to the troops at the same time as the death of Domitian. News of the death of Trajan was probably also suppressed until the position of Hadrian was secure.[111] The close control of news relating to the death of an emperor reflects a desire to contain sensitive information in order to conceal political weakness. In this light, it can be suggested that the political news which the soldiers received by official means was carefully controlled, but information passing to soldiers and their officers by unofficial means could not be so easily restricted.[112]

THE POLITICAL OPINIONS OF THE TROOPS

Despite the relative wealth of papyrological and epigraphic evidence written by serving or former members of the Roman army, there is no surviving text that can reveal the political opinions of the average soldier. However, using the evidence which remains regarding the reception of various emperors by the troops, it is possible to engage in cautious speculation on the nature of military political thinking. In particular, it may be instructive to consider the soldiers' response to various different personalities who ruled the empire during this period and the ways by which they attempted to maintain military support for their rule.

Ando has noted the differentiation in Roman minds between the office of *princeps* and the man who held it.[113] The failings of an individual emperor did not indicate the fallibility of the political system that produced him. In AD 69, the legions may have revolted against individual emperors, but they did not consider a return to republican government. While some of the soldiers considered giving the choice of new emperor to the Senate, they did not suggest giving power to the Senate itself.[114] Indeed, the willingness of the soldiers to pass the decision over to the Senate may be an attempt to give their rebellion an air of legitimacy. The oath of allegiance taken by the legions in Upper Germany to the Senate was seen as '*inane*' by the Vitellians as it failed to correspond to political reality.[115] The link between the army and the *populus Romanus* is stressed in two texts, but this most probably reflects an ideal rather than a reality.[116] In his *Res Gestae*, Augustus contrasted the record of the army of the Roman people before his reign with the victories won by his army ('*exercitus meus*'). This emphasizes the importance of his personal military leadership. The *Tabula Siarensis* describes the legions lost with Varus as an '*exercitus populi Romani*'. This description has the advantage of disassociating their loss from the overall military command of Augustus. The connection between the army and the Roman people displayed in these texts was used as a means of contrasting their military record unfavourably with that of the emperor as a military commander and they do not represent an actual political relationship between the soldiers and the populace.

It is tempting to suppose that the soldiers would have preferred a tough military emperor whose lifestyle emulated their own. Claudius was able to create an image of himself as a successful military commander by making an appearance in Britain at an opportune moment during the conquest.[117] This visit to the invasion force was followed by a flamboyant triumphal procession upon his return to Rome. However, the pursuit of military victory risked heavy casualties and the possibility of defeat. Trajan experienced humiliating reverses and a large number of casualties during his Parthian campaign. A high casualty rate would have been unpopular both within the army and populace as a whole. It is clear that military reverses and a high loss of Roman life could not always be covered up.[118]

Not all of the emperors displayed military attributes during this period. On the contrary, some of them exhibited characteristics that could have been construed as unmanly and effeminate. It is interesting to explore the reactions of the soldiers to these individuals. Despite Nero's eccentric behaviour and artistic temperament, he survived in power for fourteen years.[119] Dynastic loyalty undoubtedly played a part in this as the troops were unwilling to desert the Julio-Claudian dynasty without extreme provocation. Nero's artistic efforts were limited to Italy and Greece and were not therefore witnessed by the majority of the soldiers. This fact may well have contributed to the longevity of his reign, as it hid his erratic behaviour from the provincial armies.

92

He was careful to ensure that his bodyguards gave their support to his stage performances.[120] A recent analysis of Nero's behaviour has demonstrated that, despite the hostility of the literary accounts, Nero's actions may have made him popular with his subjects.[121] There were numerous precedents for the rowdy behaviour of aristocratic youths and Nero's exuberant behaviour allowed him to appear as a man of the people. By staying away from the provincial armies, Nero, perhaps unintentionally, prevented them from witnessing his behaviour and therefore limited the effect this would have on their opinion of him.[122]

Antoninus Pius had extremely limited military experience and did not personally embark on any military campaigns as emperor. However, he governed the empire well and had a fruitful relationship with the Senate. His success as an administrator rather than as a military commander accounted for the longevity of his reign. The emperor's competence in dealing with the Senate may have created a positive opinion of him from his military commanders which filtered down to the soldiers themselves. An emperor who ensured political stability was less likely to have to fight a civil war, which meant that there was less chance of the ensuing casualties arising from civil conflict. This must be balanced by the possibility that some soldiers could have welcomed the prospect of booty or campaigns. However, throughout this period the prospect of war also involved soldiers being forced to leave long-established billets and comforts for the uncertainties of a military campaign without a guaranteed favourable outcome.[123] The serving soldier could look forward to his *honesta missio* with generous discharge benefits and is unlikely to have supported an emperor whose actions threatened this, either by poor financial and political management or by weak wartime leadership. The soldiers most probably wanted an emperor who demonstrated his competence to rule, rewarded them for their services and brought stability to the empire.

During the Severan period, emperors who exposed the soldiers to their odd behaviour invariably experienced problems. Macrinus aroused the anger and revulsion of his troops by dressing effeminately and failing to act as a military emperor.[124] He also had financial problems and was unable to provide new recruits with the increased payment levels introduced by his predecessor. Macrinus was replaced by Elagabalus, whose physical resemblance to Caracalla aroused the support of the soldiers. His habit of dressing and behaving in a manner that the soldiers perceived as unmanly contributed to his own downfall and his cousin, despite his young age, may have played on these attributes to win military support.[125] Severus Alexander, while not prone to the erratic behaviour of his kinsman, was not the most masculine of emperors owing to his close relationship with his mother and, for this reason, could not maintain the discipline of the soldiers. The *Historia Augusta* presents him as an ideal emperor with a wealth of soldierly attributes. This probably represents the ideal of a military emperor as viewed in the context of the fourth century rather than actual reality.[126] Severus Alexander was contrasted unfavourably with the tough soldier Maximinus, who portrayed him as a timid boy unduly influenced by his mother.[127] Increasing external threats against the empire at this time put pressure on the emperor to perform militarily and this contributed to the rapid turnover of emperors at the end of the Severan dynasty. The downfall of an emperor could be caused by a failure to conform to the soldiers' ideal.

There are instances of soldiers having their own negative opinions of those close to the emperor, which were presumably formed with the aid of informal means of communication. In contrast with the rest of the army, the soldiers in Syria refused to place statues of Sejanus with their standards.[128] When Claudius' freedman Narcissus addressed the troops assembled for the invasion of Britain, he was shouted down with cries of 'Io Saturnalia', a reference to his servile origins.[129] The dislike shown by the soldiers to these individuals may have been provoked by their commanders.[130] In general, it is unlikely that the troops knew much about the careers of those who advised the emperor given that such information had little impact upon their daily lives. Their opinions towards the emperor and imperial family were of critical importance and were therefore carefully shaped by official propaganda. The suitability of the emperor to rule was of great relevance to the army. His background, dynastic connections and the circumstances regarding his accession reinforced the personal loyalty of the soldiers to him. The political knowledge of the soldiers, disseminated by official means, was probably limited to these themes rather than the wider political sphere.

ASSESSING LEVELS OF AWARENESS

Given the absence of accounts of a political nature by the soldiers themselves, it is difficult for modern scholars to assess their actual level of political awareness. However, the reactions of military units to events within the imperial family are an important indicator of the soldiers' awareness of political events in Rome and elsewhere across the empire. Three events in particular lend themselves to further analysis due to the high quality of the surviving evidence for the response of the soldiers to them, namely the deaths of Drusus, Germanicus and Geta.

The *Tabula Siarensis* reveals the response of at least some of the soldiers to the death of Germanicus' father, the elder Drusus, who died in 9 BC. Drusus established his reputation as a military commander during his campaigns in Germany where he was hailed as *imperator* by his troops.[131] His personal courage on the battlefield was believed to have been due to his desire to win the *spolia opima*, spoils taken from a dead enemy commander whom he had personally slain.[132] After the premature death of Drusus following a riding accident, his corpse was carried back to the legionary winter camp by his centurions and military tribunes.[133] The title 'Germanicus' was awarded posthumously to Drusus and was also bestowed upon his heirs.[134] It was used by his descendants including Claudius, Caligula and Nero. The power of this title to arouse the support of the soldiers of the northern legions is confirmed by the fact that it was claimed by both Vitellius and his young son in AD 69.[135] After Drusus' death, his soldiers built a *tumulus honorarium* in his memory on the bank of the Rhine.[136] The *Tabula Siarensis* clearly indicates that this was done on the initiative of the soldiers themselves.[137] They only sought Augustus' permission after they had already begun constructing the monument. The legions held games at the site on a set day each year which, on one occasion, were led by Germanicus himself.[138]

The death of Germanicus in AD 19 prompted a popular outcry regarding the suspicious circumstances surrounding his demise. This uproar impelled the Senate, at the behest of Tiberius, to publish the findings of the trial of Piso (which had continued after his suicide) and the funerary honours awarded to Germanicus. The *Senatus Consultum de Cn. Pisone Patre*, recording the outcome of the trial of Piso, and the *Tabula Siarensis* and *Tabula Hebana*, recording Germanicus' funerary honours, provide a relative wealth of evidence regarding the reactions of different elements of society to the demise of Germanicus. While much work has been done on these texts, little research has focussed on exactly what they reveal about the reaction of the army. Modern scholars have concentrated on the evidence that the documents provide for the inner workings of the Senate and the light they shed on Tacitus' representations of Tiberius and Germanicus.[139] These texts have much more to reveal, in particular concerning the role of the army in the events following Germanicus' death.

There can be little doubt that Germanicus enjoyed a high level of popularity amongst the soldiers. The troops in Lower Germany had offered to support him in a bid for power during the mutinies of AD 14, although they were probably acting out of their own self-interest.[140] The planned evacuation of his family to safety shamed the soldiers into ending their mutiny.[141] Concessions granted by Germanicus in the wake of the mutinies created a feeling of goodwill towards him among the troops, although Tiberius later cancelled these, claiming financial difficulties.[142] The campaigns in Germany led by Germanicus after the mutinies were probably aimed at boosting the morale of soldiers who had been demoralized by both the mutinies and the ensuing massacres, although the casualties arising from combat may not have been so popular. During these campaigns, Germanicus supervised the burial of the remains of the dead from the Varian disaster and recovered two of the lost eagles.[143] These actions appealed to the superstitious nature of the Roman troops. According to an anecdote recorded by Tacitus, Germanicus was not unaware of his popularity amongst his soldiers and took pains to discover the opinions of his men.[144] His popularity was not limited to his own troops as the Praetorian Guard also favoured him.[145] However, the Praetorians appear not to have been involved in agitation after his death, given that Tiberius sent two Praetorian cohorts to escort Agrippina and the ashes of Germanicus through Italy.[146] Tiberius is unlikely to have deployed the Guard in such an emotive situation if he had any doubts about their loyalty. In later years, the memory of Germanicus would inspire their support for his children.[147] Agrippina was also popular with the soldiers, in particular for her level-headed actions when panic broke out among the troops on the western bank of the Rhine.[148] The soldiers' fondness for Germanicus clearly troubled Tiberius.[149]

The funerary honours awarded to Germanicus included an arch to be constructed on the bank of the Rhine, along with another on Mount Amanus in Syria and another in Rome itself.[150] The section of the *Tabula Siarensis* concerning the arch on the Rhine shows that it was to be constructed near to the *tumulus* previously erected in memory of the elder Drusus.[151] Religious observances were also to be performed on the anniversary of Germanicus' death, similar to those carried out for Drusus. Placing the arch close to the *tumulus* of Drusus ensured that the existing memorial practices could be applied also to his son. There may also have been another motive for placing the arch on the bank of the Rhine in that, to a certain extent, it symbolized the limit of Roman control in Germany and symbolized Germanicus' military campaigns there. The arch in Syria could well have had a similar role.[152] Perhaps more importantly, there was great symbolic meaning in situating the arch at the confluence of the Rhine and Main. It is possible that remains discovered at Mainz-Kastel, the Roman base of Mogontiacum, may be those of the arch on the Rhine.[153] The possible location of the *tumulus* of Drusus has been identified at a site named the Eichelstein.[154] The close proximity of these sites to the confluence of the Rhine and Main increased both their visibility and the ease of access to them for individuals travelling on the river.

It is likely that the acts of religious observance in memory of Drusus and Germanicus carried out by both the army and local population strengthened the ties between soldiers and civilians in acts of piety towards members of the imperial family. Religious observances linked to the memory of Germanicus were not, in fact, limited to the Rhine legions. On the contrary, the Roman military religious calendar preserved on the *Feriale Duranum* indicates that the birthday of Germanicus was still being celebrated by Roman troops in Syria two centuries after his death.[155] The inclusion of Germanicus on the Roman military calendar is extraordinary given that he never became emperor and was never formally deified. It is possible that this was done on the authorization of Tiberius as an attempt to placate the troops. It does reveal, however, the deep level of affection held for his memory by soldiers across the empire and indicates his renown as a military leader long after his demise.[156]

The *Senatus Consultum de Cn. Pisone Patre* provides a rare insight into the political system of the early Principate. The document is dated 10 December AD 20. However, it has been persuasively argued that there was in fact a six-month gap between the actual events described and their publication.[157] The later decision to publish the senatorial findings of the trial of Piso may have been a response to popular agitation on the anniversary of Germanicus' death and the addition of his name to those of Gaius and Lucius at the consular and praetorian elections. There had been public anger at the delay in prosecuting Piso.[158] It is also clear that the death of Germanicus had an adverse effect on the morale of the soldiers.[159] Discontent within the legions may be indicated by the explicit order that the *Senatus Consultum de Cn. Pisone Patre* was to be set up alongside the standards in the winter camp of each legion.[160] This indicates the importance that was attached to the need to disseminate the outcome of the trial of Piso to the troops by having copies erected for display. The aim was to stifle dissent amongst the legionaries regarding the circumstances of Germanicus' death. It is also noteworthy that Piso had sent one of his lieutenants, Domitius Celer, to the winter camp of VI Ferrata to gather support for him.[161] The display of the findings of the trial of Piso in the winter quarters of each legion would have acted as both a warning and a deterrent to others who may have attempted to subvert their loyalty.

During his time in Syria, Piso had brought the province to the brink of civil war through his subversion of military discipline.[162] Piso distributed donatives in his own name and shamelessly promoted his own supporters to key positions:

> ... he had destroyed the military discipline established by the divine Augustus and maintained by Ti. Caesar Augustus, not only by allowing soldiers not to obey in the traditional manner those in command of them, but also by giving donatives in his own name from the *fiscus* of our *princeps*, a deed which, he was pleased to see, led to some soldiers being called 'Pisonians' and others 'Caesarians', and by going on to confer distinctions on those who, after usurping such a name, had shown him obedience ...[163]

On his return to Syria, Piso suborned a unit of recruits to assist him.[164] Even while travelling back to Rome, Piso's behaviour towards the soldiers of IX Hispana, who were heading for Africa, was deemed suspicious.[165] This decree praises various sections of Roman society for their loyalty throughout the whole affair including the soldiers whose allegiance was not seduced. In the wake of the death of Germanicus and the activities of Piso, the loyalty and attitude of the troops towards Tiberius and his family was obviously of prime concern. The widespread publication of the decree indicates that there was a perceived problem regarding possible discontent amongst the legions after the mysterious death of a prominent and popular member of the ruling house. Events which took place almost two centuries later demonstrate that this problem was not confined to the early Principate.

The archaeological record of northern England contains a group of inscriptions that share remarkable similarities. All of these inscriptions contain the phrase '*pro pietate ac devotione*', a term that is unique to this particular group. The chronological and geographical ranges of these inscriptions are very narrow. The most northern inscription comes from High Rochester and the most southern from Ambleside, and they were set up in AD 213, or more precisely between 1 January and 9 October of that year.[166] They are clustered around the 'frontier' zone and all come from military sites. The governor under whom these were erected, C. Julius Marcus, was evidently disgraced soon afterwards as his name has been carefully removed from several of the inscriptions. Despite the fragmentary nature of some of this group, it is clear that these inscriptions share a common theme and purpose. It appears that the military units deployed in the north of occupied Britain in AD 213 were compelled to erect inscriptions stressing their loyalty to Caracalla. The existence of this epigraphic group requires explanation.

The similarities between these inscriptions would seem to indicate that they were all set up on the orders of a single command authority, probably the governor C. Julius Marcus.[167] In some cases the phrase is lengthened to '*pro pietate ac devotione communi*', which indicates unit solidarity in the erection of the inscription. The cause of the *damnatio memoriae* of the governor is unclear. It is likely that the protestations of loyalty to Caracalla were not wholly successful. Julius Marcus could have been the last governor of an undivided Britain and his crime may have influenced Caracalla to divide the province.[168]

This group of inscriptions emphasizes two key points, namely the legitimacy of Caracalla's right to rule and the loyalty of these troops to him. The most likely cause for these declarations of allegiance is as a response to discontent amongst the troops in northern Britain. The murder of Geta in late AD 211 had angered the troops of II Parthica in Italy and the troops of northern Britain probably had similar feelings. These soldiers would have become acquainted with the imperial family during Severus' British campaign.[169] One of the inscriptions from this group comes from South Shields which had been converted into a massive supply base for this campaign. It is estimated that this supply base held enough grain to supply a force of forty thousand men for up to three months.[170] According to Herodian, Geta had jurisdiction over southern Britain during the campaign.[171] It has been suggested, on the basis of a later source referring to the martyrdom of Alban, that Geta was provided with a guard composed of men from II Parthica. This was the legion that reacted so adversely to the murder of Geta and this may explain their fondness for his memory.[172]

Herodian states that Caracalla tried to win over the support of the army in northern Britain immediately after the death of his father but was unsuccessful as the troops showed equal loyalty to both of the sons of Severus.[173] The striking physical resemblance of Geta to his father swayed the loyalty of the troops.[174] There is every reason to believe that the soldiers of northern Britain reacted angrily to the murder of Geta. They had refused to support Caracalla as sole emperor after the death of his father and there is no reason to suggest that they had changed their minds in the meantime. It appears likely that auxiliary units in the frontier region in the north of Britain were discontented and aggrieved during AD 212. The reaction of the soldiers was in contrast to the official explanation regarding the circumstances surrounding Geta's death. Caracalla portrayed the murder as an act of self-defence during an assassination attempt upon himself. An imperial procurator dedicated an altar in northern Britain in fulfilment of a vow for the safety and welfare of Caracalla, presumably when news of his 'escape' first reached Britain in AD 212.[175]

The soldiers' adverse reaction suggests that they did not believe the official version of events and held Caracalla responsible for the murder of his younger brother. Without evidence from the literary sources, it is impossible to state by what means the troops displayed their anger. The narrow geographical spread of the inscriptions would seem to indicate that only auxiliary units in northern Britain were implicated. The following year, when the disturbances had been quelled, inscriptions were set up by the units involved, probably on the orders of the governor, pledging loyalty and devotion to Caracalla.[176] Honour is also given to Caracalla's mother, Julia Domna, who is described as 'mother of the army, Senate and country'. The mention of Julia Domna in some of these inscriptions is not surprising, as pledges of devotion to Julia Domna were set up under Severus, and Caracalla may have persisted in this trend.[177]

There is evidence that reinforcements from the German provinces were sent to Britain during this period.[178] An altar to Jupiter Dolichenus was set up by a centurion from Upper Germany at Piercebridge in AD 217.[179] Three tombstones of soldiers from Upper Germany have also been discovered at the same site.[180] A fragment of an inscription from Birrens was set up by a *vexillatio* made up of men from VIII Augusta and XXII Primigenia, the legions of Upper Germany.[181] At least one of the men commemorated at Piercebridge came from the latter legion. It would have been more logical for these reinforcements to be sent to the East to support Caracalla's campaign, and therefore this unusual deployment may suggest that men of proven loyalty were transferred to units in Britain whose loyalty was in doubt.[182]

The military reaction to the deaths of Drusus, Germanicus and Geta demonstrates that soldiers were able to form political opinions that did not always agree with the official information they received. Their personal loyalty to individual members of the imperial family caused them to act on their own accord in response to events in Rome. This potential for unsanctioned political action created difficulties in managing the army. The emperor had to counteract the spread of rumours by the careful dissemination of information to the soldiers. The care taken to display the findings of the Senate regarding the death of Germanicus in a prominent position within the army camps indicates the anxiety felt in Rome about military political opinion. The events explored above demonstrate that the soldiers were aware of the personalities and qualities of members of the imperial family. This awareness manifested itself in their loyalty to them, even after death.

To a certain extent, the adverse reaction of the soldiers to the demise of prominent individuals was a product of the imperial propaganda to which they were exposed. The ideal of a united imperial family as propagated to the troops inspired their loyalty towards all the members of the dynasty. Discord and bloodshed within the imperial family undermined this concept. The importance placed on the imperial family as a unit and the protection afforded to it by the army probably incited the soldiers to demand retribution. This emotional reaction had to be managed before the soldiers became out of control and therefore steps were taken to placate them by demonstrating that justice had been done. In a similar way, the murder of Geta was incompatible with the ideal of a united Severan dynasty and incurred the wrath of the legionaries of II Parthica and auxiliaries in northern Britain. This reaction indicates that the soldiers concerned had absorbed the propaganda disseminated by Severus regarding the suitability of his dynasty to rule and demonstrates that the soldiers' political awareness could influence their actions and was therefore of great importance to the emperor.

CONCLUSION

The emperor was a distant figure to the majority of the soldiers across the empire. However, the physical distance between the emperor and his troops was overcome by his constant appearance on coins and statues, the military calendar, and on their discharge documents. If an emperor wished to maintain the loyalty of the troops, he needed to build a personal relationship with each individual soldier. This was achieved in part by the constant presence of his image and benefactions in the daily lives of the soldiers. The personal nature of this relationship meant that it is likely that the flow of information to soldiers was strictly controlled so as to do it no harm. Trouble against the emperor elsewhere in the empire would have made him seem weak in the eyes of the soldiers and information about such problems must have been restricted. The practice of displaying imperial correspondence which was of relevance to the military in the army camps was a way of both displaying political information and showing the benefits that the emperor could bestow upon loyal soldiers.

Army commanders probably had access to political information through correspondence with friends and relatives but it is unknown how much they passed on to their men. Given the demand of the *Senatus Consultum de Cn. Pisone Patre* for soldiers to be vigilant to the attitude of their commanders, perhaps they would not have shared much of their information for fear of provoking accusations of conspiracy.[183] During the fall of Perennis, the soldiers felt able to report an act of treason by their commander to the emperor himself, although it must be noted that this particular event was very unusual.[184] It was impossible for emperors to control or halt the spread of rumours through the army, which were facilitated by the movement of military personnel. However, rumour could be influenced and a favourable image of the emperor could thus be created. News of emperors acting in a military fashion while on campaign would have spread far beyond the original context of these actions.

The troops were indifferent to constitutional niceties. It is clear from the surviving evidence that they expected to be rewarded for their services through regular salary payments and occasional donatives. Failure to provide these financial inducements could lead to an emperor losing the support of the army. But the soldiers were not mere mercenaries. They wanted emperors who would provide political stability, because this decreased the possibility of civil war. Antoninus Pius did not personally lead any military campaigns yet his reign represented a period of great stability across the empire. In a similar way, the soldiers had a particular affection for dynasties, which promised long-term stability through an orderly succession. Vespasian, for example, was a particularly attractive candidate for imperial power due to the promise of future dynastic stability through his sons.

Soldiers were aware of important events within the imperial family but appear to have been relatively unaware of other political events. Their level of political awareness was dictated by the official information disseminated to them. While it has been shown that soldiers were able to communicate either in person or by letter with their comrades from other units, it is unclear how much political information was actually available to soldiers in the first place. Communication problems may well have contributed to this, but it was probably also caused by the strict control of information with the troops being told only what they needed to know to prevent them from learning any information that may have subverted their favourable image of the emperor. The shaping of military political opinion was of crucial importance in winning the support of the soldiers.

Chapter 6

The Emperor and his Soldiers

In AD 40, Gaius Caligula gathered an army on the Channel coast in preparation for an attack on Britain. He did not launch an invasion, but instead ordered his soldiers to gather shells from the shoreline. Several historians have attempted to explain this incident by detecting a hidden motive in either the emperor's orders or the literary sources.[1] Yet Caligula's behaviour on the beach was entirely consistent with his erratic actions throughout his time in Germany and Gaul, which included disguising some of his German bodyguards as hostile tribesmen, procuring hostages from a school to be pursued as enemy fugitives and a spectacularly ill-advised attempt to decimate the legions in revenge for the mutinies of AD 14.[2]

The literary sources concerning Caligula's activities in the northern provinces are predominantly hostile, but there is no evidence to suggest that he lost the support of the armies through his actions. On the contrary, it is reasonable to assume that there was strong support for him among the provincial troops. The emperor was the son of Germanicus, who continued to be admired by the soldiers long after his death. Caligula had spent much of his childhood in provincial army camps and had even acquired a nickname due to his propensity for wearing a miniature soldier's outfit. His enthusiasm for military affairs does appear to have been genuine and in missives to the Senate he contrasted his martial lifestyle with the soft-living enjoyed by the inhabitants of Rome. He was the first emperor in over fifty years to actively campaign and emphasized his connections with the army by assuming such titles as '*castrorum filius*' and '*pater exercituum*'.[3] Furthermore, his award of 400 sesterces per soldier at the Channel coast is the first recorded donative given during a campaign. Caligula may also have given additional financial rewards to individual units.[4]

Caligula's actions are a salutary reminder that the factors by which the soldiers assessed an emperor were vastly different to those used by the elite authors whose writings influence modern historical thinking. Indeed, the emperors especially detested by the senatorial order, such as Caligula, Nero and Domitian, often had significant military support. Military backing could easily overcome senatorial distaste. As Favorinus the rhetorician stated, it is wise to defer to the man who has thirty legions at his command.[5] In this chapter, I will examine how the emperor cultivated and maintained his relationship with the provincial armies. I will analyse the personal nature of the bond between the emperor and his troops to demonstrate how the individual soldier perceived his relationship with his commander-in-chief. This will be followed by an examination of how the imperial family was presented to the soldiers, particularly with regard to obtaining military support for potential successors. Representations of members of the imperial family on the material culture associated with military life, such as armour, decorations and weapons, will feature heavily in this analysis. I will then look at how the emperor presented himself while on campaign. Imperial speeches to provincial army units are of particular importance in this context. As well as verbal interaction with the soldiers, the emperor emphasized his martial attributes by assuming a soldierly lifestyle as *commilito* or 'fellow soldier', an image that emperors did not hesitate to stress in their dealings with individual soldiers. Finally, I will present an examination of the role of the emperor on the battlefield, particularly with regard to how his presence influenced the troops by encouraging them to accomplish martial feats in the hope of reward.

THE PERSONAL RELATIONSHIP BETWEEN THE EMPEROR AND HIS SOLDIERS

The ideal relationship between the emperor and his soldiers consisted of an army emotionally united in staunch support for a capable ruler. The connection between imperial power and the army was made explicit in dispatches from the emperor to the Senate, which traditionally began: 'I and the legions are in good health'.[6] Emperors emphasized their bond with the soldiers by referring to them as *commilitones* and reinforced this concept by their actions and speeches. After the establishment of the Principate, Augustus did not use the term in any of his edicts or speeches and prohibited members of the imperial family from doing so.[7] Presumably this was intended to stabilize both military discipline and the relationship between soldiers and commanders. Unofficial usage probably continued unabated and it was certainly in official use by AD 69.[8] Pliny was confident enough to address the term to Trajan in a speech before the Senate.[9] In addressing the Danubian army upon his accession, Commodus claimed that his father called him 'comrade' instead of son, and loved him and the soldiers in a similar manner.[10] According to Herodian,

Caracalla preferred to be called *commilito* rather than emperor.[11] The increasing institutionalization of the term reflects the growing dependence of imperial power on direct military support.

The title of *imperator* was first assumed by Octavian as part of his name, probably in 38 BC, as a response to Sextus Pompeius' acquisition of the name *Magnus*.[12] Emperors increasingly showed their mutual reliance on the soldiers by connecting their accessions with their acclamation by the army rather than their approval by the Senate. Claudius regarded 24 January AD 41, when he was proclaimed by the Praetorians, as his *dies imperii* rather than the following day when he was accepted by the Senate.[13] Vespasian took the day of his proclamation by the soldiers under his command, 1 July AD 69, as his *dies imperii*.[14] Although in a speech to the Alexandrians, he linked military support with the approval of the Senate:

> [I am delighted to hear that] in accord with the decrees of the most sacred Senate and with the unanimity of the most loyal troops in respect to me [you] rejoice that I have assumed the care of [public affairs].[15]

Hadrian blamed the swiftness of his accession on the eagerness of the soldiers to acclaim him as *imperator*.[16] In a papyrus letter attributed to Avidius Cassius, the writer claims to have been 'elected by the … troops'.[17] It is possible that he is imitating the political language of legitimate rulers by stating that he had military sanction for his rule. Avidius Cassius was proclaimed emperor by the soldiers under his command in Syria, although he claimed to have been elected by the troops in Pannonia.[18] The *Feriale Duranum* states that a *supplicatio* was offered annually on 13 March, which was the anniversary of the first time that Severus Alexander was acclaimed *imperator* by the troops.[19] This was the day before he was legitimately made Augustus and received the titles *Pater Patriae* and *Pontifex Maximus*. The official recognition of the importance of the soldiers' support demonstrated their personal investment in the continuing survival of the emperor.[20]

In a remarkable document, Elagabalus took this concept further by linking his political decisions to the will of the soldiers:

> For she, who wished [to give] to you a son of mine as a fitting (or future) emperor and to win favour for herself through her honourable character, and through [whom], as it behoves me to pass over the rest in silence, my most valiant and loyal [soldiers, including the] Praetorians … [have found] me [able to refuse nothing they ask] shall not remain in my bedchamber.[21]

The context of this letter lies in the emperor's renunciation of his marriage to the Vestal Virgin, Julia Aquila Severa, probably under military pressure.[22] In this instance, the influence of the soldiers was sufficient to enforce a change in the emperor's living arrangements and reflects the growing instability of Elagabalus' reign. This particular text comes from a roll of administrative documents belonging to an Egyptian *strategos*, an indication of the extent to which Elagabalus advertised his willingness to submit to the wishes of his troops. A similar desire to show concern for military opinion is manifest in Trajan's *mandata* to his provincial governors concerning military wills: 'in response to the justness of my feelings for my excellent and most loyal fellow soldiers'.[23]

The connection between the allegiance of the troops and the well-being of the emperor is made explicit in military oaths of loyalty. The *sacramentum* was sworn by a soldier upon enlistment and it appears that this oath was renewed under each new emperor.[24] Vegetius described the oath after it had become Christianized, but it is clear from his account that the original oath involved swearing never to desert, to sacrifice oneself for the state and to obey the emperor.[25] The evidence of Vegetius supports the notion that the *res publica* was also mentioned. However, the main function of the oath was to bind the soldiers to their emperor. It was renewed each year on the anniversary of the reigning emperor's accession. The soldiers also made vows annually for his welfare. Originally, these were made on 1 January but they appear to have been moved to 3 January by the reign of Trajan.[26] Pliny described the taking of these vows with his usual enthusiasm:

> We have discharged the vows, sir, renewed last year, amidst general enthusiasm and rejoicing; and have made those for the coming year, your fellow-soldiers and the provincials vying with one another in loyal demonstrations.[27]

The use of *commilitones* is of particular interest here. In communicating with Pliny, Trajan uses this term only in letters replying to news that the oath of allegiance has been taken by the soldiers, with one exception; a letter referring to the transfer of soldiers as guards at local prisons.[28] In his other letters, they are referred to as *milites*.[29] Trajan clearly wished to identify himself with the soldiers after they had successfully sworn their allegiance to him.

The joint involvement of provincials and soldiers made an important statement regarding provincial unity and loyalty. The oaths evidently represented an emotional bond for the soldiers. The inviolability of the oath was of a religious nature and the soldiers recognized a *Genius* of the *sacramentum*.[30] In his *Metamorphoses*, Apuleius tells of a soldier who lived in fear of the *Genius sacramenti* because he had lost his sword.[31] When swearing allegiance to Vespasian, the soldiers of Hordeonius Flaccus mumbled or passed over his name in silence to avoid breaking their oaths at a later date.[32] The religious power of the oath as an effective method of maintaining the loyalty of the troops should not be underestimated.[33] The frequency with which the oath was administered by new emperors suggests that it was a potent symbol of military loyalty.

The ideal relationship between the emperor and the soldiers was sustained by various factors, which linked with the military's self-interest and influenced their political decisions. Severus Alexander allegedly claimed: 'a soldier is not to be feared if he is clothed, armed and shod, and has a full stomach and something in his money belt'.[34] The financial dependence of the soldiers upon the emperor was a good reason to remain loyal.[35] Irregular payments on important occasions were more common than uniform pay raises, which occurred only under Domitian, Septimius Severus and Caracalla.[36] Pay increases had a significant and permanent economic impact, which explains their rarity. Military loyalty during periods of unrest could also bring rewards in the form of donatives. After the downfall of Sejanus, Tiberius distributed a donative to the Praetorians and also to the legions in Syria for their loyalty in not placing statues of his former prefect among the standards.[37] Nero distributed a donative to the Praetorians after both the murder of Agrippina and the Pisonian conspiracy as a reward for their continuing loyalty.[38] The soldiers had to judge for themselves where their best financial interests lay, either in remaining loyal to the emperor or supporting a rival claimant for power. During the mutinies of AD 14, the soldiers doubted that the ringleaders, Percennius and Vibulenus, could lead them because of their inability to pay the troops.[39] Yet failing to support a usurper could mean that they might miss out on a financial reward.[40]

The emperor had to find a middle way between bankruptcy and losing the support of the soldiers for failing to reward them financially. Galba lost the support of his troops by refusing to pay a donative.[41] When Septimius Severus met with the Senate after entering Rome, some of his soldiers burst in and demanded that he give them the same financial rewards as Augustus did to his troops.[42] Although he managed to extricate himself from this potentially dangerous situation by giving them a thousand sesterces each, Severus advised his sons to ensure that they gave money to the soldiers above all others.[43] Caracalla followed this advice by pledging that he only wanted money so that he could give it to his soldiers.[44] The financial motives of the soldiers influenced them to support the individual who was willing and capable of rewarding them the most. This is most clearly demonstrated by the notorious auction of the empire by the Praetorians in AD 193.[45]

Along with the financial benefits of military service, the soldiers also enjoyed legal advantages. These privileges divided soldiers from civilians and therefore reinforced the notion of a unique military identity. The granting of legal benefits by the emperor demonstrated his role as benefactor towards the army. There were a number of legal privileges available to soldiers.[46] They enjoyed the right of *in integrum restitutio*, which safeguarded their property while they were serving in the army and protected it from creditors. Property acquired during military service was covered by the privilege of *castrense peculium*, which meant that it was under the control of the soldier and not of his father. Soldiers were exempt from the normal restrictions on the creation and format of wills.[47] The marriage ban for serving soldiers demonstrates that there were some restrictions on the legal activities of the troops, although it only prevented them from engaging in a legally binding marriage and did not impinge on their sexual behaviour. Emperors could mitigate the effects of the ban. Hadrian conferred intestate rights on the illegitimate children of serving military personnel and veterans.[48] By rescinding the ban, Severus probably gained the gratitude of the soldiers and perhaps also used the occasion to emphasize the ideal of a united harmonious family unit, with particular reference to his own imperial family.[49]

The personal role of the emperor as the legal benefactor of the army was reinforced in rescripts to soldiers which demonstrated his personal intervention in their legal affairs. Caracalla gave legal advice to a group of soldiers who petitioned him on behalf of their comrade, a fugitive after murdering an individual who was probably a civilian. The emperor advised the absconder to surrender to his provincial governor and claim that his assault was not premeditated. The advantage of this course of action was that the culprit would face only military discipline rather than the full penalty for murder.[50] The personal attention of Caracalla or his advisors to this matter is striking and reveals a concern for the soldiers' welfare. On another occasion, Caracalla allowed a soldier to reopen his defence on account of 'the simple-minded ignorance of those in military service' concerning legal matters.[51]

The troops' political loyalty was encouraged by awarding individual units specific *cognomina*. These titles appealed to the pride taken by soldiers in their unit and acted as both a reward for the soldiers involved and an incentive for other units to emulate their behaviour. The soldiers' pride in these honours is demonstrated by a diploma of AD 127 which uses the title of '*pia fidelis*' for the military units in Lower Germany. This title was awarded to the legions, auxiliaries and *classis Germanica* almost forty years before by Domitian as a reward for political loyalty during the revolt of Antonius Saturninus.[52] The continuing use of this title over such a period of time indicates the pride they took in the award, as well as the power of tradition within the army.

This title, in particular, was usually awarded to loyal troops in the aftermath of political problems. In AD 215, funerary epitaphs from Apamea in Syria show that II Parthica carried the weighty title of '*Antoniniana Pia Fidelis Felix Aeterna*'.[53] It is possible that it was awarded in the aftermath of the death of Geta as a reward for ending their opposition to Caracalla.

New legions could be named after the reigning emperor, for example *II Traiana Fortis* and *XXX Ulpia Victrix*, both raised by Trajan. Commodus appears to have taken the unprecedented step of naming all of the legions and auxiliary units across the empire after himself.[54] Legionary titles could also be used to advertise specific notions which were advantageous to the reigning emperor. Severus named his three new legions in honour of his victorious Parthian campaign. The Severan emperors were particularly keen on awarding titles to military units in order to link them to the dynasty. The title '*Severiana*' was first used under Severus and was expanded to '*Severiana Alexandriana*' under Severus Alexander.[55] The increased use of honorary unit titles under the Severans indicates the rising importance they placed on winning military support and an awareness of the value of this award as perceived by the soldiers.

The special relationship between emperor and soldier persisted after the completion of military service. An edict issued by Octavian prior to the battle of Actium gave veterans, their parents and children full exemption from tribute collection and taxation, voting rights in any tribe they wished, protection from being forced to serve in the civil administration and freedom from having their homes used as a billet.[56] These privileges are an exceptional demonstration of his concern for the well-being of his veterans and their families. The edict may date to 33 BC and could therefore represent an attempt to maintain military support in the face of the imposition of heavy taxes the following year.[57] Concern for veterans' welfare was not limited to the Triumviral period. A veteran called on Augustus to defend him in court. When the emperor demurred, the veteran reminded him that: 'whenever you needed help, I did not send someone else to you but endured dangers myself everywhere on your behalf'.[58] Augustus needed no further convincing and rushed to his aid. The relationship revealed in this episode was of an intensely personal nature. It is interesting to note that, according to Macrobius, it was forged during the *Actiaco bello*.[59] Did Augustus feel a special obligation towards the men who had served him during his climactic battle for political supremacy? A group of veterans settled around Ateste bore the title of *Actiacus*, as a prominent reminder of their distinguished military service.[60] But Augustus also had to build a relationship with the former soldiers of his enemies if he was to halt the disastrous cycle of civil war. It is unsurprising, therefore, to find that he dined with one of the veterans of Antonius' Parthian campaign.[61]

In his *Res Gestae*, Augustus stressed the amounts he had personally expended in settling veterans in colonies during his reign.[62] He continued as benefactor of these colonies after their construction by sponsoring the construction of civic buildings within them.[63] Later emperors continued to take a personal interest in their veterans. Hadrian observed one of his former soldiers rubbing his back against a wall in the baths, because poverty prevented him from having someone scrub it for him, and presented him with a number of slaves and the cost of their maintenance. On a later visit, Hadrian found a group of men rubbing their backs against the wall in an attempt to obtain a similar reward from him. The bemused emperor organized the men into pairs to scrub each other.[64]

The emperor acted as the main benefactor of the soldiers and it was a position that he jealously guarded.[65] This role created and maintained a mutually beneficial relationship between the emperor and his troops. Taken to an extreme form, Caracalla claimed that: 'I am one of you, for you alone do I wish to live so that I can confer many favours on you.'[66] An important study has noted the prevalence of the use of honour as a mechanism of mutual obligation between the ruler and the ruled across the empire. This notion has particular relevance for understanding the political loyalty of the soldiers.[67] The personal nature of the relationship between the emperor and his troops ensured that it was easy for the latter to believe that their pay and privileges came directly from the emperor himself rather than the imperial bureaucracy. This is particularly well illustrated on a papyrus from Egypt where a recruit from the fleet states that he received his travel expenses from Caesar.[68] In the same way, the presence of the emperor's name on military diplomas gave the impression that he had personally authorized the honourable discharge. But the debt of gratitude from individual soldiers could not be taken for granted. Valerius Maximus records the case of Marius of Urbinum, who had risen from the ranks to reach senior equestrian posts under Augustus. Despite vowing to the emperor that he would receive a legacy in his will, when it was opened Marius had not even mentioned Augustus' name.[69] Similarly, Caligula seized the estates of *primipilares* who had failed to reward Tiberius or himself in their wills.[70] The emperor expected his officers to be grateful for their promotions.

In certain circumstances the emperor could personally intervene to help soldiers and thus earn their gratitude. A number of auxiliary units from Judaea successfully sent a joint deputation to Claudius to argue against their proposed transfer.[71] In response to a letter from Pliny, Trajan granted citizenship to the daughter of an auxiliary centurion and ensured that a copy of this order was passed to the individual concerned.[72] Promotions and the award of military decorations probably also placed the individuals concerned under some form of obligation to the emperor. The funerary inscription set up for Tiberius Claudius Maximus records that he was promoted from *vexillarius equitum legionis* to *duplicarius* by Trajan himself.[73] This sense of debt was particularly the case with the promotion of centurions whose elevation from the ranks was perceived to be under the control of the emperor.[74] The obligation that promoted men felt towards the emperor manifested itself in their political loyalty. In AD 69, various centurions in Britain were unwilling to join the Flavian cause as they owed their promotions to Vitellius.[75] Similarly, military loyalty could impose an obligation on the emperor to respond in an appropriate manner. Vespasian awarded the right of *conubium* and full citizenship to members of the Ravenna fleet, and their children in posterity, who had been instrumental in bringing the fleet over to the Flavian cause.[76] The use of personal honour and obligation can therefore be seen as a means of ensuring military allegiance to the emperor.

FAMILY BUSINESS: THE IMPERIAL HOUSE AND THE ARMY

In the Pisonian decree, it is interesting to note the emphasis placed on military loyalty to the imperial family:

> That, likewise the Senate commends the loyalty of those soldiers whose hearts were tempted in vain by the criminal activity of Cn. Piso Senior and hopes that all who were soldiers in the service of our *princeps* will continue to manifest the same loyalty and devotion to the imperial house, since they know that the safety of our empire depends on the protection of that house.[77]

In this text, allegiance to the emperor and his family takes precedence over any other form of loyalty to Rome, indeed it is alleged that the safety of the empire as a whole rests on this concept. For the soldiers, this was no idle formula. The Praetorian Prefect Burrus advised Nero against using the Guard to assassinate Agrippina as 'pledged as they were to the Caesarian house as a whole, and attached to the memory of Germanicus, would flinch from drastic measures against his issue'.[78] A similar attitude is revealed by the responses of the soldiers to the deaths of Drusus, Germanicus and Geta.[79] The survival of a ruling dynasty depended on the loyalty of the army to the emperor and his wider family.

The presentation of male imperial relatives was particularly important, in order to gather military support to safeguard the succession. Claudius often showed the infant Britannicus to his soldiers.[80] After the death of Otho,

Vitellius presented his infant son to his army during a formal parade. The toddler was wrapped in a general's cloak and was formally awarded the title of Germanicus.[81] Vitellius' display of his son was probably a reaction to the attractive proposition of dynastic stability offered by Vespasian's sons. Titus' military achievements in Judaea made his father an attractive candidate for imperial power. The elder Drusus' desire to win the *spolia opima* has likewise been viewed as a response to the pressure to gain a military reputation directed towards the young male members of Augustus' family.[82]

The involvement of women in Roman military affairs was believed to have a corrosive effect on army discipline.[83] An appropriate presentation of imperial women to the soldiers was therefore difficult to accomplish. It was only from the mid-second century that imperial consorts assumed a title linked to the army, *mater castrorum*.[84] On the imperial coinage, images showing this title usually showed the women concerned sacrificing to the legionary standards.[85] But the presentation of female members of the imperial family to the army was ongoing long before this. A drinking cup from the legionary base at Vetera is embossed with images of Augustus and Livia.[86] She is depicted as Venus and flanked by her sons Tiberius and Drusus on a bronze scabbard from Bonn.[87] Agrippina was popular with the soldiers, in particular for her level-headed actions when panic broke out among the troops on the western bank of the Rhine.[88] Caligula displayed Caesonia to the soldiers on horseback, dressed in a cloak with helmet and shield.[89] The younger Agrippina arranged for a veteran colony named after her to be planted in the town where she was born.[90] The added importance of imperial women to the army from the reign of Marcus Aurelius onwards probably reflects their increasing presence on military campaigns during this period. In AD 178, for example, three prominent female members of the imperial family were with the Danubian army.[91] Imperial women inevitably attained importance for individual soldiers. Julia Domna was equated with *Dea Caelestis* on inscriptions erected by army officers.[92] Her image is on a helmet recovered from the River Jordan and a cameo from Kassel shows her as Victoria seated on a pile of captured enemy weapons.[93] The *Feriale Duranum* commemorates a number of imperial women: Faustina, Julia Maesa, Julia Mamaea, Marciana, Matidia and an unnamed deified empress.[94]

The deliberate advertisement of the imperial family to the troops can be seen in the images displayed on the soldiers' personal equipment. As may be expected, many of these depict the emperor in a martial context. A scabbard medallion from Switzerland depicts Augustus as commander-in-chief wearing a laurel crown, cuirass and *paludamentum*.[95] The legionary *signum* from Niederbieber shows Tiberius in a cuirass holding a spear over a German captive and pile of enemy weapons.[96] The images on Roman military equipment also illustrate members of the imperial family, particularly those directly connected with the succession. These represent a conscious attempt to ensure dynastic loyalty within the army. The so-called 'sword of Tiberius' from Mainz depicts an enthroned Tiberius holding a globe, with a cuirassed Germanicus, wearing a *paludamentum*, approaching to place a small Victory figure on the globe. Mars Ultor watches Tiberius and gestures at Germanicus. This sheath is an impressive piece of metalwork and was probably created from a prototype designed for multiple productions, aimed at the higher ranks of the army.[97] The brow-band of a helmet found in the Rhine shows three imperial busts, possibly representing the younger Drusus and his two sons.[98] The cheekpiece of a helmet from Frankfurt-Hedderheim shows the bust of an imperial prince.[99] Similarly, a cheekpiece from a cavalry helmet recently discovered in Leicestershire displays a mounted emperor or prince with Victory. The context of the find indicates an early Julio-Claudian date.[100] A silver scabbard from Leiderdorp bears a medallion which displays the images of Trajan and Hadrian. Clearly this piece was designed to advertise Hadrian's links with his popular predecessor.[101]

The depiction of members of the imperial family on military decorations reinforced the benefits of loyalty to the reigning dynasty. Glass *phalerae* were mainly worn by centurions and lower ranks.[102] A series of *phalerae* from the northern provinces depict members of the Julio-Claudian house including Agrippina the elder, Tiberius, Germanicus, the younger Drusus, Caligula and Claudius.[103] The juxtaposition of characters on each *phalera* highlight particular dynastic themes, for example by depicting Tiberius with Germanicus and Drusus they display the strength of the ruling house. Furthermore, particular combinations of *phalerae* probably also emphasize particular propaganda themes. As the *phalerae* depicting Germanicus generally face towards the left, those of Agrippina to the right and those of Caligula to the front, it is possible that they were worn together as a set and formed a visual reminder of the emperor's distinguished family.[104] It is tempting to surmise that glass *phalerae* from Britain showing Claudius and his children may have been distributed by the emperor during his visit to the province.[105] The wearing of *phalerae* such as these during military parades must have had a striking visual effect and demonstrated that the rewards of army service came from the emperor and his family.

The vast majority of imperial depictions described above come from the Julio-Claudian period prior to the death of Claudius. Why are such images almost the sole preserve of this early period? I suggest that the answer lies in the relative multitude of male family members in Augustus' family who were employed in a military capacity and the succession problems which plagued the Julio-Claudian house. The outright militarism of Augustus' male relatives was not matched by any other dynasty during the period in question.[106] Titus was utilized by Vespasian as a commander in Judaea, but Domitian was completely neglected by his father in this capacity. Nor did Severus use his sons to lead independent military campaigns. The strength of Augustus' dynasty was demonstrated by the military commands held by his young relatives and this continued under Tiberius. In the absence of the emperor from active campaigning, it was safer to entrust the soldiers to dependable relatives than other individuals. Young male members of the imperial family thus acted as military surrogates for the emperor.[107] Not only did this policy have the advantage of allowing the emperor to stay in Rome, it also gave individual soldiers a far greater chance of coming into contact with a member of the ruling dynasty. That such contact was personally important to the soldiers is evident from Velleius' description of their response to Tiberius' return to the German front:

> At the sight of him there were tears of joy from the soldiers as they ran up to him and welcomed him with tremendous and unprecedented enthusiasm, eagerly taking him by the hand and unable to restrain themselves from blurting out: 'Is it really you that we see, general? Have we got you back safely?' 'I served with you in Armenia, general'. 'And I was in Raetia'. 'I received military decorations from you in Vindelicia'. 'And I in Pannonia'. 'And I in Germany'. It is difficult to express this adequately in words and indeed it may seem incredible.[108]

Augustus' shifting succession plans created a need to display family connections clearly to the soldiers, as may also have been the intention with the 'sword of Tiberius' described above.

Although military equipment was provided by the army to new recruits, soldiers paid for it through pay deductions and it became their personal property.[109] Particularly decorative items of equipment were therefore worthy prizes for martial endeavour and functioned as devices to instil and display military loyalty to the ruling regime.[110] Weapons were given as a reward for valour on the battlefield.[111] The spectacular silver cavalry parade helmet from Xanten, which is embossed with a laurel wreath and the head of an unidentified prince, may come from a similar context as an ostentatious object awarded for personal merit.[112] The frequent presence of male members of the ruling family with the provincial armies in the northern provinces during the early Principate presented an opportunity for ceremonial occasions at which these individuals could personally distribute rewards to the soldiers. Silver *denarii* minted at Lugdunum 15–10 BC, which depict Augustus receiving laurel branches from Tiberius and Drusus, are likely to have been given as donatives.[113] The scabbard plaque from Bonn depicting Livia, Tiberius and Drusus may be linked to the same occasion, as could a cameo double portrait of the two men which probably belonged to an officer.[114]

The depiction of significant individuals on these objects turned their owners into advertisements for the benefits of loyalty to the ruling regime. It also highlighted the generosity of the imperial family in bestowing such prestigious items on their soldiers. A number of weapon nameplates and shield bosses have been recovered from the Wetterau bearing the text *Imp(eratore) Com(modo) Aug(usto)*. These were probably distributed as a reward for loyalty during unrest in the region c. AD 185–6.[115] Premature mortality and dynastic squabbles eventually depleted the numbers of male imperial relatives available for military service and decreased the number of opportunities for the personal distribution of imperial rewards. The use of dynastic images on *phalerae* by Caligula and Claudius was probably intended to highlight their relationship to Germanicus.

The strong dynastic loyalty of the soldiers meant that an individual with a family link to the dynasty would invariably take precedence over a usurper with no connection at all.[116] In Josephus' account, the soldier who discovered Claudius hiding in the palace after the murder of Caligula shouted to his comrades: 'Here's a Germanicus', linking his suitability to rule with his relationship with Germanicus and ultimately the elder Drusus.[117] Claudius Pompeianus was twice offered imperial power after the death of Commodus.[118] His marriage to the daughter of Marcus Aurelius was of greater importance than his otherwise relatively humble origins. A relief panel from the Arch of Marcus Aurelius reused on the Arch of Constantine shows Marcus addressing a barbarian chief in the presence of soldiers and legionary standards. One modern scholar has identified the figure standing behind the emperor as Pompeianus clad in military garb.[119] If such a dynastic link did not exist, it could easily be manufactured. Nymphidius Sabinus claimed to be an illegitimate son of Gaius Caligula.[120] By AD 195 Severus had falsely claimed imperial descent all the way back to Nerva. His victory at Ctesiphon was celebrated on the centennial anniversary of Trajan's accession. On the same day, Caracalla was made Augustus and Geta entitled Caesar.[121] He sought to portray himself as the son of Marcus Aurelius and brother of Commodus.[122] Severus personally oversaw Commodus' deification and in AD 201 bestowed the name of *Colonia Aelia Capitolina Commodiana Pia Felix* on Jerusalem.[123] The title '*Antoniniana*' is widely attested in use by both legions and auxiliary units during the reign of Caracalla. It has been demonstrated that this title was bestowed during the reign of Septimius Severus and was probably used to link the Severans with the previous Antonine dynasty.[124] In a similar fashion, Elagabalus and Severus Alexander both claimed to be the illegitimate sons of

Caracalla and, as his reign progressed, Elagabalus' public image increasingly resembled that of Caracalla.[125]

THE EMPEROR ON CAMPAIGN

In Rome, the emperor could only come into contact with soldiers of the city cohorts and occasional military messengers from the provinces. To display himself to the provincial armies, he had to go on campaign. Dio of Prusa compared a king who did not visit his soldiers with a shepherd who did not know those who shared in guarding the flock with him and did not stay awake with them.[126] It was a concept of sufficient importance for otherwise non-military emperors, like Claudius, to participate in military expeditions, although his involvement was carefully arranged to associate himself with the glory of military conquest.[127] Imperial campaigns did not always entail overseeing actual combat operations; Hadrian's extensive provincial tour was advertised on the coinage as EXPEDITIO AVG despite its peaceful nature.[128] The presence of the emperor among his troops allowed him to elaborate and reinforce crucial themes concerning his self-representation which had been iterated through official propaganda. The importance of this contact is evidenced in Trajan's decision to spend over eighteen months after his accession reviewing the German and Danubian frontier armies before returning to Rome.[129]

Hadrian's behaviour during his provincial tour was a practical demonstration of his image as *commilito*, which was particularly crucial given his lack of desire for further imperial expansion, in stark contrast to his predecessor. To this end, Hadrian acted as a restorer of military discipline, by clearing the camp of unnecessary clutter and luxurious items, and dressing in an unostentatious manner, avoiding unnecessary personal ornamentation and going bareheaded regardless of the weather. He travelled on horseback or even on foot, marching up to twenty miles in full armour. Hadrian shared the basic military diet of bacon, cheese and vinegar, which he consumed in the open, presumably so that he could be observed to be doing so.[130] The practice of eating the same food as the soldiers was not limited to Hadrian. Pescennius Niger also ate soldierly fare outside his tent in the presence of his troops. He conscientiously avoided seeking shelter from inclement weather, if it was not also available to the rest of his army.[131] Tiberius, Septimius Severus and Severus Alexander dined openly in the same manner.[132]

Imperial concern for wounded soldiers was also likely to have proven popular with their comrades. A detachment of German soldiers passing through Rome were reluctant to desert Galba because he had taken great pains to care for them when they were ill.[133] Trajan ripped up his own clothing to make bandages and Severus Alexander is alleged to have provided the sick with comfortable billets at his own expense.[134] Such behaviour reached its natural conclusion with Caracalla, who seems to have fully adopted the persona of a soldier. He shared in routine military duties including hard menial labour like digging ditches or bridging rivers and made a point of being the first to begin the work. Furthermore, his food was of a simple nature and he even dined using wooden utensils. The emperor only ate bread that was sourced locally, and thus also available to his men. He marched on foot with the soldiers and sometimes carried the legionary standards, a considerable feat of strength as well as comradeship. Caracalla also neglected to change his clothes or wash on a regular basis, mimicking the behaviour of his troops.[135]

Personal contact with the provincial armies gave the emperor an opportunity to emphasize his role as the source of their privileges and benefits. During the siege of Jerusalem, Titus suspended military operations in order to hold a pay parade. At the end of hostilities, he personally awarded decorations to worthy individuals in the presence of the entire army. Afterwards, a sacrifice and banquet were held.[136] Scene 44 on Trajan's Column shows Trajan distributing rewards to his soldiers. A military diploma from Britain dated to 17 July AD 122 records the discharge of soldiers from an unprecedented fifty separate units stationed in the province. The inclusion of two governors on the diploma is also unusual and suggests that some of the discharges were delayed until Hadrian's visit. It is likely that the soldiers were personally discharged in a single ceremony by the emperor himself.[137] The *exercitus* series of coins minted under Hadrian that show the different provincial armies were probably produced to be distributed to the troops by the emperor.[138] Hadrian's personal discharge of British soldiers would have increased his reputation among veterans and perhaps in wider society outside of the army camps through their later assimilation into civilian communities.

Imperial parades were often accompanied by a speech in the form of an *adlocutio*, addresses to the troops were made from a special platform, which was specifically included in the layout of an army camp, and the image of the *adlocutio* was sufficiently important for it to be included on the imperial coinage.[139] Assessing the validity of extant imperial military speeches is extremely difficult.[140] There are numerous practical difficulties in addressing large crowds and it is unlikely that a single individual could be heard by an entire army. Hadrian's speeches at Lambaesis were addressed to individual units, rather than the African army as a whole. Nor is it plausible that anyone present would have memorized a speech in its entirety. We may question the historicity of recorded speeches, especially as there is an established genre of battle speeches evident in the classical sources.[141] Very often battle exhortations are literary constructs rather than accurate descriptions of an imperial address. They reflect what a particular author believed should have been said, rather than the emperor's actual words. On practical grounds, it is more realistic that an emperor repeated a number of key sentiments to different sections of the army, or distributed his speech to the centurions to be read to their men, rather than delivering a single speech.

I will examine a number of examples of imperial orations to soldiers in times of crisis, in order to explore the themes deployed to maintain the soldiers' support. It is impossible to have complete confidence in the speeches recorded by classical authors, but the text of Hadrian's speeches at Lambaesis is more reliable as it was inscribed by soldiers themselves. Although not set in a period of crisis, Hadrian's speeches provide an intriguing example of the key themes which the soldiers remembered. The text is far shorter than the actual speeches must have been and is formed from a selection of excerpts, presumably edited by the governor to cast the imperial visit in a favourable light.

The first speech under consideration was made by Marcus Aurelius to his Danubian troops when news broke of Avidius Cassius' revolt.[142] The emperor began his oration by calling them 'fellow soldiers' and proceeded to describe how the treachery of a friend had forced him into yet another war. He emphasized his reluctance to fight and claimed to be willing to surrender his power for the good of the State, but stated that Cassius would not permit this. The emperor then compared Cassius' army unfavourably to his own and concluded by stating his wish to forgive the usurper. The speech is designed to persuade the soldiers that the emperor has no responsibility or wish for the inevitable bloodshed to follow. This sentiment was likely to have had a positive reception by the soldiers. It also forestalled any lingering support for Avidius Cassius by promising him mercy. Although a possible literary construct, this speech accords well with the emperor's later actions, particularly in his dismay at Cassius' death.

The second speech was made by Commodus after the death of his father.[143] It was set within a ceremonial context, on the parade ground after an imperial sacrifice with the new emperor surrounded by his father's *comites*. Commodus stressed the love which his father held equally for him and the soldiers, and his personal familiarity with the troops. He noted that he was the first emperor to have been born to the purple. Finally, he urged the soldiers to continue doing their duty so as to discourage further barbarian incursions and please the recently deceased Marcus Aurelius. Commodus' speech is conspicuously aimed at securing military support for his accession by linking him closely with his father.

Severus' oration to his Danubian troops at the start of his bid for power included several themes utilized in the previous speeches.[144] He dwelt on his duty in saving Rome from a 'bad' emperor. The prowess of the Danubian legions is emphasized, in contrast to the worthlessness of the Praetorian Guard. In reference to rumours concerning Niger's usurpation, Severus belittled the mental and physical attributes of the Syrians, who would prove no match for his own soldiers. Severus' speech on his decision to fight Albinus reiterates a number of points.[145] He claimed that he had been personally wronged by Albinus, who had no respect for the gods or for the previous promises he had made, and to whom Severus had shown nothing but friendship. He painted Albinus as the aggressor, guilty of both cowardice and treachery. Severus concluded his address by highlighting the soldiers' victories and superiority over the enemy. There are marked similarities between Severus' speeches and Marcus Aurelius' oration, not least the emperors' reluctance to fight, which is overcome by their sense of duty and the treachery of their opponent, and the superiority of the soldiers who form their audience. On this basis, it is possible that Severus or Herodian were consciously using Aurelius' speech as a model.

The speeches made by Hadrian to the various army units based in Africa in AD 128 were recorded in a shortened form on a monument sited on the parade ground of the legionary fort at Lambaesis.[146] The speech to the soldiers of *legio III Augusta* was evidently a source of continuing pride as part of the inscription was recut when the legion was reformed in AD 253.[147] Unit pride was deliberately cultivated in the emperor's comments. In one section, he tells Viator, the commander of his horse guard, to perform on the parade ground of another unit rather than on that of the *ala* he has just seen train and who evidently need no such demonstration.[148] Hadrian's speeches demonstrated his knowledge of military tactics and soldierly skills and he was not afraid to criticize mistakes. By scrutinizing the training manoeuvres of his soldiers, the emperor showed his interest in their affairs and his desire for military efficiency: 'Had anything been lacking, I would note it; had anything stood out, I would mention it.'[149] Hadrian's apparent mastery of the details of army life is impressive, from selecting the best type of stones for building a wall to complicated equestrian drills.

The emperor reinforced the military chain of command by praising his officers, particularly the legate Catullinus but also the individual auxiliary unit commanders. The former was granted an ordinary consulship two years later and it is tempting to believe that the performance of his troops in Africa was the cause for his elevation.[150] Hadrian's address to the senior centurions is particularly interesting both for the importance he attached to them and his grasp of the problems they faced in executing their duties. The emperor empathized with their manpower shortages, dispersed locations and the fact that their troops had constructed two substantial forts within recent memory.[151] He praised the senior centurions for not allowing any of these problems to interfere with the training of their men. Within the context of Hadrian's self-presentation to the army, it is noteworthy that he refers to Trajan as 'my model', a clear attempt to link his policies with his predecessor.[152] These speeches are an exercise in bonding with the soldiers and Hadrian uses *vos* more than any other word.[153]

With the exception of Caracalla, who seems to have had a genuine enthusiasm for army life, it is tempting to suspect that much of the behaviour which emperors exhibited on campaign was deliberately 'stage managed' to attract the admiration of the common soldiers. According to Pseudo-Hyginus, the emperor's residence while on campaign was completely surrounded by his Praetorian Guard and cavalry. His senior officers, including *comites* and the Praetorian Prefect, were situated directly adjacent to him.[154] Even if this layout is only theoretical, it is reasonable to assume that the emperor's elite guards would have been encamped closest to him. Imperial encounters with the provincial troops could therefore be restricted to occasions that were favourable to the emperor. The difficulties faced by a member of the imperial family in achieving genuine contact with ordinary soldiers can be seen in Germanicus' actions in wearing a disguise to mingle with his men around their campfires.[155] Clearly Germanicus felt it to be impossible to ascertain their real opinions by any other means.

THE EMPEROR ON THE BATTLEFIELD

The emperor could most clearly demonstrate his martial prowess on the battlefield itself. During the period in question it was extremely rare for an emperor to personally engage in combat. Personal weaknesses exposed in battle were hard to suppress and fuelled hostile propaganda. Marcus Antonius alleged that Octavian had disappeared during the Battle of Mutina and reappeared the following day without his horse or purple cloak. It is surely no coincidence that he exhibited conspicuous bravery in the next engagement by shouldering a legionary eagle when the standard bearer was seriously wounded.[156] In this context, it is interesting to note conflicting accounts of Severus' conduct during the Battle of Lugdunum. According to Herodian, the emperor chose to flee and, after being knocked off his horse, disposed of his cloak to avoid being detected.[157] In Dio's account, Severus lost his horse in battle and tore off his cloak to fight alongside his soldiers.[158] This episode is the only attestation of Severus' personal involvement in battle during the civil wars. The discrepancy between the two accounts probably represents the influence of official propaganda in covering up his shameful flight.

Yet despite the potential for personal embarrassment, by deliberately exposing himself to danger the emperor could motivate the soldiers while demonstrating his own martial *virtus*. A recent study has argued that sieges provided a particularly useful arena for such behaviour because of a static enemy, high visibility and reasonably controlled circumstances.[159] Psychologically, the emperor's self-exposure showed that the enemy were not to be feared. The inevitable artillery onslaught on his person would rouse the soldiers' anger against his attackers and thus motivate them for combat. Aside from these limited exposures to danger, Maximinus was the first emperor to deliberately fight alongside his soldiers in battle, a fact that he advertised by ordering large illustrations of his feats to be displayed in front of the Senate.[160] Maximinus' personal involvement in combat probably stemmed from his need to win support after the end of the Severan dynasty, particularly by contrasting his own bravery with that of his predecessor.[161] Commodus' actions in fighting as a gladiator in the arena had created a precedent for emperors to display their martial *virtus* through actual combat. Caracalla is alleged to have challenged enemy leaders to single combat.[162] In fighting as a soldier, Maximinus pushed the emperor's role as *commilito* to its logical conclusion, particularly after Caracalla had developed his relationship with the soldiers to an extreme level.[163]

The most important artistic representations of the emperor and his army during the period in question are Trajan's Column, the Great Trajanic Frieze and the Column of Marcus Aurelius. It is interesting to note that one particular scene, namely the presentation of severed heads by soldiers to the emperor, can be found on each of these monuments.[164] Modern scholars have explained these scenes as representations of a particular aspect of martial behaviour exhibited by auxiliary soldiers of Gallic or Germanic extraction.[165] The taking of heads was certainly an established practice in Iron Age warfare as a demonstration of a warrior's prowess.[166] The significance of severed heads continued unabated in Gaul during the Roman period. An altar to Mars from Apt, dedicated by individuals with Celtic names, was strategically placed over a burial of eight or nine human skulls.[167] But the identification of this behaviour as a limited ethnic practice is the result of a pronounced romanocentric bias in some modern scholarship, which associates what historians view as barbaric behaviour with non-Romans. This is evident in the mistaken belief that, on Trajan's Column, the emperor shows his personal distaste when presented with the severed heads.[168] Severed heads do not appear solely in ancient Gallic and Germanic iconography. They are also objects of significance in Etruscan art.[169] Moreover, the first Roman numismatic depiction of a Gaul is in the form of a severed head, held by a triumphant Roman cavalryman.[170]

It can be reasonably assumed that the scenes depicted on the Great Trajanic Frieze and the columns of Trajan and Marcus Aurelius had direct imperial approval. It is highly unlikely that consent would be granted for the advertisement of a practice that was perceived to be barbaric. This is particularly the case with Trajan's Column, as one study has argued that one of Trajan's motives in choosing the particular themes depicted was to demonstrate his control over the army and allay civilian fears of the military.[171] I suggest that the image of soldiers presenting severed enemy heads to their emperor had a specific meaning that was important enough to warrant its inclusion on all three monuments.

It can be posited that heads were severed in combat for three main reasons. First, they were taken in order to terrorize the enemy. Frontinus includes four descriptions of the use of severed heads as objects of terror in his *Stratagems*.[172] He records that, during the siege of Tigranocerta, Domitius Corbulo had the head of a captured nobleman shot by a ballista into the city, where it conveniently fell into the middle of a council meeting and induced the defenders to make a rapid surrender. Scene 56 on Trajan's Column depicts legionaries building a road with Dacian heads mounted on poles behind them.[173] In 46 BC, Caesar displayed the heads of soldiers who had rioted during the games in Rome, presumably *pour encourager les autres*.[174] In the ditch outside the west gate of the fort at Colchester were found six skulls, perhaps originally displayed in order to intimidate the local population.[175] During Domitian's purge in Germany after the crushing of Saturninus' revolt, the Senate were informed of the victims' identities only by the severed heads that were sent to Rome by the emperor.[176] The emperor's reliance on severed heads rather than imperial dispatches was probably intended to terrorise and intimidate the senators in Rome. Septimius Severus had the heads of Pescennius Niger and Clodius Albinus sent to Byzantium and Rome respectively.[177] In a letter that accompanied Albinus' head to Rome, Severus explained that 'he had sent Albinus' head to be displayed in public so that the Roman people could see for themselves the measure of his temper and his anger with Albinus' friends'.[178] Not only severed heads, but also the mutilated bodies left behind were objects of terror. Plutarch describes the horror attached to headless corpses in consular robes, which were strewn over the Forum after the accession of Otho.[179]

The second motive in severing heads from corpses was as a means of identification, especially for political enemies. This practice began during the Republican proscriptions.[180] After the death of Caesar, a mob mistakenly paraded the head of Helvius Cinna, rather than Cornelius Cinna, through Rome.[181] Dio describes a man who was sentenced to death by Commodus but faked his own death and disappeared. His ultimate fate was unknown despite the fact that 'a great number of heads purporting to be his were brought to Rome'.[182] In the purge after the failed revolt of Scribonianus against Claudius, the bodies of those executed in Rome were displayed on the Gemonian stairs alongside the heads of those who were killed in the provinces.[183] The public display of the decapitated remains of a usurper proved definitively that their cause was lost. Inextricably linked with the role of the severed head as a means of identification was the potential they offered for reward. Marcus Antonius gleefully awarded an extra bonus to the centurion who brought him the severed head and hand of Cicero.[184] The heads of Piso and Vinius, killed along with Galba, were ransomed to their relatives for burial.[185]

For soldiers, aside from the practical value of severed heads as objects of terror or means of identification, they could also serve as trophies to emphasize personal valour. The fate of Galba's corpse is particularly instructive on this point:

> He was killed beside the lake of Curtius and was left lying just as he was until a common soldier, returning from a distribution of grain, threw down his load and cut off the head. Then, since there was no hair by which to grasp it, he put it under his robe, but later thrust his thumb into the mouth and so carried it to Otho.[186]

In Plutarch's account, the soldier was encouraged by his comrades not to carry the head covertly but to display it as a symbol of his valour and so it was impaled on a spear and paraded through Rome.[187] Likewise after the Battle of Munda, some of Caesar's legionaries erected a palisade on which Pompeian heads were prominently displayed.[188] A relief from an arch at Arles shows a severed head alongside other spoils of war.[189] The imagery of the severed head as a war trophy was evidently of importance to the soldiers themselves.[190] A human skull was buried alongside a cavalry parade helmet in a pit outside the fort at Newstead, in circumstances which suggest a ritual deposition.[191] A tombstone recovered from Lancaster in 2005 belongs to a cavalryman named Insus and depicts him on horseback riding down a barbarian whose head he carries.[192] It is to be wondered whether the relief illustrates a particular event from Insus' military career, as in the case of Tiberius Claudius Maximus discussed below.

It can be argued that one of the key roles of the emperor on the battlefield was to observe his soldiers. This was not only so that he could commit reserve units to threatened positions, but also as an incentive for them to perform well. Soldiers were believed to fight better when they were watched by their commander-in-chief.[193] According to Dio, Tiberius watched the attack on Seretium in AD 9 from a platform 'since this would encourage his men to fight with more spirit'.[194] Similarly, Titus watched assaults on the Temple at Jerusalem from the fortress of Antonia so that individual soldiers could be rewarded or punished as their conduct deserved.[195] A general serving under Domitian ordered his troops to write their own names as well as those of their centurions on their shields, in order for particularly brave or cowardly individuals to be identified.[196]

Inevitably this sense of being watched strengthened the bond between the emperor and his soldiers, as Pliny's praise of Trajan makes clear:

> Thus you can call nearly all your soldiers by name, and know the deeds of bravery of each one, while they need not recount the wounds they received in their country's service, since you were there to witness and applaud.[197]

The funerary inscription of a Batavian cavalryman records how he swam the Danube in full armour and fired two arrows in quick succession, the second of which transfixed the first, under the gaze of Hadrian.[198] The role of the emperor as a military observer was relatively straightforward in static situations, such as sieges or set-piece battles, where the emperor could view the panorama as a whole. Alternatively, a tour of the battlefield after combat had ceased would indicate which units and individuals had been particularly hard pressed. But there were situations where the emperor could not be present to witness the valour of individual soldiers. It is in this context that the significance of the severed heads presented to the emperor can be found. They functioned as trophies to demonstrate the valour of the soldiers who presented them. In 214 BC, Tiberius Sempronius Gracchus instructed his troops to remove the heads of enemy combatants as a proof of their personal courage.[199] The emperor Julian encouraged his soldiers by offering a bounty for every head brought to him as a means of inspiring his army.[200]

The cavalryman Tiberius Claudius Maximus brought the head of Decebalus to Trajan and was rewarded with promotion to the rank of decurion.[201] At the time of his most distinguished exploit, Maximus was serving as an *explorator* which necessarily entailed service away from the main army. Although the exact identity of the soldiers who present heads to emperors on the imperial reliefs are unclear, in all cases it is possible that they were individuals who could have fought at a distance from the imperial presence. The soldiers in scene 66 on the Column of Marcus Aurelius are clearly auxiliaries, and the depiction of a cavalry engagement in the previous scene suggests that they are dismounted cavalrymen carrying trophies from the skirmish. The men in scenes 24 and 72 on Trajan's Column are also auxiliaries, although it is not possible to prove that they are dismounted cavalrymen. Nevertheless, it may be significant that in scene 24 cavalrymen ride past below the emperor and are dressed in an identical manner to the individuals presenting severed heads. The individuals on slab 6 of the Great Trajanic Frieze can be positively identified as cavalrymen on the basis of their distinctive helmets.[202] Furthermore, these figures lend credence to the notion that the heads were taken during engagements that the emperor could not witness in person. In this particular scene, the mounted emperor charges from the left into the barbarian enemy, who recoil towards the right. The emperor is followed closely by his standard bearers. Yet the soldiers carrying heads move from the right towards Trajan. This arrangement could have been designed to show that these individuals had been operating behind enemy lines.

The importance of the iconography of the severed head as a war trophy is further emphasized by the treatment of Decebalus' head. The Dacian king committed suicide before he could be captured.[203] Tiberius Claudius Maximus removed his head as proof that he was dead. Yet there is a clear ambiguity in the official version of Decebalus' death. On his tombstone, Maximus styles himself as the captor of the Dacian king. An inscription to Apollo and Diana from Cyrene, dedicated in AD 107, celebrates Trajan's capture of Decebalus.[204] In scene 145 on Trajan's Column, Maximus is shown reaching down from his horse as if to seize the blade from the king before he can kill himself. This is in stark contrast to the relief on Maximus' tombstone, where the cavalryman wields a sword ready to behead Decebalus.[205] On Trajan's Column, Decebalus next appears in scene 147 as a severed head being shown to the soldiers by Trajan and an unidentified individual, probably one of his *comites*. The emperor then sent the head to Rome, where it was thrown on the Gemonian stairs, as a visual symbol of his victory.[206] The official version of the fate of Decebalus was therefore vague on two particular points: whether he was captured alive and who exactly took his head. His capture was a more positive outcome than his pre-emptive suicide, both for Trajan and Maximus. Furthermore, the imaginary survival of the king allowed the emperor himself to present his head as a personal war trophy. The imperial coinage displayed Trajan, *Pax* and *Dea Roma* trampling on Decebalus' head. It was an appropriate image for the most prominent soldier–emperor of the second century to display his martial prowess to the Roman people.[207]

The presentation of severed heads to the emperor was highly symbolic of the relationship between the soldiers and their commander-in-chief. In displaying their trophies to the emperor, the individuals asserted his right to command and demonstrated their need for his recognition. A modern parallel from the Second World War is instructive:

Our men brought back a Japanese rifle, an officer's shoulder strap and a steel helmet. Sometimes they brought back even more convincing exhibits as did the Gurkhas who presented themselves before their general, proudly opened a large basket, lifted from it three gory heads, and laid them on his table. Then they politely offered him for dinner the freshly caught fish which filled the rest of the basket.[208]

The presentation of these trophies was made by soldiers who operated at a distance from their general, in order to prove that they had engaged the enemy and as an affirmation of their personal courage, in much the same way as Tiberius Claudius Maximus. This image was a visual representation of the emperor's command over his soldiers and their willingness to commit violent acts on his behalf and as such was repeatedly incorporated into the major imperial reliefs concerning warfare during the early empire.[209]

CONCLUSION

Imperial Rome was not a warrior society and the emperor did not need to act as a warrior chieftain, exhibiting a personal pre-eminence in combat, in order to bind his troops to him. But nor was he simply a distant figurehead for the armies to follow. Rather, the emperor was an active participant in an evolving relationship with his soldiers. The imperial image was undoubtedly well known in the army camps, but the emperor was also a real person whose generosity was particularly advantageous for them. The privileges and benefits of military service appeared to flow from him and their ensuing obligation ultimately circumvented the many layers of military hierarchy which separated the common soldier from his emperor.

The Pisonian decree and other evidence demonstrate that the Julio-Claudian Principate was not founded on the principle of one-man rule, but instead was the imposition of a ruling dynasty. The succession of a new emperor was potentially a time of crisis and the adhesion of the army to the imperial family was therefore of paramount importance. Participation in military campaigns provided an opportunity for the emperor to display his family to the troops, which strengthened military bonds to the dynasty as a whole. The increasing importance of imperial women reflects a need to inculcate the army's allegiance to the wider imperial family rather than a single prospective heir, whose succession could be ruled out by premature mortality or political disloyalty. Speeches to the soldiers emphasized key themes relating to imperial propaganda, as well as acting as a means of securing military support during political crises.

But most importantly, the presence of the emperor among the provincial armies allowed him to demonstrate his status as *commilito*. In both word and deed, he emphasized his self-identification with the troops. Imperial oversight of their activities in training and battle was of particular importance for individual soldiers and was worthy of commemoration for future generations. In return, the emperor could count on military support to sustain his rule. Some of the factors that appealed to the soldiers were highly visible, as in the case of tough soldier–emperors like Trajan. But other emperors relied on more subtle means of gathering military support. Despite his effeminate traits, Elagabalus represented himself as being part of an established dynasty which had a strong relationship with the army. Regardless of his personal attributes and circumstances, no emperor could afford to ignore the support base provided by the soldiers. The secret that Tacitus exposed in his account of the civil wars of AD 69 had long been a barely concealed fact: 'a well hidden secret of the Principate had been revealed: it was possible, it seemed, for an emperor to be chosen outside Rome'.[210]

Conclusion

The coming of the Principate devolved supreme military power on to a single man. The need to consult the Senate on military issues was a polite fiction, for the emperor was 'Lord of war and peace'.[1] The symbiotic relationship between the emperor and his soldiers was evident from the outset, with the retention of the Praetorian Guard as an indicator that Augustus and his successors intended to retain perpetual command over the army.[2] The bodyguard formally allotted to protect Republican proconsuls now permanently served the emperor. The impact of this innovation on the social fabric of Rome was muted at first by their deployment in Italian towns and it was only with the concentration of the Guard in Rome under Tiberius that large numbers of soldiers were stationed in the city. Throughout the period in question, the number of soldiers in Rome gradually increased. Inevitably, there was considerable rivalry between the different military formations protecting the emperor, which occasionally escalated into outright violence.

The close proximity of the Guard strengthened their relationship with the emperor. They were on hand to benefit immediately from his benefactions and lend their support in times of crisis. But they also posed a potential threat to the security of the emperor if their loyalty was seduced by an usurper. For this reason, the emperor jealously guarded his relationship with the Praetorians and would brook no interference in his monopoly. For practical reasons, the emperor delegated command of the Guard to his Praetorian prefects. These men were usually chosen for their personal qualities according to the whims of individual emperors. The collegiality of the prefecture discouraged treasonous activities and it was rare for a prefect to replace the emperor in the affections of the soldiers. The emperor constantly emphasized his role as supreme military commander through his daily issuing of the watchword and his appearance on discharge diplomas. Yet although the loyalty of the Guard was essential for the emperor's safety, the Praetorians were unable to enforce the rule of an emperor who had lost the backing of the provincial troops.

Outside of Rome, the army was scattered along the frontier regions of the empire. Strategic priorities encouraged the concentration of military units in certain key areas, which promoted the creation of regional identities and threatened the cohesion of the army. To curb this potential fragmentation, army life was regulated by a strict framework of rituals which united the soldiers in loyalty to the emperor and imperial house. The *sacramentum* and military calendar emphasized the empire-wide soldierly community. Furthermore, the transfer of officers between units across the empire promoted uniformity in tactics and training.

According to official propaganda, the emperor was responsible for imposing discipline over his soldiers. Yet in reality, it was his army commanders who dealt with delinquent behaviour. The legal sources attest that when an emperor did become involved in military legal affairs, it was usually to mitigate the consequences for individual soldiers. Ill-discipline could lead to outright mutiny. But these were usually small-scale strikes responding to service conditions or the conduct of campaigns. Mutinies only posed a threat to the emperor if they spread between military units or when the emperor happened to be with the soldiers concerned, thus exposing himself to physical danger. For the most part, it was the army officers and commanders who bore the brunt of the soldiers' disciplinary problems.

On a daily basis the immediate instigators of military discipline were the centurions. Their position in the army was anomalous. They were the primary infantry leaders, yet were socially distinct to the tribunes and senior officers and formed a significant group within the army. The importance of the centurions had been recognized by Julius Caesar and they formed the professional backbone of the imperial army. Talented centurions could rise to the highest level of the imperial administration and the status of *primipilaris* was cherished even more than equestrian rank. The desire to obtain the post of *primus pilus* was an incentive for centurions to remain loyal, as advancement appeared to be at the discretion of the emperor. Winning the support of the centurions was crucial in maintaining the soldiers' loyalty. For this reason, centurions were transferred into units of questionable loyalty during times of political crisis.

Augustus' reign witnessed a profound shift in what it meant to command soldiers. The scope for independent command was drastically curtailed and generals served under the auspices of the emperor. But enthusiasm among the upper classes for military service remained. Distinguished exploits were still recognized and rewarded, albeit with less prestigious honours than those available to their Republican predecessors. The men chosen for military commands were generally non-specialists, except in times of emergency when individuals of proven worth could be recalled in extraordinary circumstances. There was no specialist career path for potential generals, as the concept of specialization was alien to the Roman administrative mindset. Army officers were chosen for their personal qualities and connections rather than for relevant skills. Loyalty was undoubtedly uppermost in the emperor's mind when selecting his generals as, potentially, the most dangerous threat to his position came from his immediate subordinates.

Maintaining military support entailed shaping the soldiers' political opinions. The information which the soldiers received came through both official and unofficial channels. Certain themes were of particular interest to the troops, such as the provision of new benefits, and were disseminated throughout the army as a matter of necessity. Other information, such as plots against the emperor, must have been carefully restricted to prevent them from damaging the emperor's reputation. The soldiers' image of the emperor was carefully constructed through the distribution of his image on statues and coins, as well as his constant appearance on the military calendar and official documents.

The emperor's military virtues were reinforced by his personal behaviour as *commilito* when on campaign. The ideal soldierly emperor shared his soldiers' hardships, ate the same food and emulated every aspect of their lifestyle. In his words and actions he emphasized the personal importance of the soldiers to him. The imperial army was imbued with a tradition of loyalty to the emperor and his family. This is evident in the *Feriale Duranum* where imperial individuals are commemorated centuries after their demise. It can also be seen in military responses to the deaths of members of the imperial family. The soldiers were not mere mercenaries serving whoever paid them the most, but rather invested emotionally in the emperor and the perpetuation of his dynasty. Antonius mocked Octavian for owing everything to his name, but the concept held true for a number of later emperors, such as Caligula and Elagabalus, who maintained the support of the soldiers through their dynastic connections despite their erratic personal behaviour.[3] The importance of a dynastic link is revealed by the false genealogies created by members of the Severan dynasty, which reached back over a century.

The political management of the imperial army was accomplished remarkably well. There were only two prolonged periods of civil war during the period in question. Mutinies, although probably common, were almost invariably highly localized and posed no threat to the emperor. The vast majority of army officers remained loyal to the emperor. I have emphasized the presence of 'buffer layers' within the army, namely the army commanders and the legionary legates. The commanders' responsibility for the daily management of their troops protected the emperor from the soldiers' wrath. Harsh disciplinary measures or failed campaigns were blamed on individual commanders without impinging on the emperor's prestige as commander-in-chief. The legionary legates were directly appointed by the emperor. This ensured that their allegiance was to the emperor, rather than their immediate superior and prevented governors from building up political groups among the officers in the provinces.

Yet the political equanimity exhibited by the soldiers for the vast majority of the period in question does not mean that their views were of no consequence. On the contrary, the army formed the major support base for the emperor's rule. This is evident in Septimius Severus' deathbed advice to his sons: 'Be harmonious, enrich the soldiers, and scorn all other men'.[4] As a group, the soldiers retained the potential to march on Rome and raise their own candidate to supreme power. No emperor could survive without the support of the army. It is little wonder then, that for the upper classes and provincials alike, soldiers were the most visible instruments of imperial oppression. In reality, Roman soldiers were not the good shepherds whom Dio of Prusa imagined guarding the flock of the empire, but the wolves.[5]

Military Units in Rome

A number of different military units were based in Rome under the Principate. This appendix presents an overview of the origins and nature of the various formations in the city. The reader is advised to consult it in conjunction with the first chapter of this book.

The Praetorian Guard was created by Augustus and it has been suggested that he had a legitimate right to do so as a proconsul entitled to a *praetorium*.[1] Nevertheless, the permanent presence of soldiers in Rome could upset senatorial sensibilities and therefore caution was exercised by minimizing the appearance of a military autocracy, notably by the civilian dress worn by soldiers on the Palatine.[2] Augustus created nine cohorts, perhaps to avoid comparison with a legion, of which only three were stationed in Rome itself with the rest deployed around Italy.[3] There is evidence that three more cohorts were added under Augustus but the composition of the Guard reverted to nine cohorts by AD 23 when they were concentrated in one camp in Rome by Sejanus.[4] The number of cohorts rose again to twelve under Caligula or Claudius and to sixteen under Vitellius, who also raised the cohorts to military strength, presumably to create more vacancies to fill with his own men.[5] Vespasian reduced the Guard to nine cohorts and Domitian later set the number of cohorts to ten, where it remained until the Guard was finally disbanded by Constantine. The strength of each cohort was increased to around 1500 men under Commodus or Septimius Severus.

During the early Principate, Tacitus records that the Guard was recruited from Etruria, Umbria and Latium.[6] By the late second century, members of the Guard were recruited from Italy, Spain, Macedonia and Noricum.[7] Until the early third century, the epigraphic record confirms that the Guard was predominantly of Italian origin.[8] On coming to power, Severus disbanded the existing Guard and replaced them with his own legionaries. From this point on, the Guard was recruited mainly from the Danubian provinces, although Italian recruits were not formally excluded. Prior to the Severan reform, the Guard was imbued with an exclusive status by prohibiting legionaries from transferring into its ranks. The only exceptions to this rule were Vitellian legionaries who replaced the cashiered Othonian Praetorians.[9]

The Praetorian centurionate was composed entirely of men who had risen from the ranks of the Guard and had seen service in the legions or in other city formations before returning to their former unit. Small numbers of directly commissioned centurions also entered the Guard, presumably as a result of influential patrons, but legionary centurions who had risen from the ranks were denied entry.[10] The consequence of this rigid entry procedure was that, for the first two centuries of its existence, membership was kept pure and distinctly separate from that of the legions. This may have been a mistake, as it denied the provincial soldiery any hope of entry into the Guard under normal circumstances.

In contrast to service in the legions, Praetorians were originally enrolled for twelve years, lengthened to sixteen years in AD 5 with a discharge bonus of 5000 denarii.[11] From 27 BC they received double the pay of the legionaries. By AD 14, this had risen to 720 denarii per year compared to 225 denarii received in the legions.[12] It is little wonder therefore that the provincial soldiery were envious of the status and lifestyle afforded to the Praetorian Guard. The mutineers of AD 14 contrasted their own harsh terms of service with the relative luxury enjoyed by members of the Guard.[13] The military quality of the Praetorians was in some doubt, given their prolonged exposure to soft living. Tacitus describes their grumbling when compelled to participate in a military campaign and Vitellius claimed that they were lazy, indolent and corrupted by the pleasures of city life.[14] It is claimed that some even hired substitutes to complete duties which they found particularly onerous.[15]

Yet military service in Rome may not have been as rosy as the picture painted by the literary sources suggests. Demographic research demonstrates that the military units in the city had unusually high mortality rates. In the second century AD, 58 per cent of Guard recruits did not complete their seventeen-year term of service. By the third century, 45 per cent did not complete a thirteen-year term of service. High mortality rates were not confined to the Guard alone. The *equites singulares Augusti* suffered an attrition rate of around 60 per cent in a twenty-year term of service and more than 50 per cent of the *Germani* attested in the epigraphic record died before reaching the age of 25.[16] Some of these losses may have been incurred during combat operations, particularly during the Antonine and Severan periods. However, the fate of the *Germani* suggests an alternative possibility; that the high mortality rate of soldiers serving in Rome was caused by their exposure to disease within the city.[17] There is some support for this theory from the literary sources. Vitruvius claimed that northerners were particularly susceptible to fevers and the Gauls and Germans billeted in Rome by Vitellius suffered great losses due to disease.[18] Regardless of the exact cause of these high mortality rates, the average soldier had a greater chance of survival serving in the provinces than in Rome.

The Praetorian Guard was supported by the urban cohorts who were under the command of the *praefectus urbi*.[19] The three urban cohorts were numbered consecutively with the Praetorian cohorts as X, XI and XII, which suggests that they were originally part of the structure of the Guard, perhaps representing the three cohorts stationed in Rome by Augustus. The formal separation of the two units was completed by the end of Augustus' reign when separate provision was made for them in his will.[20] By the middle of the first century AD, urban cohorts were established at Ostia and Puteoli. Vespasian also deployed urban cohorts at Lugdunum and Carthage. A fourth cohort was established in Rome during the Flavian period. Members of the urban cohorts were paid 375 denarii annually for a twenty-year term of service. Their pay was increased to 500 and 1250 denarii by Domitian and Caracalla respectively.[21] The vast majority of recruits to the urban cohorts were of Italian origin.[22] The lack of any change in recruitment under Severus indicates that the urban cohorts did not represent a threat to him. The role of the urban cohorts appears to have been restricted to maintaining law and order within the city and they did not have any significant role in the security arrangements around the emperor.

In a similar way, the *vigiles* appeared to have played no significant military role.[23] In 22 BC Augustus had created a force of 600 state slaves to fight fires in Rome. By AD 6, the *vigiles* encompassed seven cohorts with a total of around 3920 men under the command of the *praefectus vigilum*. Two cohorts were stationed at Ostia and Portus, where fire could potentially have devastating consequences on Rome's food supply. In Rome, the *vigiles* were provided with barracks and fourteen *excubitoria*, which aided their primary purpose in rapidly containing and fighting fires.[24]

The Praetorian Guard, urban cohorts and *vigiles* were linked by the movement of their centurions. Soldiers promoted from the ranks of the Guard could progress to the command of a century in a legion. Alternatively, they could serve as a centurion in the *vigiles*, urban cohorts and Guard in turn before progressing to the legions and the primipilate in some cases. Centurions who had held a post in the legions could return to the Rome cohorts and begin the sequence with a post in the urban cohorts; presumably the legionary centurionate was seen as the equivalent of a post in the *vigiles*. Centurions who had held this sequence of posts referred to themselves as *trecenarii*, which set them apart from their peers who had not commanded centuries in the Rome units.[25] Tribunes could also pass through each of the Rome units in turn, although other career paths were possible including a direct transfer to the tribunate of the Guard after the post of *primus pilus*.

On a lower level, soldiers from the urban cohorts could transfer into the Guard if they proved to be worthy candidates. Hadrian is recorded as telling an ardent young recruit to prove himself in the urban cohorts in the hope of a transfer.[26] The movement of personnel between the units in Rome encouraged uniformity in discipline and command style as well promoting familiarity with the duties and procedures used by the different formations.

The *Germani corporis custodes*, established under Augustus and cashiered by Galba, were the only irregular unit stationed in Rome.[27] They are also noteworthy for being the only unit which was completely divorced from the structure of the army. The exact number of *Germani* in Rome is unknown, but the figure of 500–1000 individuals suggested by Bellen seems to be unreasonably high.[28] Suetonius refers to them as both a cohors and a *numerus* in different parts of his work and this terminology cannot be used to infer their numerical status.[29] They appear to have been predominantly called *Germani*, reflecting their ethnic origin.[30] The absence of a formal military designation emphasized their status as a unit outside of the framework of the army. The *Germani* were recruited primarily from the Batavi, Baetasii and Ubii.[31]

These areas also furnished recruits for the *equites singulares Augusti*. There has been a tendency among some modern scholars to equate the *Germani* with this later unit on the basis of their shared ethnic origin.[32] However, there are a number of reasons to dispute this claim and the evidence suggests that the two units were completely separate. The *equites singulares* were selected from the provincial cavalry units whereas the *Germani* were chosen from the tribes themselves and there is no evidence to suggest that they had seen any previous Roman military service. According to Suetonius, Caligula went to Germany with the intention of directly selecting new recruits for the *Germani*.[33] Their role as ethnic soldiers is further reinforced by their dismissal from Rome as a possible security risk after the defeat of Varus.[34] There is also no evidence that any of the *Germani* were promoted to positions within other military units.

Another indication that they were significantly different from the *equites singulares Augusti* is the fact that they were commanded not by regular army officers, but by individuals selected personally by the emperor. Both Caligula and Nero appointed former gladiators to this role and, while it has been suggested that the position was a reward for popularity, it seems that physical strength was the main factor in such appointments.[35] Personal strength would have been a worthy asset when commanding a unit which had not been exposed to military discipline and where recruits may have found this personal attribute worthy of admiration and respect. Rather than acting as the predecessors of the *equites singulares Augusti*, the *Germani* were actually the descendants of the ethnic bodyguards who protected senior figures during the late Republic. They were bound to the emperor through personal loyalty to the Julio-Claudian dynasty, which was enhanced by substantial cash payments.[36] The termination of the dynasty after the death of Nero ensured that they were ignominiously discharged by Galba.

After the cashiering of the *Germani*, the Flavian emperors employed their own horsemen as bodyguards, although it is unclear whether these were attached to the Praetorian Guard or had served Vespasian and Titus in the East. It was probably Trajan who formed the *equites singulares Augusti* as a counterweight to the Guard, who had reason to be hostile towards him after he executed some of their comrades.[37] This unit of 1000 horsemen was based in the *Castra Priora* on the Caelian Hill. A second camp, *Castra Nova*, was built by Severus who also doubled their strength. In contrast to the Guard before the Severan reform, they were recruited from the provincial armies and therefore the *equites singulares Augusti* were a true military elite in that a transfer to their ranks was a real possibility for promising cavalrymen from the provincial armies. Recruits came mostly from the German and Danubian provinces with emphasis shifting to the latter by the third century, in line with the recruitment of the Guard.[38] The means by which candidates were chosen from the provincial armies is unclear. Veterans were commissioned as legionary centurions and this unit therefore provided a valuable link between the provincial soldiers and the troops in Rome.[39]

Other soldiers were also present in or near Rome. Troops must regularly have passed through the city on official business or on leave. At the time of the death of Nero, for example, a large number of soldiers from a variety of different provinces were gathered at Rome in preparation for a campaign against the Alani.[40] Severus deployed II Parthica at Albano, significantly increasing the number of soldiers in Italy. In Rome itself, provincial soldiers would have been present as *frumentarii*. The exact role of these men has provoked much discussion among modern scholars.[41] They were housed in the *Castra Peregrina* on the Caelian Hill under the command of the *princeps peregrinorum*. *Frumentarii* appear in the literary sources as spies, assassins and security agents acting on behalf of the emperor.[42] This has led a number of scholars to suggest that they acted as an intelligence service for the emperor, by gathering information and eliminating his opponents.[43] However, it has been demonstrated that the majority of *frumentarii* were originally recruited into their local legions and, when they died in Rome, were always commemorated by colleagues from the same legion or province.[44]

The local recruitment and provincial identity of the *frumentarii* suggests that they were ordinary legionaries selected by the provincial governor for special duties and formed part of his *officium consularis*. Their role consisted of carrying messages between Rome and the provinces. While staying in Rome, the *frumentarii* could be used for special tasks designated by the emperor, some of which are recorded in the literary sources. Service as a *frumentarius* offered promotion in the *castra*, legions or the *officium consularis*. The *frumentarii* acted as a valuable conduit of information between the provinces and Rome, which could be exploited by both the provincial governors and the emperor.

Abbreviations

AE	*L'Année épigraphique* (Paris, 1893–).
ANRW	Temporini, H. *et al.* (eds), *Aufstieg und Niedergang der römischen Welt* (Berlin, 1972–).
BGU	*Berliner griechische Urkunden (*Ägyptische *Urkunden aus den königlichen Museen zu Berlin* (Berlin, 1895–).
BMCRE	Mattingly, E. H. *et al.* (eds) *Coins of the Roman Empire in the British Museum*, Vols. 1–6 (1923–66).
CIL	Mommsen, Th. *et al.* (eds) *Corpus Inscriptionum Latinarum* (Berlin, 1863–).
CJ	Krueger, P. (ed.) *Codex Iustinianus; Corpus Iuris Civilis* Vol. II (Berlin, 1877).
Dig.	Mommsen, Th. (ed.) *Digesta; Corpus Iuris Civilis* vol. I (Berlin, 1872).
FIRA	Riccobono, S. *et al.* (eds) *Fontes iuris Romani anteiustiniani* (3 volumes, Florence, 1940–3).
IGBulg	Mikailov, G. (ed.) *Inscriptiones Graecae in Bulgaria repertae* (Sofia, 1956–87).
ILAlg	Gsell, A. *et al.* (eds) *Inscriptions Latines de l'Algérie* (Paris, 1922–76).
ILS	Dessau, H. (ed.) *Inscriptiones Latinae Selectae* (Berlin, 1892–1916).
P. Bub.	Hagedorn, D. *et al.* (eds) *Die verkohlten Papyri aus Bubastos* (Opladen, 1989–98).
P. Dura	Welles, C. B. *et al.* (eds) *The Excavations at Dura-Europos. Final Report V 1. The Parchments and Papyri* (New Haven, 1959).
P. Mich.	Winter, J. G. *et al.* (eds) *Papyri in the University of Michigan Collection* (Ann Arbor, 1931–99).
P. Vindob.	Boswinkel, E. *et al.* (eds) *Einige Wiener Papyri* (Leiden, Amsterdam, 1942–76).

RGDA	*Res Gestae Divi Augusti.*
RIB	Collingwood, R. G. & Wright, R. P. (eds) *The Roman Inscriptions of Britain*, Vol. I *Inscriptions on Stone* (Oxford, 1965).
RIC	Mattingly, E. H., Sydenham, A. *et al.* (eds) *The Roman Imperial Coinage* (London, 1923–94).
RMR	Fink, R. O. *Roman Military Documents on Papyrus* (Cleveland, 1971).
RPC	Burnett, A. *et al. Roman Provincial Coinage* (London, 1992–).
RRC	Crawford, M. H. *Roman Republican Coinage* (Cambridge, 1974).
SB	Preisigke, F. *et al.* (eds) *Sammelbuch griechischer Urkunden aus* Ägypten (Strassburg, Heidelberg, Wiesbaden, 1915–).
SCPP	*enatus Consultum de Cn. Pisone Patre*
SEG	Hondius, J. J. *et al.* (eds) *Supplementum Epigraphicum Graecum* (1923–).
Sel. Pap.	Hunt, A. S. & Edgar, C. C. (eds) *Select Papyri* Vol. I: *Non-Literary Papyri, Private Affairs* (Cambridge, MA, 1932); Vol. II *Official Documents* (Cambridge, MA, 1934).
Tab. Vindol. I	Bowman, A. K. & Thomas, J. D. *Vindolanda: The Latin Writing Tablets* (Gloucester, 1983).
Tab. Vindol. II	Bowman, A. K. & Thomas, J. D. *The Vindolanda Writing Tablets* (London, 1994).
Tab. Vindol. III	Bowman, A. K. & Thomas, J. D. *The Vindolanda Writing Tablets* (London, 2003).

Editions Used

LITERARY SOURCES

Aelius Aristides *Orationes*	Brill translation by C. A. Behr (1981)
Cassius Dio	Loeb translation by E. Cary (1955)
Fronto, *Epistulae*	Loeb translation by C. R. Haines (1919–20)
Herodian	Loeb translation by C. R. Whittaker (1969)
Josephus, *Antiquitates Judaicae*	Exeter University Press translation by T. P. Wiseman (1991)
Josephus, *Bellum Judaicum*	Loeb translation by J. St. J. Thackeray (1927)
Onasander, *Strategikos*	Loeb translation by W. A. Oldfather *et al.* (1923)
Pliny, *Epistulae*	Loeb translation by B. Radice (1969)
Pliny, *Panegyricus*	Loeb translation by B. Radice (1969)
Plutarch	Loeb translation by B. Perrin (1926)
Polybius	Penguin translation by I. Scott-Kilvert (1979)
Seneca, *De beneficiis*	Loeb translation by J. Basore (1928)
Suetonius	Penguin translation by R. Graves, revised by M. Grant (1979)
Tacitus, *Agricola*	Penguin translation by H. Mattingly, revised by S. A. Handford (1970)
Tacitus, *Annales*	Loeb translation by J. J. Jackson (1981)
Tacitus, *Historiae*	Penguin translation by K. Wellesley (1964, revised 1995)
Velleius Paterculus	Loeb translation by F. W. Shipley (1924)

INSCRIPTIONS

RGDA	Cambridge University Press translation by A. Cooley (2009)
SCPP	In Griffin, M. (1997) 'The Senate's Story' *JRS* 87 pp. 249–63

OTHER

Tab. Vindol. I	Bowman, A. K. & Thomas, J. D. *Vindolanda: The Latin Writing Tablets* (Gloucester, 1983).
Tab. Vindol. II	Bowman, A. K. & Thomas, J. D. *The Vindolanda Writing Tablets* (London, 1994).
Tab. Vindol. III	Bowman, A. K. & Thomas, J. D. *The Vindolanda Writing Tablets* (London, 2003).

Bibliography

Adams, J. N. (1999) 'The poets of Bu Njem: language, culture and the centurionate' *Journal of Roman Studies* 89 pp. 109–34.

Aldhouse-Green, M. (2001) *Dying for the Gods: Human Sacrifice in Iron Age and Roman Europe* Stroud.

Alföldy, G. (1969) *Fasti Hispanienses: Senatorische Reichsbeamte und Offiziere in den Spanischen Provinzen des römischen Reiches von Augustus bis Diokletian* Wiesbaden.

Allison, P. M. (2006) 'Mapping for gender: interpreting artefact distribution in 1st and 2nd century AD forts in Roman Germany' *Archaeological Dialogues* 13 pp. 1–20.

Alston, R. (1994) 'Roman military pay from Caesar to Diocletian' *Journal of Roman Studies* 84 pp. 113–23.

Alston, R. (1995) *Soldier and Society in Roman Egypt: A Social History* London.

Amit, M. (1965) 'Les moyens de communication et la defense de l'empire Romain' *Parola del passato* 20 pp. 207–22.

Ando, C. (2000) *Imperial Ideology and Provincial Loyalty in the Roman Empire* Berkeley.

Ando, C. (2007) 'The army and the urban elite: a competition for power' in P. Erdkamp (ed.) *A Companion to the Roman Army* Oxford pp. 359–78.

Applebaum, A. (2007) 'Another look at the assassination of Pertinax and the accession of Julianus' *Classical Philology* 102 pp. 198–207.

Ash, R. (1997) 'Severed heads: Individual portraits and irrational forces in Plutarch's Galba and Otho' in J. Mossman (ed.) *Plutarch and his intellectual world* London pp. 189–213.

Ash, R. (1999) *Ordering Anarchy: Armies and Leaders in Tacitus' Histories* London.

Ashby, T. & Baillie Reynolds, P. K. (1923) 'The Castra Peregrinorum' *Journal of Roman Studies* 13 pp. 152–67.

Austin, N. J. E. & Rankov, N. B. (1995) *Exploratio: Military and Political Intelligence in the Roman World from the Second Punic War to the Battle of Adrianople* London.

Badian, E. (1989) 'History from square brackets' *Zeitschrift für Papyrologie und Epigraphik* 79 pp. 59–70.

Baillie Reynolds, P. K. (1923) *The Vigiles of Imperial Rome* Oxford.

Ball, W. (2000) *Rome in the East: The transformation of an empire* London.

Beard, M. (1980) 'A British dedication from the city of Rome' *Britannia* 11 pp. 313–4.

Beard, M. (2007) *The Roman Triumph* Cambridge.

Beard, M. (2008) *Pompeii: The Life of a Roman Town* London.

Bellen, H. (1981) *Die germanische Leibwache der römischen Kaiser des julisch-claudischen Hauses* Wiesbaden.

Benefiel, R. (2001) 'A new Praetorian laterculus from Rome' *Zeitschrift für Papyrologie und Epigraphik* 134 pp. 221–32.

Bennett, J. (2001) *Trajan: Optimus Princeps* London.

Bennett, J. (2006) 'New evidence from Ankara for the collegia veteranorum and the albata decursio' *Anatolian Studies* 56 pp. 95–101.

Bennett, J. (2007) 'Two new centurions of the Legio IIII Scythica' *Latomus* 66 pp. 404–13.

Berriman, A. & Todd, M. (2001) 'A very Roman coup: the hidden war of imperial succession AD 96–8' *Historia* 50 pp. 312–31.

Bidwell, P. (1985) *The Roman Fort of Vindolanda at Chesterholm, Northumberland* London.

Birley, A. R. (1981) *The Fasti of Roman Britain* Oxford.

Birley, A. R. (1990) 'Officers of the second Augustan legion in Britain' in R. J. Brewer (ed.) *The Second Augustan Legion and the Roman Military Machine* Cardiff pp. 103–24.

Birley, A. R. (1998) 'A new tombstone from Vindolanda' *Britannia* 29 pp. 299–306.

Birley, A. R. (1999) *The African Emperor Septimius Severus* (2nd edition), Oxford.

Birley, A. R. (2000) 'Senators as generals' in G. Alföldy, B. Dobson and W. Eck (eds) *Kaiser, Heer und Gesellschaft in der Römischen Kaiserzeit. Gedenkschrift für Eric Birley* Stuttgart pp. 97–119.

Birley, A. R. (2001) *Hadrian: The Restless Emperor* London.

Birley, A. R. (2003) 'The commissioning of equestrian officers' in J. J. Wilkes (ed.) *Documenting the Roman Army: Essays in Honour of Margaret Roxan* London pp. 1–18.

Birley, A. R. (2005) *The Roman Government of Britain* Oxford.

Birley, A. R. (2007) 'Making emperors: imperial instrument or independent force?' in P. Erdkamp (ed.) *A Companion to the Roman Army* Oxford pp. 379–94.

Birley, E. (1934) 'A new inscription from Chesterholm' *Archaeologia Aeliana (4th Series) 11* pp. 127–37.

Birley, E. (1935) 'Marcus Cocceius Firmus: an epigraphic study' *Proceedings of the Society of Antiquaries of Scotland* 70 pp. 363–77.

Birley, E. (1939) 'The Beaumont inscription, the Notitia Dignitatum and the garrison of Hadrian's Wall' *Transactions of the Cumberland & Westmorland Antiquarian and Archaeological Society* 39 pp. 190–226.

Birley, E. (1953a) 'The origins of legionary centurions' in *Roman Britain and the Roman Army* Kendal pp. 104–24.

Birley, E. (1953b) 'Senators in the emperors' service' *Proceedings of the British Academy* 39 pp. 197–214.

Birley, E. (1961) 'Britain after Agricola and the end of the ninth legion' in *Roman Britain and the Roman Army* Kendal pp. 20–30.

Birley, E. (1964) 'Promotions and transfers in the Roman army II: the centurionate' *Carnuntum Jahrbucher 1963/4* pp. 21–33.

Birley, E. (1966) 'The Roman inscriptions of York' *Yorkshire Archaeological Journal* 41 pp. 726–34.

Birley, E. (1967) 'Troops from the two Germanies in Roman Britain' *Epigraphische Studien* 4 pp. 103–7.

Birley, E. (1978) 'The religion of the Roman army 1895–1977' *ANRW* 2.16.2 pp. 1506–41.

Birley, E. (1984) 'A centurion of Leg VI Victrix and his wife' *Zeitschrift für Papyrologie und Epigraphik* 57 pp. 230–2.

Birley, E. (1988a) 'Promotions and transfers in the Roman army: senatorial and equestrian officers' in *The Roman Army: Papers 1929–1986* Amsterdam pp. 93–113.

Birley, E. (1988b) 'The equestrian officers of the Roman army' in *The Roman Army: Papers 1929–1986* Amsterdam pp. 147–64.

Birley, E. (1989) 'Some legionary centurions' *Zeitschrift für Papyrologie und Epigraphik* 79 pp. 114–28.

Black, E. W. (1984) 'The Antonine Itinerary: aspects of government in Roman Britain' *Oxford Journal of Archaeology* 3 pp. 109–21.

Bodel, J. (2001) *Epigraphic evidence: ancient history from inscriptions* London.

Bonfante, L. (1984) 'Human sacrifice on an Etruscan funerary urn' *American Journal of Archaeology* 88 pp. 531–9.

Boorstein, M. (2007) 'Eerie souvenirs from the Vietnam War' *Washington Post*, Tuesday, 3 July 2007.

Boschung, D. (1987) 'Römische Glasphalerae mit Porträtbüsten' *Bonner Jahrbücher* 187 pp. 193–258.

Botermann, H. (1968) *Die Soldaten und die römische Politik in der Zeit von Caesars Tod bis zum Begründung des Zweiten Triumvirats* Munich.

Bowman, A. K. (1970) 'A letter of Avidius Cassius?' *Journal of Roman Studies* 60 pp. 20–6.

Bowman, A. K. (1994) 'The Roman imperial army: letters and literacy on the northern frontier' in A. K. Bowman & G. Woolf (eds) *Literacy and Power in the Ancient World* Cambridge pp. 109–25.

Bowman, A. K. & Thomas, J. D. (1991) 'A military strength report from Vindolanda' *Journal of Roman Studies* 81 pp. 62–73.

Breeze, D. (1969) 'The organisation of the legion: the first cohort and the equites legionis' *Journal of Roman Studies* 59 pp. 50–5.

Breeze, D. J. (1988) 'Why did the Romans fail to conquer Scotland?' *Proceedings of the Society of Antiquaries of Scotland* 118 pp. 3–22.

Breeze, D. J. (1997) 'The regiments stationed at Maryport and their commanders' in R. J. A. Wilson (ed.) *Roman Maryport and Its Setting: Essays in Honour of Michael G. Jarrett* Maryport pp. 67–89.

Breeze, D. & Dobson, B (1969) 'The Rome cohorts and the legionary centurionate' *Epigraphische Studien* 8 pp. 100–17.

Brilliant, R. (1963) *Gesture and Rank in Roman Art* New Haven.

Brunt, P. A. (1973) 'The fall of Perennis: Dio-Xiphilinus 72.9.2' *Classical Quarterly* 23 pp. 172–77.

Brunt, P. A. (1975) 'The administrators of Roman Egypt' *Journal of Roman Studies* 65 pp. 124–47.

Brunt, P. A. (1976) 'Conscription and volunteering in the Roman army' *Scripta Classica Israelica* 1 pp. 90–115.

Brunt, P. A. (1977) 'The lex de imperio Vespasiani' *Journal of Roman Studies* 67 pp. 95–116.

Brunt, P. A. (1983) 'Princeps and equites' *Journal of Roman Studies* 73 pp. 42–75.

Brunt, P. A. (1988) 'The army and the land in the Roman Revolution' in *The Fall of the Roman Republic and Other Essays* Oxford pp. 240–80.

Brunt, P. A. (1990a) 'Laus imperii' in *Roman Imperial Themes* Oxford pp. 288–323.

Brunt, P. A. (1990b) 'Tacitus on the Batavian Revolt' in *Roman Imperial Themes* Oxford pp. 33–52.

Bruun, C. (2004) 'The legend of Decebalus' in L. De Ligt *et al.* (eds) *Roman Rule and Civic Life: Local and Regional Perspectives. Proceedings of the Fourth Workshop of the International Network Impact of Empire* Amsterdam pp. 153–75.

Busch, A. W. (2007) 'Militia in urbe: the military presence in Rome' in L. De Blois and E. Lo Cascio (eds) *The Impact of the Roman Army (200 BC – AD 476)* Leiden pp. 315–41.

Campbell, B. (1975) 'Who were the viri militares?' *Journal of Roman Studies* 65 pp. 11–31.

Campbell, B. (1984) *The Emperor and the Roman Army (31 BC – AD 235)* Oxford.

Campbell, B. (1987) 'Teach yourself how to be a general' *Journal of Roman Studies* 77 pp. 13–29.

Campbell, B. (1994) *The Roman Army 31 BC – AD 337: A Sourcebook* London.

Campbell, B. (2002) *War and Society in Imperial Rome 31 BC – AD 235* London.

Campbell, D. B. (1986) 'What happened at Hatra? The problem of the Severan siege operations' in P. Freeman & D. Kennedy (eds) *The Defence of the Roman and Byzantine East* BAR International Series 297 pp. 51–76.

Caprino, C. (1955) *La Colonna di Marco Aurelio* Rome.

Carroll, M. (2006) *Spirits of the Dead: Roman Funerary Commemoration in Western Europe* Oxford.

Champlin, E. (2003) *Nero* Cambridge, Mass.

Chilver, G. E. F. (1957) 'The army in politics AD 68–70' *Journal of Roman Studies* 47 pp. 29–35.

Chrissanthos, S. G. (2001) 'Caesar and the mutiny of 47 BC' *Journal of Roman Studies* 91 pp. 63–75.

Christol, M. & Drew-Bear, T. (1987) *Un castellum romain près d'Apamée de Phrygie* Wien.

Clarke, S. (2000) 'In search of a different Roman period: the finds assemblage at the Newstead military complex' in G. Fincham, G. Harrison, R. Holland & L. Revill (eds) *TRAC 99: The Ninth Annual Proceedings of the Theoretical Roman Archaeology Conference* Oxford pp. 22–9.

Clay, C. (2004) 'Iconoclasm in Roman Chester: the significance of the mutilated tombstones from the north wall' *Journal of the British Archaeological Association* 157 pp. 1–16.

Conole, P. & Milns, R. D. (1983) 'Neronian frontier policy in the Balkans: The career of Ti. Plautius Silvanus' *Historia* 32 pp. 183–200.

Corcoran, S. (1996) *The Empire of the Tetrarchs: Imperial Pronouncements and Government AD 284–324* Oxford.

Cornell, T. (1993) 'The end of Roman imperial expansion' in J. Rich & G. Shipley (eds) *War and Society in the Roman World* London pp. 139–70.

Cotton, H. M. (1981) 'Military tribunates and the exercise of patronage' *Chiron* 11 pp. 229–38.

Coulston, J. C. (2000) 'Armed and belted men: the soldiery in imperial Rome' in J. Coulston and H. Dodge (eds) *Ancient Rome: The Archaeology of the Eternal City* Oxford pp. 76–118.

Coulston, J. C. N. (2003) 'Overcoming the barbarian: depictions of Rome's enemies in Trajanic monumental art' in L. De Blois *et al.* (eds) *The Representation and Perception of Roman Imperial Power: Proceedings of the Third Workshop of the International Network Impact of Empire* Amsterdam pp. 389–424.

Coulston, J. C. (2007) 'Art, culture and service: the depiction of soldiers on funerary monuments of the 3rd century AD' in L. De Blois and E. Lo Cascio (eds) *The Impact of the Roman Army: Economic, Social, Political, Religious and Cultural Aspects (200 BC – AD 476)* Leiden pp. 529–61.

Crawford, M. H. (1974) *Roman Republican Coinage* (2 vols), Cambridge.

Crawford, M. H. (1996) *Roman Statutes* London.

Cunliffe, B. (2002) *Iron Age Communities in Britain* London

Cunliffe, B. (2003) *Danebury Hillfort* Stroud.

Curle, J. (1911) *A Roman Frontier Post and Its People: The Fort of Newstead in the Parish of Melrose* Glasgow.

Damon, C. (2006) 'Constructing a narrative' in D. S. Potter (ed.) *A Companion to the Roman Empire* Oxford pp. 23–44.

Daniels, C. & Harbottle, B. (1980) 'A new inscription of Julia Domna from Newcastle' *Archaeologia Aeliana (5th Series) 8* pp. 65–74.

D'Arms, J. H. (1988) 'Pompeii and Rome in the Augustan age and beyond: the eminence of the Gens Holconia' in R. I. Curtis (ed.) *Studia Pompeiana et Classica in Honor of Wilhelmina F. Jashemski* New Rochelle, NY pp. 51–73.

Davies, G. (1985) 'The significance of the handshake motif in classical art' *American Journal of Archaeology* 89 pp. 627–40.

Davies, P. J. E. (1997) 'The politics of perpetuation: Trajan's Column and the art of commemoration' *American Journal of Archaeology* 101 pp. 41–65.

Davies, R. W. (1968) 'Fronto, Hadrian and the Roman army' *Latomus* 27 pp. 75–95.

Davies, R. W. (1969) 'Joining the Roman army' *Bonner Jahrbücher* 169 pp. 208–32.

Davies, R. W. (1970) 'The Roman military medical service' *Saalburg Jahrbuch* 27 pp. 84–104.

Davies, R. W. (1974) 'A report of an attempted coup' *Aegyptus* 54 pp. 179–96.

Davies, R. W. (1976) 'Centurions and decurions of Cohors XX Palmyrenorum' *Zeitschrift für Papyrologie und Epigraphik* 20 pp. 253–75.

Dessau, H. (1912) 'British centurions' *Journal of Roman Studies* 2 pp. 21–4.

Devijer, H. (1976) *Prosopographia militiarum equestrium quae fuerunt ab Augusto AD Gallienum* Leuven.

Devijver, H. (1992) 'Bears, bison – and the Roman army' in *The Equestrian Officers of the Roman Army II* Stuttgart pp. 140–7.

Dobson, B. (1972) 'Legionary centurion or equestrian officer: a comparison of pay and prospects' *Ancient Society* 3 pp. 193–207.

Dobson, B. (1974) 'The significance of the centurion and primipilaris in the Roman army and administration' *ANRW* II.1 Berlin pp. 392–434.

Dobson, B. (1978) *Die Primipilares* Bonn.

Dobson, B. (1993) 'The centurionate and social mobility during the Principate' in D. Breeze & B. Dobson (eds) *Roman Officers and Frontiers* Stuttgart pp. 201–17.

Dobson, B. (2000) 'The primipilares in army and society' in G. Alfoldy, B. Dobson and W. Eck (eds) *Kaiser, Heer und Gesellschaft in der Römischen Kaiserzeit. Gedenkschrift für Eric Birley* Stuttgart pp. 139–52.

Dobson, B. & Mann, J. C. (1973) 'The Roman army in Britain and Britons in the Roman army' *Britannia* 4 pp. 191–205.

Dolmans, M. & Thunissen, C. (2002) *Het oudste Leiderdorp ligt onder je voeten. Leiderdorp uit archeologische en historische bron* Leiderdorp.

Dorutiu, E. (1961) 'Some observations on the military funeral altar of Adamklissi' *Dacia* 5 pp. 345–63.

Duncan-Jones, R. (1990) *Structure and Scale in the Roman Economy* Cambridge.

Durry, M. (1938) *Les Cohortes Prétoriennes* Paris.

Dušanić, S. (2003) 'The imperial propaganda of significant day-dates: two notes in military history' in J. J. Wilkes (ed.) *Documenting the Roman Army: Essays in Honour of Margaret Roxan* London pp. 89–100.

Eadie, J. (1996) 'One hundred years of rebellion: the eastern army in politics, AD 175–272' in D. L. Kennedy (ed.) *The Roman Army in the East* Ann Arbor pp. 135–51.

Eaton, J. (2011). The political significance of the imperial watchword in the early empire. *Greece & Rome*, 58(1) pp. 48–63.

Eaton, J. (2017) 'The political role of the legionary centurions' in A. Parker (ed.) Ad *Vallum: Papers on the Roman Army and Frontiers in Celebration of Dr Brian Dobson* BAR British Series 631 pp. 11–18.

Echols, E. (1958) 'The Roman city police: origin and development' *Classical Journal* 53 pp. 377–84.

Eck, W. (2002) 'Imperial administration and epigraphy: in defence of prosopography' in A. K. Bowman *et al.* (eds) *Representations of Empire: Rome and the Mediterranean World* Oxford pp. 133–52.

Ehrenberg, V. & Jones, A. H. M. (1949) *Documents Illustrating the Reigns of Augustus and Tiberius* Oxford.

Ezov, A. (2007) 'The centurions in the Rhine legions in the second and early third century' *Historia* 56.1 pp. 46–81.

Ferguson, N. (2006) *The War of the World: History's Age of Hatred* London.

Fields, N. (2005) 'Headhunters of the Roman army' in A. Hopkins & M. Wyke (eds) *Roman Bodies* London pp. 55–65.

Fink, R. O. (1971) *Roman Military Records on Papyrus* Ann Arbor.

Fink, R. O., Hoey, A. S. & Snyder, W. F. (1940) 'Feriale Duranum' *Yale Classical Studies* 7 pp 1–222.

Fishwick, D. (1991) *The Imperial Cult in the Latin West: Studies in the Ruler Cult of the Western Provinces of the Roman Empire* Volume 2.1 Leiden.

Fishwick, D. (2004) *The Imperial Cult in the Latin West: Studies in the Ruler Cult of the Western Provinces of the Roman Empire: The Provincial Centre* Volume 3.3 Leiden.

Flower, H. L. (2001) 'A tale of two monuments: Domitian, Trajan and some Praetorians at Pozzuoli' *American Journal of Archaeology* 105 pp. 625–48.

Franke, T. (1991) *Die Legionslegaten der römischen Armee in der Zeit von Augustus bis Traian* Bochum.

Freis, H. (1967) *Die Cohortes Urbanae* Epigraphische Studien 2, Köln.

Frenz, H. G. (1989) 'The honorary arch at Mainz-Kastel' *Journal of Roman Archaeology* 2 pp. 120–5.

Gagos, T. & Potter, D. S. (2006) 'Documents' in D. S. Potter (ed.) *A Companion to the Roman Empire* Oxford pp. 45–74.

Galinsky, K. (1996) *Augustan Culture* Princeton.

Galsterer, H. (1990) 'A man, a book and a method: Sir Ronald Syme's Roman Revolution after fifty years' in K. A. Raaflaub & M. Toher (eds) *Between Republic and Empire: Interpretations of Augustus and his Principate* Berkeley pp. 1–20.

Galsterer, H. (1999) 'Das Militär als Träger der lateinischen Sprach- und Schriftkultur' in H. von Hesberg (ed.) *Das Militär als Kulturträger in römischer Zeit* Köln pp. 37–50.

Gilliam, J. F. (1940) 'The ordinarii and ordinati of the Roman army' *Transactions of the American Philological Association* 71 pp. 127–48.

Gilliam, J. F. (1954) 'The Roman military feriale' *Harvard Theological Review* 47 pp. 183–96.

Gilliam, J. F. (1957) 'The appointment of auxiliary centurions (PMich.164)' *Transactions of the American Philological Association* 88 pp. 155–68.

Gilliver, K. (1993) 'The de munitionibus castrorum: text and translation' *Journal of Roman Military Equipment Studies* 4 pp. 33–48.

Gilliver, K. (1996) 'Mons Graupius and the role of auxiliaries in battle' *Greece & Rome* 43 pp. 54–67.

Gilliver, K. (2007) 'Display in Roman warfare: the appearance of armies and individuals on the battlefield' *War in History* 14 pp. 1–21.

Ginsburg, M. (1940) 'Roman military clubs and their social functions' *Transactions of the American Philological Association* 71 pp. 149–56.

Goldsworthy, A. (1996) *The Roman Army at War 100 BC – 200 AD* Oxford.

Goldsworthy, A. (1999) 'Community under pressure: the Roman army at the siege of Jerusalem' in A. Goldsworthy & I. Haynes (eds) *The Roman Army as a Community* Portsmouth pp. 197–210.

Gónzalez, J. (1988) 'The first oath pro salute Augusti found in Baetica' *Zeitschrift für Papyrologie und Epigraphik* 72 pp. 113–27.

Gónzalez, J. (1999) 'Tacitus, Germanicus, Piso and the Tabula Siarensis' *American Journal of Philology* 120 pp. 123–42.

Gordon, A. E. (1952) *Quintus Veranius, consul AD 49: a study based upon his recently identified sepulchral inscription* Berkeley.

Gradel, I. (2002) *Emperor Worship and Roman Religion* Oxford.

Grant, A. E. (2007) *Roman Military Objectives in Britain under the Flavian Empire* BAR British Series 440.

Griffin, M. (1997) 'The Senate's story' *Journal of Roman Studies* 87 pp. 249–63.

Griffin, M. (2001) *Nero: The End of a Dynasty* London.

Hansen, M. H. (1993) 'The battle exhortation in ancient historiography: fact or fiction?' *Historia* 42 pp. 161–80.

Harker, A. (2008) *Loyalty and Dissidence in Roman Egypt: The Case of the Acta Alexandrinorum* Cambridge.

Harris, W. V. (1989) *Ancient Literacy* Cambridge, Mass.

Harris, W. V. (2006) 'Readings in the narrative literature of Roman courage' in S. Dillon & K. Welch (eds) *Representations of War in Ancient Rome* Cambridge pp. 300–20.

Harrison, S. (2006) 'Skull trophies of the Pacific War: transgressive objects of remembrance' *Journal of the Royal Anthropological Institute* 12 pp. 817–36.

Harto Trujillo, M. L. (2008) *Las arengas militares en la historiografía Latina* Madrid.

Hauken, T. (1998) *Petition and Response: An Epigraphic Study of Petitions to Roman Emperors 181–249* Bergen.

Haynes, H. (2006) 'Survival and memory in the Agricola' *Arethusa* 39 pp. 149–70.

Haynes, I. (2002) 'Britain's first information revolution: the Roman army and the transformation of economic life' in P. Erdkamp (ed.) *The Roman Army and the Economy* Amsterdam pp. 111–26.

Haynes, I. (2013) *Blood of the Provinces: The Roman Auxilia and the Making of Provincial Society from Augustus to the Severans.* Oxford.

Hebblewhite, M. (2017) *The Emperor and the Army in the Later Roman Empire.* Abingdon, Oxon.

Hekster, O. (2001) 'All in the family: the appointment of emperors designate in the second century AD' in L. De Blois (ed.) *Administration, Prosopography and Appointment Policies in the Roman Empire: Proceedings of the First Workshop of the International Network Impact of Empire* Amsterdam pp. 35–49.

Hekster, O. (2003a) 'Coins and messages: audience targeting on coins of different denominations?' in L. De Blois et al (eds) *The Representation and Perception of Roman Imperial Power: Proceedings of the Third Workshop of the International Network Impact of Empire* Amsterdam pp. 20–35.

Hekster, O. (2003b) *Commodus: An Emperor at the Crossroads* Leiden.

Hekster, O. (2005) 'Captured in the gaze of power: visibility, games and Roman imperial representation' in R. Fowler & O. Hekster (eds) *Imaginary Kings: Royal Images in the Ancient Near East, Greece and Rome* Munich pp. 157–76.

Hekster, O. (2007a) 'Fighting for Rome: the emperor as a military leader' in L. De Blois and E. Lo Cascio (eds) *The Impact of the Roman Army (200 BC–AD 476)* Leiden.

Hekster, O. (2007b) 'The Roman army and propaganda' in P. Erdkamp (ed.) *A Companion to the Roman Army* Oxford pp. 339–58.

Helgeland, J. (1978) 'Roman army religion' *ANRW* 16.2 pp. 1470–1505.

Henig, M. (1974) *A Corpus of Roman Engraved Gemstones from British Sites* Oxford.

Herrmann, P. (1968) *Der römische Kaisereid* Göttingen.

Herz, P. (2002) 'Sacrifice and sacrificial ceremonies of the Roman imperial army' in A. Baumgarten (ed.) *Sacrifice in Religious Experience* Leiden pp. 81–100.

Herz, P. (2007) 'Finances and costs of the Roman army' in P. Erdkamp (ed.) *A Companion to the Roman Army* Oxford pp. 306–22.

Hewitt, K. V. (1983) 'The coinage of L. Clodius Macer AD 68' *Numismatic Chronicle* 143 pp. 64–80.

Hill, P. R. (1997) 'The Maryport altars: some first thoughts' in R. J .A. Wilson (ed.) *Roman Maryport and Its Setting: Essays in Honour of Michael G. Jarrett* Maryport pp. 92–104.

Hind, J. G. F. (2003) 'Caligula and the spoils of the Ocean: a rush for riches in the far North-West?' *Britannia* 34 pp. 272–4.

Hoffmann, B. (1995) 'The quarters of the legionary centurions of the Principate' *Britannia* 26 pp. 107–51.

Hoffmann, B. (2004) 'Tacitus, Agricola and the role of literature in the archaeology of the first century AD' in E. W. Sauer (ed.) *Archaeology and Ancient History: Breaking Down the Boundaries* London pp. 151–65.

Holder, P. A. (1980) *Studies in the Auxilia of the Roman Army from Augustus to Trajan* BAR International Series 70.

Holder, P. A. (1999) 'Exercitus Pius Fidelis: The army of Germania Inferior in AD 89' *Zeitschrift für Papyrologie und Epigraphik* 128 pp. 237–50.

Holmes, R. (2003) *Acts of War: The behaviour of men in battle* London.

Holmes, R. (2004) *Tommy: The British Soldier on the Western Front 1914–18* London.

Hope, V. M. (2001) *Constructing Identity: The Roman funerary monuments of Aquileia, Mainz and Nimes* Oxford.

Hope, V. M. (2003) 'Trophies and tombstones: commemorating the Roman soldier' *World Archaeology* 35 pp. 79–97.

Hopkins, K. (1983) *Death and Renewal* Cambridge.

Howe, L. L. (1942) *The Pretorian Prefect from Commodus to Diocletian (AD 180–305)* Chicago.

Isaac, B. (1995) 'Hierarchy and command structure in the Roman army' in Y. Le Bohec (ed.) *La Hierarchie (Rangordnung) De L'Armee Romaine sous le Haut-Empire* pp. 23–31 Paris.

Isaac, B. H. & Roll, I. (1976) 'A milestone of AD 69 from Judaea: The elder Trajan and Vespasian' *Journal of Roman Studies* 66 pp. 15–9.

Isserlin, R. M. (1997) 'Thinking the unthinkable: human sacrifice in Roman Britain?' in Meadows, K., Lemke, C. and Heron, J. (eds) *TRAC 96: Proceedings of the Sixth Annual Theoretical Roman Archaeology Conference, University of Sheffield, March 1996*. Oxford pp. 91–100.

James, S. (1999) 'The community of the soldiers: a major identity and centre of power in the Roman empire' in P. Barker *et al.* (eds) *TRAC 98: Proceedings of the eighth annual Theoretical Roman Archaeology Conference* Oxford pp. 14–25.

James, S. (2006) 'Engendering change in our understanding of the structure of Roman military communities' *Archaeological Dialogues* 13 pp. 31–6.

Jarrett, M. G. (1994) 'Non-legionary troops in Britain Part I: the units' *Britannia* 25 pp. 35–77.

Jones, A. H. M. (1956) 'Numismatics and history' in R. A. G. Carson (ed.) *Essays in the Roman Coinage Presented to Harold Mattingly* Oxford pp. 13–33.

Jones, B. W. (1993) *The Emperor Domitian* London.

Kajanto, I. (1970) 'Tacitus' attitude to war and the soldier' *Latomus* 29 pp. 699–718.

Keaveney, A. (2007) *The Army in the Roman Revolution* London.

Kemmers, F. (2006) *Coins for a Legion: An Analysis of the Coin Finds from the Augustan Legionary Fortress and Flavian Canabae Legionis at Nijmegen* Mainz.

Kennedy, D. L. (1978) 'Some observations on the Praetorian Guard' *Ancient Society* 9 pp. 275–301.

Kennedy, D. L. (1983) 'C. Velius Rufus' *Britannia* 14 pp. 183–96.

Kennedy, D. L. (1986) 'Europaean soldiers and the Severan siege of Hatra' in P. Freeman & D. Kennedy (eds) *The Defence of the Roman and Byzantine East* BAR International Series 297 pp. 397–409.

Keppie, L. (1983) *Colonisation and Veteran Settlement in Italy 47–14 BC* London.

Keppie, L. (1984) *The Making of the Roman Army: From Republic to Empire* London.

Keppie, L. (1994) 'Roman inscriptions and sculpture from Birrens: a review' *Transactions of the Dumfriesshire and Galloway Natural History and Antiquarian Society* 69 pp. 35–51.

Keppie, L. (1996) 'The Praetorian Guard before Sejanus' *Athenaeum 84* pp. 101–24.

Koeppel, G. (1969) 'Profectio und adventus' *Bonner Jahrbücher* 169 pp. 130–94.

Kraay, C. (1952) 'Revolt and subversion: the so-called military coinage of AD 69 re-examined' *Numismatic Chronicle* 12 pp. 78–86.

Kuttner, A. L. (1995) *Dynasty and Empire in the Age of Augustus: The Case of the Boscoreale Cups* Berkeley.

Kyle, D. G. (1998) *Spectacles in Death in Ancient Rome* London.

Le Bohec, Y. (1989) *La Troisième Légion Auguste* Paris.

Lee, A. D. (1993) *Information and Frontiers: Roman Foreign Relations in Late Antiquity* Cambridge.

Lee, A. D. (1996) 'Morale and the Roman experience of battle' in A. B. Lloyd (ed.) *Battle in Antiquity* London pp. 199–217.

Lendon, J. E. (1997) *Empire of Honour: The Art of Government in the Roman World* Oxford.

Lendon, J. E. (2004) 'The Roman army now' *Classical Journal* 99 pp. 441–9.

Lendon, J. E. (2005) *Soldiers and Ghosts: A History of Battle in Classical Antiquity* New York.

Lendon, J. E. (2006) 'Contubernalis, commanipularis and commilito in Roman soldiers' epigraphy: drawing the distinction' *Zeitschrift für Papyrologie und Epigraphik* 157 pp. 270–6.

Lepper, F. & Frere, S. (1988) *Trajan's Column: A New Edition of the Cichorius Plates* Gloucester.

Levick, B. (1982) 'Propaganda and the imperial coinage' *Antichthon* 16 pp. 104–16.

Levick, B. (1985) 'L. Verginius Rufus and the four emperors' *Rheinisches Museum für Philologie* 128 pp. 318–46.

Levick, B. (1999) 'Messages on Roman coins: types and inscriptions' in G. M. Paul (ed.) *Roman Coins and Public Life under the Empire* Ann Arbor pp. 41–60.

Levick, B. (2007) *Julia Domna: Syrian Empress* London.

Levithan, J. (2007) 'Emperors, sieges and intentional exposure' in E. Bragg, L. Hau and E. Macauley-Lewis (eds) *Beyond the Battlefields: New Perspectives on Warfare and Society in the Graeco–Roman World* Newcastle pp. 25–45.

Linderski, J. (2002) 'Romans in the province of Pesaro and Urbino' *Journal of Roman Archaeology* 15 pp. 577–80.

Lörincz, B. (1982) 'Zur Datierung des Beinamens Antoniniana bei Truppenkörpern' *Zeitschrift für Papyrologie und Epigraphik* 48 pp. 142–8.

MacMullen, R. (1960) 'Inscriptions on armour and the supply of arms in the Roman empire' *American Journal of Archaeology* 64 pp. 23–40.

MacMullen, R. (1984) 'The legion as a society' *Historia* 33 pp. 440–56.

Malloch, S. J. V. (2001) 'Gaius on the Channel coast' *Classical Quarterly* 51 pp. 551–6.

Malone, S. J. (2006) *Legio XX Valeria Victrix: Prosopography, Archaeology and History* Oxford.

Mann, J. C. (1983a) 'Trecenarius' *Zeitschrift für Papyrologie und Epigraphik* 52 pp. 136–40.

Mann, J. C. (1983b) *Legionary Recruitment and Veteran Settlement during the Principate* London.

Mann, J. C. (1985) 'Epigraphic consciousness' *Journal of Roman Studies* 75 pp. 204–6.

Mann, J. C. (1988) 'The organisation of the frumentarii' *Zeitschrift für Papyrologie und Epigraphik 74* pp. 149–50.

Marshall, A. J. (1975) 'Tacitus and the governor's lady: a note on Annals iii. 33–4' *Greece & Rome* 22 pp. 11–8.

Mattern, S. P. (1999) *Rome and the Enemy: Imperial Strategy in the Principate* Berkeley.

Mattingly, H. (1952) 'The military class in the coinage of the civil wars of AD 68–69" *Numismatic Chronicle* 12 pp. 72–7.

Maxfield, V. A. (1981) *The Military Decorations of the Roman Army* London.

Maxfield, V. A. (1986) 'Pre-Flavian forts and their garrisons' *Britannia* 17 pp. 59–72.

Bibliography

McDonnell, M. (2006) *Roman Manliness: Virtus and the Roman Republic* Cambridge.

Messer, W. S. (1920) 'Mutiny in the Roman army: the Republic' *Classical Philology* 15 pp. 158–75.

Metcalf, W. E. (2006) 'Roman imperial numismatics' in D. S. Potter (ed.) *A Companion to the Roman Empire* Oxford pp. 35–44.

Millar, F. (1964) *A Study of Cassius Dio* Oxford.

Millar, F. (1977) *The Emperor in the Roman World (31 BC – AD 337)* London.

Millar, F. (1982) 'Emperors, frontiers and foreign relations, 31 BC to AD 378' *Britannia* 13 pp. 1–23.

Millar, F. (1988) 'Imperial ideology in the Tabula Siarensis' in J. Acre & J. Gónzalez (eds) *Estudios sobre la Tabula Siarensis* Madrid pp. 11–9.

Mirković, M. (1994) 'Beneficiarii consularis in Sirmium' *Chiron* 24 pp. 345–401.

Mitchell, S. (1976) 'Requisitioned transport in the Roman Empire: a new inscription from Pisidia' *Journal of Roman Studies* 66 pp. 106–31.

Morgan, G. (2006) *69 AD The Year of Four Emperors* Oxford.

Mosser, M. (2003) *Die Steindenkmäler der Legio XV Apollinaris* Wien. Mrozewicz, L. (1984) 'Victoria Aug(usta) Panthea Sanctissima' *Zeitschrift für Papyrologie und Epigraphik* 57 pp. 181–8.

Nicolay, J. (2007) *Armed Batavians: Use and Significance of Weaponry and Horse Gear from Non-military Contexts in the Rhine Delta (50 BC to AD 450)* Amsterdam.

Nicols, J. (1978) *Vespasian and the Partes Flavianae* Wiesbaden.

Nock, A. D. (1952) 'The Roman army and the Roman religious year' *Harvard Theological Review* 45 pp. 187–252.

Noreña, C. F. (2001) 'The communication of the emperor's virtues' *Journal of Roman Studies* 91 pp. 146–68.

Noy, D. (2000) *Foreigners at Rome: Citizens and Strangers* London.

Nippel, W. (1984) 'Policing Rome' *Journal of Roman Studies* 74 pp. 20–9.

Nippel, W. (1995) *Public Order in Ancient Rome* Cambridge.

Okamura, L. (1988) 'Social disturbances in late Roman Gaul: deserters, rebels and Bagaudae' in T. Yuge and M. Doi (eds) *Forms of Control and Subordination in Antiquity* pp. 288–302 Leiden.

Ortisi, S. (2007) 'Roman military in the Vesuvius area' in L. De Blois and E. Lo Cascio (eds) *The Impact of the Roman Army (200 BC – AD 476)* Leiden pp. 343–53.

Osgood, J. (2006) *Caesar's Legacy: Civil War and the Emergence of the Roman Empire* Cambridge.

Parker, R. (1983) *Miasma: Pollution and Purification in early Greek Religion* Oxford.

Passerini, A. (1939) *Le Coorti Pretorie* Rome.

Patterson, J. (1993) 'Military organization and social change in the later Roman Republic' in J. Rich (ed.) *War and Society in the Roman World* London pp. 92–112.

Pegler, A. (2000) 'Social organisations within the Roman army' in G. Fincham *et al.* (eds) *TRAC 99: Proceedings of the ninth annual Theoretical Roman Archaeology Conference* Oxford pp. 37–43.

Peretz, D. (2005) 'Military burial and the identification of Roman fallen soldiers' *Klio* 87 pp. 123–38.

Petrocelli, C. (2008) *Onasandro: Il generale, Manuale per l'esercizio del comando, introduzione, tradizione e note* Bari.

Phang, S. E. (2001) *The Marriage of Roman Soldiers (13 BC – AD 235): Law and family in the imperial army* Leiden.

Phang, S. E. (2007) 'Military documents, languages and literacy' in P. Erdkamp (ed.) *A Companion to the Roman Army* Oxford pp. 286–305.

Phang, S. E. (2008) *Roman Military Service: Ideologies of Discipline in the Late Republic and Early Principate* Cambridge.

Pitts, L. F. & St. Joseph, J. K. (1985) *Inchtuthil: The Roman Legionary Fortress Excavations 1952–1965* Britannia Monograph Series 6 London.

Pollard, N. (2000) *Soldiers, Cities & Civilians in Roman Syria* Ann Arbor.

Potter, D. S. (1987) 'The Tabula Siarensis, Tiberius, the Senate and the Eastern Boundary of the Roman Empire' *Zeitschrift für Papyrologie und Epigraphik* 69 pp. 269–76.

Potter, D. S. (1996) 'Emperors, their borders and their neighbours: the scope of imperial *mandata*' in D. L. Kennedy (ed.) *The Roman Army in the East* (JRA Supplement 18) Ann Arbor pp. 49–65.

Potter, D. S. (1999) 'Political theory in the Senatus Consultum de Cn. Pisone Patre' *American Journal of Philology* 120 pp. 65–88.

Potter, D. S. (2006) 'The transformation of the empire 235–337 CE' in D. S. Potter (ed.) *A Companion to the Roman Empire* Oxford pp. 153–73.

Raaflaub, K. A. (1980) 'The political significance of Augustus' military reforms' in W. S. Hanson & L. J. F. Keppie (eds) *Roman Frontier Studies 1979: Papers presented to the 12th International Congress of Roman Frontier Studies* Oxford pp. 1005–25.

Rainbird, J. S. (1986) 'The fire stations of imperial Rome' *Papers of the British School at Rome 54* pp. 147–69.

Ramsay, R. M. (1925) 'The speed of the Roman imperial post' *Journal of Roman Studies* 15 pp. 60–74.

Rankov, B. (1987) 'M. Oclatinius Adventus in Britain' *Britannia 18* pp. 243–9.

Rankov, B. (1990) 'Frumentarii, the Castra Peregrina and the provincial officia' *Zeitschrift für Papyrologie und Epigraphik* 80 pp. 176–82.

Rankov, B (1994) *The Praetorian Guard* Oxford.

Rankov, B. (2006) 'Les frumentarii et la circulation de l'information entre les empereurs Romains et les provinces' in L. Capdetrey & J. Nelis-Clément (eds) *La circulation d'information dans les états antiques* Paris pp. 129–40.

Rea, J. (1993) 'A letter from the emperor Elagabalus' *Zeitschrift für Papyrologie und Epigraphik* 96 pp. 127–32.

Reynolds, J. (1982) *Aphrodisias and Rome* London.

Rich, J. W. (1999) 'Drusus and the spolia opima' *Classical Quarterly* 49 pp. 544–55.

Richier, O. (2004) *Centuriones ad Rhenum: les centurions legionnaires des armées romaines du Rhin* Paris.

Richmond, I. (1967) 'Adamklissi' *Papers of the British School at Rome* 22 pp. 29–39.

Rives, J. B. (1999) *Germania* Oxford.

Rivet, A. L. & Jackson, K. (1970) 'The British section of the Antonine Itinerary' *Britannia* 1 pp. 34–82.

Robertson, A. S. (1956) 'The numismatic evidence of Romano-British coin hoards' in R. A. G. Carson (ed.) *Essays in the Roman Coinage Presented to Harold Mattingly* Oxford pp. 262–83.

Roller, M. B. (2001) *Constructing Autocracy: Aristocrats and Emperors in Julio-Claudian Rome* Princeton.

Rose, C. B. (1997) *Dynastic Commemoration and Imperial Portraiture in the Julio-Claudian Period* Cambridge.

Rosenstein, N. (2006) 'Aristocratic values' in N. Rosenstein & R. Morstein-Marx (eds) *A Companion to the Roman Republic* Oxford pp. 365–82.

Rowe, G. (2002) *Princes and Political Cultures: The New Tiberian Senatorial Decrees* Ann Arbor.

Roxan, M. (1996) 'An emperor rewards his supporters: the earliest extant diploma issued by Vespasian' *Journal of Roman Archaeology* 9 pp. 247–56.

Roxan, M. & Eck, W. (1993) 'A military diploma of AD 85 for the Rome cohorts' *Zeitschrift für Papyrologie und Epigraphik* 96 pp. 67–74.

Roymans, N. (2004) *Ethnic Identity and Imperial Power: The Batavians in the Early Roman Empire* Amsterdam.

Rubin, N. (1985) 'Unofficial memorial rites in an army unit' *Social Forces* 63 pp. 795–809.

Sabin, P. (2000) 'The face of Roman battle' *Journal of Roman Studies* 90 pp. 1–17.

Saddington, D. B. (2003) 'An Augustan officer on the Roman army: militaria in Velleius Paterculus and some inscriptions' in J. J. Wilkes (ed.) *Documenting the Roman Army: Essays in honour of Margaret Roxan* London pp. 19–29.

Saddington, D. B. (2007) 'Classes: the evolution of the Roman imperial fleets' in P. Erdkamp (ed.) *A Companion to the Roman Army* Oxford pp. 201–17.

Salazar, C. F. (2000) *The Treatment of War Wounds in Graeco-Roman Antiquity* Leiden.

Saller, R. P. (1980) 'Promotion and patronage in equestrian careers' *Journal of Roman Studies* 70 pp. 44–63.

Saller, R. P. (1982) *Personal Patronage under the Early Empire* Cambridge.

Saller, R. P. & Shaw, B. D. (1984) 'Tombstones and Roman family relations in the Principate: civilians, soldiers and slaves' *Journal of Roman Studies* 74 pp. 124–56.

Samet, E. D. (2005) 'Leaving no warriors behind: the ancient roots of a modern sensibility' *Armed Forces and Society* 31 pp. 623–49.

Saxer, R. (1967) 'Untersuchungen zu den Vexillationen der römischen Kaiserheeres von Augustus bis Diokletian' *Epigraphische Studien* 1 pp. 1–147.

Scheidel, W. (1996) *Measuring Sex, Age and Death in the Roman Empire: Explorations in Ancient Demography* Ann Arbor.

Scheidel, W. (2007) 'Marriages, families and survival: Demographic aspects' in P. Erdkamp (ed.) *A Companion to the Roman Army* Oxford pp. 417–34.

Severy, B. (2003) *Augustus and the Family at the Birth of the Roman Empire* London.

Shay, J. (2003) *Achilles in Vietnam: Combat trauma and the undoing of character* New York.

Sheldon, R. M. (2005) *Intelligence Activities in Ancient Rome: Trust in the Gods, but Verify* New York.

Shils, E. A. & Janowitz, M. (1948) 'Cohesion and disintegration in the Wehrmacht in World War II' *Public Opinion Quarterly* 12.2 pp. 280–315.

Shotter, D. (2003) 'The murder of Flavius Romanus at Ambleside: a possible context' *Transactions of the Cumberland and Westmorland Antiquarian and Archaeological Society* 3 pp. 228–31.

Shotter, D. (2007) 'Cicero and the Treveri: new light on an old pun' *Greece & Rome* 54 pp. 106–10.

Sidebottom, H. (1993) 'Philosophers' attitudes to warfare under the Principate' in J. Rich & G. Shipley (eds) *War and Society in the Roman World* London pp. 241–64.

Silberberg-Peirce, S. (1986) 'The many faces of the Pax Augusta: images of war and peace in Rome and Gallia Narbonensis' *Art History* 9 pp. 306–24.

Sinnigen, W. G. (1962) 'The origins of the frumentarii' *Memoirs of the American Academy in Rome* 27 pp. 211–24.

Sinnigen, W. G (1965) 'The Roman secret service' *Classical Journal* 61 pp. 65–72.

Slim, W. J. (1999) *Defeat into Victory: Battling Japan and India 1942–1945* London.

Smith, C. J. (1998) 'Onasander on how to be a general' in M. Austin *et al.* (eds) *Modus Operandi: Essays in honour of Geoffrey Rickman* London pp. 151–66.

Speidel, M. A. (1992) 'Roman army pay scales' *Journal of Roman Studies* 82 pp. 87–106.

Speidel, M. A. (2001) 'Specialisation and promotion in the Roman imperial army' in L. De Blois (ed.) *Administration, Prosopography and Appointment Policies in the Roman Empire: Proceedings of the First Workshop of the International Network Impact of Empire* Amsterdam pp. 50–61.

Speidel, M. P. (1970) 'The captor of Decebalus: a new inscription from Philippi' *Journal of Roman Studies* 60 pp. 142–53.

Speidel, M. P. (1978) *Guards of the Roman Armies: An essay on the singulares of the provinces* Bonn.

Speidel, M. P. (1984a) 'Europeans – Syrian elite troops at Dura-Europos and Hatra' in M. P. Speidel *Roman Army Studies* I Amsterdam pp. 301–9.

Speidel, M. P. (1984b) 'Germani corporis custodes' *Germania 62* pp. 31–45.

Speidel, M. P. (1985) 'Furlough in the Roman army' *Yale Classical Studies* 28 pp. 283–93.

Speidel, M. P. (1992a) 'Becoming a centurion in Africa: brave deeds and the support of the troops as promotion criteria' in *Roman Army Studies* II pp. 124–8 Stuttgart.

Speidel, M. P. (1992b) 'Centurions promoted from beneficiarii?' *Zeitschrift für Papyrologie und Epigraphik* 91 pp. 229–32.

Speidel, M. P. (1992c) 'The framework of an imperial legion' in R. J. Brewer (ed.) *The Second Augustan Legion and the Roman Military Machine* pp. 125–43 Cardiff.

Speidel, M. P. (1993) 'Commodus the God-Emperor and the army' *Journal of Roman Studies* 83 pp. 109–14.

Speidel, M. P. (1994a) *Riding for Caesar: The Roman Emperors' Horse Guards* London.

Speidel, M. P. (1994b) 'The tribunes' choice in the promotion of legionary Centurions' *Zeitschrift für Papyrologie und Epigraphik* 100 pp. 469–70.

Speidel, M. P. (1998) 'The Risingham Praetensio' *Britannia* 29 pp. 359–9.

Speidel, M. P. (2006a) *Emperor Hadrian's speeches to the African army: a new text* Mainz.

Speidel, M. P. (2006b) 'Trajan's comites guard and Tacitus' Germania' *Chiron* 36 pp. 135–40.

Stäcker, J. (2003) *Princeps und miles: Studien zum Bindungs-und Nahverhältnis von Kaiser und Soldat im 1. und 2. Jahrhundert n. Chr.* Hildesheim.

Stoll, O. (1995) "Die Fahnenwache in der Römischen armee" *Zeitschrift für Papyrologie und Epigraphik* 108 pp. 107–18.

Summerly, J. (1990) *Studies in the Legionary Centurionate* (unpublished PhD thesis) Durham.

Sumner, G. V. (1970) 'The truth about Velleius Paterculus: prolegomena' *Harvard Studies in Classical Philology* 74 pp. 257–97.

Sutherland, C. H. V. (1959) 'The intelligibility of Roman imperial coin types' *Journal of Roman Studies* 49 pp. 46–55.

Swan, V. G. (1992) 'Legio VI and its men: African legionaries in Britain' *Journal of Roman Pottery Studies* 5 pp. 1–33.

Swan, V. G. (1997) "Vexillations and the garrisons of Britannia in the second and early third centuries: A Ceramic Point of View" in W. Groenman-van Waateringe *et al.* (eds) *Roman Frontier Studies 1995* pp. 289–94 Oxford.

Swan, V. G. (2008) 'Builders, suppliers and supplies in the Tyne-Solway region and beyond' in P. Bidwell (ed.) *Understanding Hadrian's Wall* Kendal pp. 49–82.

Syme, R. (1939a) 'Review of Les Cohortes Prétoriennes' *Journal of Roman Studies* 29 pp. 242–8 (= *Roman Papers* VI (1991) Oxford pp. 25–34).

Syme, R. (1939b) *The Roman Revolution* Oxford.

Syme, R. (1958a) 'Imperator Caesar: a study in nomenclature' *Historia* 7 pp. 172–88 (= *Roman Papers* I (1979) Oxford pp. 361–77).

Syme, R. (1958b) *Tacitus* (2 vols), Oxford.

Syme, R. (1962) 'The wrong Marcius Turbo' *Journal of Roman Studies* 52 pp. 87–96 (= *Roman Papers* II (1979) Oxford pp. 541–56).

Syme, R. (1964) 'Pliny and the Dacian Wars' *Latomus* 23 pp. 750–9 (= *Roman Papers* VI (1991) Oxford pp. 142–9).

Syme, R. (1968) 'People in Pliny' *Journal of Roman Studies* 58 pp. 135–51 (= *Roman Papers* II (1979) pp. 694–723).

Syme, R. (1971) *Emperors and Biography: Studies in the Historia Augusta* Oxford.

Syme, R. (1977) 'The march of Mucianus' *Antichthon* 11 pp. 78–92 (= *Roman Papers* III (1984) Oxford pp. 998–1013).

Syme, R. (1978) 'Donatus and the like' *Historia* 27 pp. 588–603 (= *Roman Papers* III (1984) Oxford pp. 1105–19).

Syme, R. (1980) 'Guard Prefects of Trajan and Hadrian' *Journal of Roman Studies* 70 pp. 64–80 (= *Roman Papers* III (1984) Oxford pp. 1276–302).

Syme, R. (1988) 'Antonine government and governing class' in *Roman Papers* V Oxford pp. 668–88.

Talbert, R. J. A. (1984) *The Senate of Imperial Rome* Princeton.

Thomas, J. D. & Davies, R. W. (1977) 'A new military strength report on papyrus' *Journal of Roman Studies* 67 pp. 50–61.

Thorley, J. (2002) 'The Ambleside Roman gravestone' *Transactions of the Cumberland and Westmorland Antiquarian and Archaeological Society* 2 pp. 51–58.

Tomlin, R. S. O. & Annis, R. G. (1989) 'A Roman altar from Carlisle Castle' *Transactions of the Cumberland and Westmorland Antiquarian and Archaeological Society* 89 pp. 77–92.

Touati, A. L. (1987) *The Great Trajanic Frieze* Stockholm.

Tritle, L. (2000) *From Melos to My Lai: War and Survival* London.

Tritle, L. (2004) 'Xenophon's portrait of Clearchus: a study in post-traumatic stress disorder' in C. Tuplin (ed.) *Xenophon and His World: Papers from a conference held in Liverpool in July 1999* pp. 325–39 Stuttgart.

Tuck, S. L. (2005) 'The origins of Roman imperial hunting imagery: Domitian and the redefinition of *virtus* under the Principate' *Greece & Rome* 52 pp. 221–45.

Uzzi, J. D. (2005) *Children in the visual arts of Imperial Rome* Cambridge.

Vervaet, F. J. (2002) 'Domitius Corbulo and the senatorial opposition to the reign of Nero' *Ancient Society* 32 pp. 135–93.

Vervaet, F. J. (2003) 'Domitius Corbulo and the rise of the Flavian dynasty' *Historia* 52 pp. 436–64.

Voisin, J. L. (1984) 'Les Romains, chasseurs de têtes' in Y. Thomas (ed.) *Du châtiment dans la cite: Supplices corporels et peine de mort dans la monde antique* Rome pp. 241–93.

Walker, D. R. (1988) 'The Roman coins' in B. Cunliffe (ed.) *The Temple of Sulis Minerva at Bath Volume II: The Finds from the Sacred Spring* Oxford pp. 281–358.

Weingartner, J. J. (1992) 'Trophies of war: US troops and the mutilation of Japanese war dead 1941–1945' *The Pacific Historical Review* 61 pp. 53–67.

Wellesley, K. (1975) *The Long Year AD 69* London.

Wells, C. (1972) *The German Policy of Augustus* Oxford.

Wheeler, E. L. (1996) 'The laxity of Syrian legions' in D. L. Kennedy (ed.) *The Roman Army in the East* pp. 229–76.

Whitehorne, J. (2004) 'Petitions to the centurion: a question of locality?' *Bulletin of the American Society of Papyrologists* 41 pp. 155–69.

Whittaker, D. R. (1964) 'The revolt of Papirius Dionysius AD 190' *Historia* 13 pp. 348–69.

Wigg, D. G. (1997) 'Coin supply and the Roman army' in W. Groenman-van Waateringe *et al.* (eds) *Roman Frontier Studies 1995* Oxford pp. 281–8.

Williams, M. F. (1997) 'Four mutinies: Tacitus 'Annals' 1.16–30; 1.31–49 and Ammianus Marcellinus 'Res Gestae' 20.4.9–20.5.7; 24.3.1–8' *Phoenix* 51 pp. 44–74.

Wong, L. (2005) 'Leave no man behind: recovering America's fallen warriors' *Armed Forces and Society* 31 pp. 599–622.

Woodman, A. J. (2006) 'Mutiny and madness: Tacitus Annals 1.16–49' *Arethusa* 39 pp. 303–29.

Woods, D. (2000) 'Caligula's sea shells' *Greece and Rome* 47 pp. 80–7.

Woolf, G. (1996) 'Monumental writing and the expansion of Roman society in the early empire' *Journal of Roman Studies* 86 pp. 22–39.

Wooliscroft, D. J & Hoffmann, B. (2006) *Rome's First Frontier: The Flavian Occupation of Northern Scotland* Stroud.

Yavetz, Z. (1969) *Plebs and Princeps* Oxford.

Ziólkowski, A. (1993) 'Urbs direpta, or how the Romans sacked cities' in J. Rich and G. Shipley (eds) *War and Society in the Roman World* London pp. 69–91.

Ziólkowski, M. (1992) 'Epigraphical and numismatic evidence of Disciplina' *Acta Antiqua Academiae Scientiarum Hungaricae* 33 pp. 347–50.

Notes

PRELIMS
1. Campbell (1984).

INTRODUCTION
1. Plut. *Galba* 1.3–4.
2. Patterson (1993) pp. 102–3.
3. In 44 BC, Antonius' legions mocked his promised donative of 100 denarii in comparison to the 500 denarii offered by Octavian: App. *B Civ.* 3.31.
4. Caes. *B. Hisp.* 17.
5. Described in Osgood (2006) pp. 43–60.
6. Appian *BC* 3.12, 40.
7. Botermann (1968) p. 30.
8. Nic. Dam. 29.115.
9. Ibid. 18.56.
10. Dio Cass. 51.20; *RG* 13; Verg. *Aen.* 1.293–6.
11. Suet. *Aug.* 49. The political significance of Augustus' army reforms is discussed in Raaflaub (1980).
12. The histories of individual legions are described in Keppie (1984) pp. 205–15. Note also the interesting description in Dio Cass. 55.23–4.
13. Concerning the military situation in AD 23, Tacitus states that auxiliary units account for just under half of the army: Tac. *Ann.* 4.5.
14. On the evolution of the imperial fleets, see Saddington (2007).
15. For the Rome cohorts, see Appendix 1.
16. Suet. *Dom.* 21.
17. Campbell (1984). Stäcker (2003) has had little impact on academia. Hekster (2007a) focuses on the emperor's self-representation as military leader. For the later empire, see Hebblewhite (2017).
18. For example, Chilver (1957).
19. A. R. Birley (2007).
20. See E. Birley (1953a), (1964), Dobson (1978), (1993), (2000).
21. Devijer (1976).
22. For example: Alföldy (1969), A. R. Birley (2005).
23. An overview of the literary sources for the imperial period can be found in Damon (2006) pp. 24–31.
24. Herod. 1.2.5, 2.15.7.

25. Dio Cass. 53.19.1–3.
26. Suet. *Claud.* 41.
27. See below p. 52.
28. For a more realistic description of Severus Alexander's chaotic reign, see Syme (1971) pp. 146–62.
29. See Bodel (2001). Many of these points also apply to the use of papyri. Recommendations on the correct use of ancient documents can be found in Gagos and Potter (2006) pp. 54–60.
30. A point cogently made in Mann (1985) p. 206.
31. Woolf (1996) p. 22.
32. The phrase is borrowed from the title of Badian (1989).
33. See Metcalf (2006) pp. 41–3.
34. See below pp. 89–9.
35. Syme (1968) p. 145.

CHAPTER 1

1. Coulston (2000) p. 81.
2. The reader is advised to refer to Appendix 1 (see p. 132) for a description of the relevant military formations.
3. See the dedications to *Concordia* erected jointly by soldiers from two different legions at Carlisle and Corbridge: *RIB* 1125 and *Britannia* 20 (1989) p. 331 no. 4.
4. Joseph. *AJ* 19.186–9.
5. See Flower (2001) p. 636.
6. Phang (2001) pp. 153, 159–64.
7. Dio Cass. 75.2.6.
8. HA *Did. Jul.* 6.5.
9. *CIL* VI 32582, 32543. Discussed in Noy (2000) p. 219.
10. The petition from the villagers of Scaptopara presented to Gordian by a Praetorian may be an example of this phenomenon. See below pp. 14–15.
11. See Coulston (2007).
12. Dio Cass. 80.4.2–5.1.
13. *Tab. Vindol.* III 650. See Speidel (2006b).
14. In a similar way, the tombstone of the *Germani* mimicked those of the Praetorian Guard, perhaps as a way of claiming equivalent status; Coulston (2000) p. 96.
15. Speidel (1994a) p. 140. Namely Jupiter Optimus Maximus, Juno, Minerva, Mars, Victory, Hercules, Fortuna, Mercury, Felicitas, Salus, the Fates, the Campestres, Silvanus, Apollo, Diana, Epona, the Suleviae Mothers and the Genius of the *equites singulares*.
16. E. Birley (1935).

17. Holmes (2004) pp. 116–7.
18. Dio Cass. 72.12.5–72.14.4; Herodian 1.12–3.
19. Whittaker (1964) pp. 366–7.
20. Herodian 2.4.1. Note also Juv. *Sat.* 16 referring to the impotence of civilians in the face of military oppression.
21. Epictetus *Disc.* 4.13.5.
22. Suet. *Otho* 6.
23. HA *Marc.* 25.4; *Avid. Cass.* 7.4.
24. It is worth quoting Syme (1980) p. 64 on this point: 'Apart from seasons of disturbance, the holders of this useful and necessary office tend to evade notice in written history.'
25. Syme (1939a) p. 247.
26. Tac. *Ann.* 4.59.
27. Ibid. 15.72.
28. Tac. *Hist.* 1.46.
29. Dio Cass. 71.5.2–3 (Bassaeus Rufus); 71.12.3 (Tarrutenius Paternus); HA *Comm.* 6.12–3, Herodian 1.12.3 (Aurelius Cleander).
30. *Corpus Papyrorum Latinarum* 238/*P. Berlin* 8.334.
31. Pliny *Pan.* 86.
32. Ulpius Julianus and Julianus Nestor: Dio Cass. 78.15.1.
33. See Rankov (1987) for Adventus' remarkable career.
34. HA *Macr.* 12.4–5; Dio Cass. 78.14.1.
35. Four out of twenty-two known Severan prefects were certainly lawyers: Aemilius Papinianus, Valerius Patruinus, Opellius Macrinus and Domitius Ulpianus. The *Historia Augusta* claims that Julius Paulus was prefect under Elagabalus but this appears to be false: HA *Sev. Alex.* 26.5–6; *Pesc. Nig.* 7.4.
36. See Howe (1942) pp. 32–40 on the evolving civil powers of the prefects.
37. Ibid. pp. 49–50.
38. Dio Cass. 80.2.2.
39. For example: Cornelius Fuscus, Marcius Turbo, Gavius Maximus and Furius Victorinus.
40. *Vigiles*: Sertorius Macro, Ofonius Tigellinus, Plotius Firmus, Bassaeus Rufus and Rustius Rufinus; *Frumentarii*: Oclatinius Adventus, Ulpius Julianus and Julianus Nestor.
41. Ostorius Scapula, Seius Strabo and Lusius Geta.
42. Julius Alexander, Julius Ursus, Laberius Maximus, Petronius Secundus, Sulpicius Similis, Petronius Mamertinus, Furius Victorinus, Baienus Blassianus, Veturius Macrinus, Longaeus Rufus, Aemilius Saturninus, Maecius Laetus, Geminius Chrestus and Domitius Honoratus.

Notes

43. The military aspects of the Egyptian prefecture are discussed in Brunt (1975) pp. 131–2.
44. Tac. *Ann.* 4.39; Dio Cass. 69.18.4.
45. Tac. *Hist.* 1.87.
46. Suet. *Dom.* 6.1; Tac. *Hist.* 2.86, 3.42.
47. Dio Cass. 68.9.2.
48. *CIL* V 648.
49. HA *Marc.* 14.5.
50. Dio Cass. 71.3.5.
51. Ibid. 71.5.2–3.
52. Ibid. 71.33.3.
53. HA *Did. Jul.* 6.4, 8.1.
54. Suet. *Titus* 6.
55. Suet. *Tib.* 48.2.
56. Tac. *Ann.* 4.7.
57. Dio Cass. 68.3.3.
58. Aur. Vict. *Caes.* 11.
59. Dio Cass. 68.3.2. Tacitus' description of the Praetorian riot under Otho is likely to have been influenced by the events of AD 97: Tac. *Hist.* 1.80–5.
60. Dio Cass. 68.3.4.
61. Berriman & Todd (2001) pp. 326–9. Syme hinted at this possibility: Syme (1958b) p. 35.
62. On hearing of the outbreak of Saturninus' revolt in AD 89, Trajan marched his legion from Spain to the Rhine and was rewarded with a consulship: Plin. *Pan.* 14.3–5.
63. Herodian 2.2.9.
64. Perennis was sufficiently powerful to give legionary commands to his sons and, in one province at least, replace senatorial officers with equestrians, who would presumably feel under obligation to him: Herodian 1.9.1; HA *Comm.* 6.1–2.
65. Plutarch *Galba* 8. Galba suspected that some of the officers of the Guard had been loyal to him and dismissed a number of soldiers on account of their support for Sabinus: Tac. *Hist.* 1.25, Suet. *Galba* 16.
66. Suet. *Galba* 14.
67. Herodian 3.11.4.
68. Dio Cass. 76.15.4. For the overzealous nature of his guards see Herodian 3.11.3.
69. HA *Ant. Pius* 8.7.
70. HA *Comm.* 6.6–7.
71. Tac. *Ann.* 11.33, 37.

72. Ibid. 12.42.
73. Herodian 1.9.10.
74. The issue becomes more complex after the period in question, as prefects were increasingly valuable to the emperor for their non-military responsibilities (a fact which became apparent during the Severan period). This eventually led to the complete divorce of the prefects from any involvement in the military sphere. See Howe (1942) pp. 52–64 for the evolution of the prefecture.
75. See Eaton (2011)
76. Caligula: *BMCRE* I p. 151 nos. 33–5, *RIC* I p. 111 no. 40; Nero *BMCRE* I pp. 218–9 nos. 122–6, p. 259–60 nos. 303–4; *RIC* I p. 159 nos. 95–6, p. 174 nos. 386, 388.
77. *BMCRE* III p. 497, *RIC* II p. 457 nos. 908–11.
78. *BMCRE* IV p. 744 nos. 298–9, p. 830, 832; *RIC* III p. 389 no. 207, p. 390 no. 220, p. 423 no. 496, p. 432 no. 580, p. 433 no. 590.
79. *BMCRE* I p. 165 no. 5, p. 166 nos. 8–10.
80. Suet. *Claud.* 10.
81. Suet. *Aug.* 101.2; *Tib.* 48.2, 76. Caligula doubled this legacy of his own volition: Dio Cass. 59.2.3.
82. Suet. *Claud.* 10.4; Dio Cass. 60.12.4.
83. Plin. *Pan.* 25.2.
84. Tac. *Hist.* 1.5.4.
85. Herodian 2.7.1–2.
86. Marcus Aurelius refused to award a donative after Verus' Parthian campaign because it would have necessitated higher taxes for the soldiers' civilian relatives. The potential political fallout of this refusal was mitigated by the substantial donative which had been given on their joint accession: Dio Cass. 71.3.3.
87. HA *Marc.* 7.9–10. See B. Campbell (1984) p. 170.
88. Dio Cass. 74.1.2, 8.3.
89. Ibid. 74.11.3.
90. Herodian 2.6.14.
91. Ibid. 2.6.9–11; Dio Cass. 74.11.2–6.
92. Applebaum (2007) pp. 201–3.
93. Dio Cass. 74.11.5.
94. Herodian 2.6.9.
95. Ibid. 2.10.4. The accusation of deception refers to Julianus' inability to pay the promised donative.
96. Ibid. 2.13.6–7.
97. Severus: Dio Cass. 76.1.1. Caracalla: Herodian 4.4.7.
98. Dio Cass. 46.46.7; HA *Sev.* 7.6.

99. Suet. *Aug.* 56.4.
100. Dio Cass. 78.17.4.
101. *ILS* 206.
102. *IGBulg* 659. For a full commentary on the Scaptopara text see Hauken (1998) pp. 74–139.
103. Suet. *Nero* 7.2.
104. *Fragmenta Vaticana* no. 195.
105. B. Campbell (1984) pp. 110–1.
106. Tac. *Ann.* 11.35.
107. Dio Cass. 74.24.1.
108. Ibid. 64.15; Plut. *Otho* 17.10; Suet. *Otho* 12.2; Tac. *Hist.* 2.49.4.
109. Suet. *Otho* 4.2.
110. Tac. *Hist.* 1.24.
111. Ibid. 1.5.
112. Suet. *Galba* 16.1; Tac. *Hist.* 1.25. Four tribunes were also cashiered by Galba, two from the Praetorian cohorts and one each from the urban cohorts and *vigiles*: ibid. 1.20.
113. Ibid. 1.36. The Praetorians were also able to select their own prefects and the relief of the unofficial tax levied by centurions on soldiers requesting leave was approved: ibid. 1.46.
114. Plut. *Otho* 3; Suet. *Otho* 8.2. See Tac. *Hist.* 1.80–5 for the riot and its aftermath.
115. Tac. *Ann.* 11.35, 14.7.
116. Note the argument of a Praetorian tribune for killing Nymphidius Sabinus: 'Shall we, then, sacrifice Galba after Nero, and choosing the son of Nymphidia as our Caesar, shall we slay the scion of the house of Livia, as we have slain the son of Agrippina? Or shall we inflict punishment on Nymphidius for his evil deeds, and thereby show ourselves avengers of Nero, but true and faithful guardians of Galba?': Plut. *Galba* 14.3.
117. Tac. *Hist.* 3.24.
118. Ash (1999) p. 87.
119. Tac. *Ann.* 6.3.
120. HA *Hadr.* 23.8.
121. Tac. *Hist.* 1.74; Suet. *Galba* 16.2.
122. HA *Did. Jul.* 8.5; Herodian 2.13.1.
123. Durry (1938) p. 399.

CHAPTER 2

1. Aelius Aristides *Or.* 26.75.
2. Livy 44.39.5. See also Tac. *Hist.* 3.84 '… the special glory of the soldier lay in his barracks, for this was his country and this his home'.

3. This may have been more than a geographical approximation. It has recently been argued that the footwear from Roman military sites which has been attributed to female owners may in fact have been worn by boys living in the camps; James (2006) pp. 34–5.
4. On the enlistment process see R. W. Davies (1969).
5. James (1999) pp. 19–21. In Petron. *Sat.* 82, Encolpius is unmasked as a civilian, despite carrying a sword and claiming to be a soldier, because he is wearing slippers.
6. See: *AE* 1974 570 (a joint dedication by serving soldiers and veterans of XI Claudia); *P. Dura* 30 (recording the marriage of a soldier witnessed by his comrades and a veteran who wrote on behalf of the bride); *P. Dura* 31 (sale document recording the purchase of a vineyard by a veteran which was witnessed by soldiers and drawn up in the winter quarters of his former unit).
7. Smaller army groups were often influenced by their more powerful neighbours: see Tac. *Hist.* 1.11.
8. Ibid. 3.24–5. See also 2.37, 3.35.5.
9. Herodian 6.7.3.
10. Dio Chrys. *Or.* 1.28.
11. *D* 29.1.1.1. See B. Campbell (1984) p. 226.
12. In contrast to the rest of the army, only the Syrian legions were frequently described in terms of their laxity and general ill discipline: see Wheeler (1996). Yet even in light of the evident literary *topos*, there are indications of real disciplinary problems: the situation described at Dura-Europos in *P. Dur.* 55/*RMR* no. 90 corresponds neatly with one of the problems listed in Fronto *Principia Historiae* 12 (Loeb II p. 209) 'wandering off from their garrisons'.
13. For example: Suet. *Tib.* 19, *Vesp.* 8; Plin. *Pan.* 18; HA *Hadr.* 10.3; HA *Macr.* 12. Augustus' disciplinary reforms, including the revival of archaic punishments, were intended to prevent a return to the political factionalism of late Republican armies: Suet. *Aug.* 24. Conversely, Otho criticised the severity of Galba's disciplinary measures: Tac. *Hist.* 1.37.
14. Fronto AD *Verum Imp.* 2.1.20 (Loeb II pp. 23–4). See R. W. Davies (1966).
15. Fronto *De Bello Parthico* 2 (Loeb II p. 23).
16. Phang (2008) p. 127.
17. Herodian 2.4.4.
18. Dio Cass. 75.1.1; Herodian 2.12.2.
19. *RIC* II p. 367 no. 232, p. 436 nos. 746–7, *BMCRE* III p. 318 no. 602.
20. *BMCRE* III p. 466 no. 1488.
21. *RIC* III p. 108 no. 604.

22. *RIC* III p. 124 no. 769, *BMCRE* IV p. 270 nos. 1675–6.
23. Britain: *Britannia* 10 (1979) p. 346 no. 7 (Chesters), *JRS* 49 (1959) pp. 136–7 no. 6 (Bertha), *RIB* 990 (Bewcastle*), RIB* 1127–8 (Corbridge), *RIB* 1723 (Great Chesters), *RIB* 1978 (Castlesteads), *RIB* 2092 (Birrens); Africa: *ILS* 3810 (Lambaesis), *CIL* VIII 9832, 10657, *AE* 1955 no. 41 (Volubilis), *AE* 1957 122 (Lambaesis), *AE* 1960 no. 264 (Ghadames), E. Birley (1978) p. 1515 (Gemellae).
24. See Eaton (2017).
25. Examples – FIDES EXERCITVVM: *RIC* 3 p. 293 nos. 997–9; CONCORDIA EXERCITVVM: *BMCRE* 4 p. 618 no. 1394; MATRI CASTRORVM: *BMCRE* 4 p. 534 nos. 929–31.
26. The theme could also have been used to persuade a civilian audience that the emperor had restored military discipline.
27. Plin. *Ep.* 10.22, 30. The emphasis on troop deployment reflects the concern of the emperor in preventing the use of soldiers in illicit and subversive activities, for example the activities of Lucius Capito, procurator of Asia, who was condemned for utilising soldiers who were not under his command; Tac. *Ann.* 4.15. See also Suet. *Tib.* 19 for the punishment of a legionary commander who sent soldiers to accompany his freedman on a hunting trip.
28. Plin. *Ep.* 10.29 requests clarification regarding the punishment of two slaves who had enlisted in the army and taken the oath of allegiance but had not been enrolled in a unit.
29. Millar (2001) p. 317.
30. Suet. *Aug.* 89.
31. *Dig.* 49.16.12.1.
32. Ibid. 49.16.3. Hadrian had previously decreed that soldiers should rarely be called away from the standards: *Dig.* 22.5.3.6.
33. Plin. *Ep.* 6.31.6.
34. *Dig.* 49.16.10; see also *CJ* 12.35.1 (in this case Caracalla refused the request).
35. See below p. 59.
36. Joseph. *BJ* 5.128.
37. Tac. *Ann.* 1.35, 4.4.
38. Tac. *Ann.* 1.20. In similar circumstances, Minicius Justus was relieved of the camp prefecture of VII Claudia and rushed to Vespasian to protect him from the troops: *Hist.* 3.7.
39. Tac. *Ann.* 15.67.
40. Tac. *Ann.* 13.17, 35–6; Fronto AD *Verum Imp.* 2.1.20 (Loeb II p. 149); Dio Cass. 73.8.2.
41. Ibid. 13.35.

42. Joseph. *BJ* 5.109–29; Titus later demonstrated his *severitas* by executing a cavalryman for losing his horse to the enemy: see Ibid. 6.153–6.
43. Tac. *Agr.* 16; *Hist.* 1.60. The tension between soldiers and their commanders is most visible during the chaotic events of AD 69 owing to mutual suspicion and hostility: see Ibid. 1.36, 2.23, 4.34–5.
44. Tac. *Agr.* 7.
45. Ibid. 28.
46. Dio Cass. 80.4.2–5.1.
47. *P. Dur.* 55/*RMR* no. 90.
48. Plin. *Pan.* 18. Vitellius relaxed discipline as a means of winning the support of the soldiers: Tac. *Hist.* 1.52. Note also Tacitus' comment on Antonius Primus' decision to allow his men to select their own centurions: 'these were the methods of an agitator who sought to ruin discipline': ibid. 3.49.
49. Tac. *Ann.* 11.20.
50. Lendon (2005) pp. 177–8.
51. Caes. *B Gall.* 5.44.
52. McDonnell (2006) p. 387. For the shifting meaning of *virtus* in relation to the senatorial order, see below pp. 61–2.
53. For example: *BMCRE* III p. 337 no. 774; *BMCRE* V p. 179 nos. 142–3.
54. McDonnell (2006) pp. 149–54.
55. See below pp. 116–17.
56. Dio Cass. 77.13.1.
57. Livy 8.7.1–8.2; see also 8.30.1–35.9 for a master of horse narrowly avoiding a similar fate for launching an attack without authorisation.
58. Joseph. *BJ* 5.125.
59. Frontinus included a section on restraining demands for battle from the troops: *Str.* 1.10.
60. Caes. *B Gall.* 7.47, *B Civ.* 1.45; Tac. *Agr.* 33; *Hist.* 1.63, 2.23,26, 3.19, 4.34–5, Joseph. *BJ* 5.127–8.
61. Tac. *Hist.* 3.32–3 (sack of Cremona); Joseph. *BJ* 6.260–6 (burning of the Temple at Jerusalem). On the sacking of cities see A. Ziółkowski (1993).
62. Caes. *B Civ.* 2.13; Suet. *Vesp.* 6.
63. The need to display *virtus* discouraged shameful behaviour: Caes. *B Gall.* 7.80, Onasander *Strategikos* 32.7; Polyaenus *Strat.* 8.23.16. Conversely, nocturnal darkness hid disgraceful activities: Caes. *B Civ.* 1.67, 2.31; Tac. *Hist.* 4.36. On honour and shame in the Roman army see Lendon (1997) pp. 243–52.
64. Joseph. *BJ* 6.68–71.
65. Similarly, Frontin. *Str.* 1.11.17–8 advises that troops should be encouraged to fight by exposing the feebleness of enemy prisoners to them.

66. See below p. 121.
67. Phang (2008) pp. 242–6.
68. Onasander *Strategikos* 9.2–3; Polyaenus *Strat.* 3.9.35; Tac. *Hist.* 4.26.
69. Tac. *Ann.* 11.20; see also 13.53.
70. I suspect that the construction of Hadrian's Wall was based on a similar rationale.
71. See Joseph. *BJ* 3.72–6 for the importance of Roman military training.
72. Lambaesis: *ILS* 2847; march: HA *Hadr.* 10.4.
73. Onasander *Strategikos* 13; 14.1–4; 23; Frontin. *Str.* 2.7–8; 3.12, 16; Polyaenus *Strat.* 2.1.3, 6–8; 3.4, 8, 11–2, 15; 3.9.34; 4.3.3, 9.6, 14, 20; 5.12.5, 24, 25; 7.21.7. On military handbooks see B. Campbell (1987).
74. Hence XIIII Gemina won renown for its conduct in Britain during the revolt of Boudicca: Tac. *Hist.* 2.11.
75. The mutineers in Pannonia were unable to combine three legions into one because of the soldiers' unit pride: Tac. *Ann.* 1.18.
76. Caes. *B Gall.* 1.40, 42.
77. Joseph. *BJ* 5.502–3. Antonius Primus adopted a similar tactic at Cremona: Tac. *Hist.* 3.27. *ILS* 5795 records a competition between auxiliaries and marines. Tacitus imagined Agricola's soldiers and marines boasting to each other about their feats of endurance: *Agr.* 25. Unit rivalry could easily escalate into actual fighting: see Tac. *Hist.* 1.64.2; 2.28, 68 and see above pp. 2–5.
78. See below pp. 108–109.
79. Joseph. *BJ* 5.41. *CIL* III 30 & *AE* 1923 83 record a *primus pilus* of XII Fulminata who was demoted to an ordinary centurionate in X Fretensis, perhaps as a result of the former's disgrace. See Goldsworthy (1999) pp. 200–1.
80. *CIL* XIII 5201, 11514 (two tombstones with XXI Rapax erased). See also Clay (2004) on mutilated tombstones of XX Valeria Victrix.
81. Le Bohec (1989) pp. 451–3.
82. Tac. *Ann.* 1.46–7.
83. Lendon (1997) p. 265.
84. Dio Cass. 40.18.
85. Tert. *Apol.* 16.8. See Ando (2000) pp. 259–69 for a discussion on the significance of the cult of the standards.
86. Disgrace: Caes. *B Civ.* 3.74, Tac. *Hist.* 3.17 (standard bearers disgraced). Protecting the eagle: Caes. *B Gall.* 4.25, 5.37; Frontin. *Str.* 2.8.1–5; Tac. *Hist.* 2.43, 3.17.
87. Stoll (1995). The shrine that housed the standards could also act as a place of refuge: Tac. *Ann.* 1.39.4; Herodian 4.4.5.

88. *Natalis aquilae*: *CIL* II 6183. *Rosaliae signorum*: Hoey (1937). *Primipili*: *CIL* VIII 2634.
89. Joseph. *BJ* 6.316.
90. Suet. *Aug.* 94, 96; *Vit.* 9; Tac. *Ann.* 2.17.
91. See below p. 79. Note also Tiberius' donative to the Syrian legions for not displaying Sejanus' statue next to the standards: Suet. *Tib.* 48.2. Sejanus had previously warned that the soldiers would erect portraits of Agrippina among the standards: Tac. *Ann.* 5.4.4.
92. App. *Illyr.* 12.25.
93. Most famously on the cuirass of the *Prima Porta* statue; see Galinsky (1996) pp. 155–8.
94. *RGDA* 29.2; Ovid *Fasti* 5.593–94.
95. Dio Cass. 55.10.4. See Rich (1998) on the temple of Mars Ultor.
96. Tac. *Ann.* 1.41.1.
97. Dio Cass. 60.8.7.
98. Ibid. 68.9.3.
99. Tac. *Ann.* 1.42.
100. Amm. Marc. 15.5.17.
101. See below p. 79.
102. See below p. 117.
103. On the ceremonial nature of the morning reports see Phang (2007) p. 292.
104. Herz (2002) pp. 84–5.
105. *Tab. Vindol.* II 166–77.
106. Tac. *Ann.* 15.9; Suet. *Galb.* 6.2. See M. P. Speidel (1985).
107. Veg. *Mil.* 2.19.
108. Tac. *Hist.* 1.46.
109. Gilliam (1954) pp. 187–9. For the significance of the *Feriale Duranum*, see below p. 90.
110. Caes. *B. Civ.* 1.72, 3.90.
111. Suet. *Aug.* 25.
112. Joseph. *BJ* 5.316.
113. Fronto *Principia Historiae* 14 (Loeb II p. 213).
114. Vell. Pat. 2.97.4.
115. *ILS* 216.
116. Agricola committed his auxiliaries to battle at Mons Graupius rather than risk his legionaries, reflecting a clear distinction in the perceived worth of the different army branches: see Tac. *Agr.* 35 and Gilliver (2007).
117. See R. W. Davies (1970) and Salazar (2000) pp. 74–83.
118. See below pp. 116–17.

119. *Dig.* 49.16.13.3.
120. *CJ* 12.35(36).6.
121. Modestinus 27.1.8.2–5.
122. Fair treatment for wounded soldiers may also have boosted recruitment: see B. Campbell (1984) p. 314.
123. *Dig.* 29.1.1.
124. Joseph. *BJ* 6.188.
125. Onasander *Strategikos* 36.1–2.
126. Tac. *Ann.* 4.73.3.
127. Tac. *Hist.* 2.45.
128. Tac. *Ann.* 1.62.
129. Titus favourably contrasted the release obtained by a glorious death on the battlefield with the fate of being entombed as a civilian corpse: Joseph. *BJ* 6.46–7. On the retrieval of the dead as a fundamental concept for the modern American and Israeli armies, see Samet (2005) p.626; Wong (2005) p. 599.
130. Cic. *Phil.* 14.12.33.
131. Hope (2003) p. 90.
132. Suet. *Aug.* 14.
133. Dio Cass. 69.14.3.
134. A modern parallel can be seen in the Israeli Defence Force which prohibits units from conducting services or erecting commemorative monuments for individual soldiers, in order to maintain morale. The commemoration of fallen soldiers is strictly regulated; see Rubin (1985) p. 796.
135. The mound was soon destroyed by the enemy, demonstrating the structure's lack of permanence; Tac. *Ann.* 2.7.3–4.
136. On the treatment of Roman prisoners of war in the east see Ball (2000) pp. 114–23.
137. Hor. *Carm.* 3.5.5–12.
138. Dio Cass. 68.12.1.
139. The *tropaeum* is discussed in detail by Richmond (1967).
140. Unfortunately, the name of the reigning emperor has not survived and there is continuing debate as to whether the monument was erected during the reign of Domitian or Trajan. On the basis of the nomenclature of the listed soldiers and the known movements of military units on the Danube, a strong case has been made for attributing the altar to the reign of Domitian; Dorutiu (1961).
141. *Tabula Siarensis*, fr. i, col. a, lines 26–8.
142. Dorutiu (1961) p. 361. It could be argued that the presence of the emperor's name and title on the altar precludes the possibility of

unauthorized construction. However, the military letter-cutter who inscribed the text on the altar would have been familiar with applying the emperor's title to the vast majority of his work, including building and dedicatory inscriptions, without requiring direct imperial permission to do so.

143. Julius Caesar was praised for vowing not to cut his hair until his fallen soldiers had been avenged: Polyaenus *Strat.* 8.23.23. Avenging the dead was a strong factor in motivating troops to fight: Caes. *B Gall.* 7.28; Tac. *Ann.* 1.49.3. For revenge or 'payback' in combat see Tritle (2000) pp. 131–2.

144. A similar sentiment is expressed by Trajan's retrieval of Fuscus' lost standards; see above p. 29.

145. Tac. *Hist.* 1.56; see also 1.26, 52, 80 for further suggestions that mutinies were generally caused by a minority of unruly soldiers.

146. Veg. *Mil.* 3.4.

147. See above p. 26 on the dangers of *otium*.

148. Tac. *Ann.* 1.16, 31.

149. Frontin. *Str.* 9. On Republican mutinies see Messer (1920), Keaveney (2007) pp. 71–92.

150. *Dig.* 49.16.3.4, 3.6, 3.22, 6.1, 6.8.

151. Ibid. 49.16.3.19–21.

152. In a rescript, Severus Alexander upheld the loss of benefits imposed on soldiers who were dishonourably discharged: *CJ* 12.35.3.

153. Suet. *Iul.* 70; Plut. *Caes.* 51; App. *B Civ.* 2.93; Dio Cass. 42.53; Tac. *Ann.* 1.42. See Chrissanthos (2001) on the historicity of this event.

154. Polyaenus *Strat.* 8.23.15.

155. Tac. *Ann.* 1.42.2. Livy 28.27.3–4 attributes a similar ploy in Scipio's speech during the mutiny at Sucro; see Woodman (2006) pp. 321–2.

156. HA *Sev. Alex.* 52.3, 53.10–54.4.

157. Tac. *Hist.* 2.29.

158. Tac. *Ann.* 1.40.3–41.3; Dio Cass. 57.5.6.

159. Tac. *Ann.* 1.35.4–5; Dio Cass. 57.5.2. Junius Blaesus also suggests that the mutineers kill him: Tac. *Ann.* 18.3.

160. Tac. *Hist.* 3.10.

161. HA *Avid. Cass.* 4.

162. Parker (1983) p. 23 citing Xen. *An.* 5.7.13–35; Curt. 10.9.11.

163. Suet. *Aug.* 24.2; *Calig.* 48.1–2 (unsuccessful); *Galba* 12.2; Tac. *Hist.* 1.5–6, 37; HA *Macr.* 12.2; Amm. Marc. 24.3.1–2. On decimation see Phang (2008) pp. 123–9.

164. Polyb. 6.37–8.

165. Tac. *Ann.* 1.29. The lunar eclipse that preceded this convinced some of the soldiers that the mutiny was a religious transgression: Ibid. 1.28. The revolt of Scribonianus ended abruptly due to soldierly superstition: Suet. *Claud.* 13.2. On the religious significance of the *sacramentum,* see below p. 106.
166. Tac. *Ann.* 1.44.
167. Tac. *Hist.* 1.82.
168. Evidenced by demands from Caesarian soldiers to be decimated after periods of mutinous behaviour: Caes. *B Civ.* 3.74; App. *B Civ.* 2.13.94.
169. Some of Octavian's troops mutinied after Actium at Brundisium for an immediate discharge and payment of bounties: Suet. *Aug.* 17. Soldiers were prone to acting on unsubstantiated rumours: Caes. *B Gall.* 1.39 Tac. *Ann.* 1.22; *Hist.* 1.51, 80–5.
170. Caligula's actions on the Channel coast are often seen as a direct response to a serious mutiny among his soldiers. However, I am inclined to see Caligula as the sole impetus for not invading Britain. During his time in Gaul and Germany, Caligula showed great enthusiasm for military affairs but a marked reluctance to win glory legitimately by engaging in actual combat, see below p. 103.
171. Dio Cass. 76.12.3–5.
172. M. P. Speidel (1984a) proposed that the 'Europaeans' were in fact the garrison of Dura-Europos, based on a tentative reconstruction of an extremely fragmentary inscription (*AE* 1934 278). This theory has been refuted by Kennedy (1986) pp. 402–3.
173. Dio Cass. 76.10.2.
174. D. B. Campbell (1986) p. 56. Severus later regretted killing Laetus: HA *Sev.* 15.6.
175. Tac. *Ann.* 1.46–7.
176. Ibid. 1.16–7; Dio Cass. 57.4.
177. Tac. *Ann.* 1.17, 31.4.
178. See Brunt (1976) pp. 95–6.
179. Mutinies could be quelled by referring the soldiers' grievances to a higher authority: Tac. *Ann.* 1.19.3–4, 36; Dio Cass. 57.4.3.
180. Tac. *Hist.* 2.28, 23, 26, 28–30; the frequency with which Caesarian troops communicated with him via their centurions and tribunes suggests a deliberate attempt to provide an outlet for their grievances and opinions without recourse to mutiny: Caes. *B Civ.* 1.64; *B Gall.* 1.41, 7.17.
181. 'I levy my soldiers, I don't buy them.' Tac. *Hist.* 1.5.4. According to Tacitus, even a small gesture would have been enough to appease the troops.

182. See above pp. 15–17.
183. Tac. *Hist.* 1.59, 64, 2.27, 66, 4.19.
184. See Roymans (2004) pp. 227–34 on the Batavians' self-image.
185. Tac. *Hist.* 4.36.10, 59.15.
186. Soldiers who deserted en masse but returned within a specific period of time were demoted and dispersed to other units. This was probably intended to break up a potentially seditious group: *Dig.* 49.16.3.9.
187. Tac. *Ann.* 1.18.2; see Woodman (2006).
188. See below p. 105.

CHAPTER 3

1. The main studies of the auxiliary centurionate are Gilliam (1957) and Holder (1980).
2. The annual salary of an auxiliary centurion was 3750 sesterces prior to Domitian's pay raise and rose in proportion to later pay increases: M. A. Speidel (1992) pp. 104–5.
3. Ibid. p. 102.
4. Hoffmann (1995) p. 1.
5. Dobson (1972) pp. 200–2.
6. Social fraternisation between military tribunes and centurions was not encouraged; see Plin. *Ep.* 6.31 on the wife of a tribune who had an affair with a centurion and was thought to have brought shame on her rank by doing so.
7. The career paths of *primipilares* have been studied by Dobson (1974), (1978).
8. Suet. *Cal.* 44.
9. Ibid. pp. 148–50.
10. See above pp. 6–7.
11. Tac. *Hist.* 3.6.
12. Ibid. 4.2.
13. Ibid. 4.68.
14. *CIL* III 14349.2.
15. Dio Cass. 69.19.
16. *CIL* VIII 24587.
17. HA *Ant. Pius* 8.7; *AE* 1971 65.
18. *CIL* IX 1582, 1583; X 1127; XIV 4389.
19. *Tab. Vindol.* II 344.
20. Tac. *Ann.* 14.31.
21. Dio Cass. 73.2.4.
22. Juv. *Sat.* 16.17–9.
23. Grünewald (2004) pp. 114–5.

24. *RIB* 152 (Bath), 583 (Ribchester); *Tab. Vindol.* II 250.
25. Plin. *Ep.* 10.77–8.
26. *Tab. Vindol.* II 250, III 653 (a letter addressed to another *centurio regionarius*).
27. Whitehorne (2004).
28. See Tac. *Ann.* 2.65 (centurion sent to feuding kings in Thrace by Tiberius); Ibid. 15.5 (Corbulo sent centurion to Vologeses); *Hist.* 2.58 (centurions sent to Moorish kings to win support for Vitellius). The centurion Velius Rufus was dispatched to Parthia to escort the Commagenian princes to Rome; *ILS* 9200. See Kennedy (1983) for a full discussion of his career.
29. Aulus Pudens: Mart. *Epig.* 1.31, 4.29, 5.48, 6.58, 7.11, 9.81, 13.69.
30. Although Martial claimed that his work was read by tough centurions: Ibid. 11.3.
31. *Tab. Vindol.* II 255.
32. Adams (1999).
33. See below pp. 81–2.
34. Any analysis of the origins of a specific body of Roman military personnel can be based only on the surviving epigraphic material, particularly cases which can be securely dated. In the case of the centurionate, there are five lists of names which can be used to ascertain the origins of the centurions of a particular unit at a specific date: the centurial stones from Hadrian's Wall c. AD 122, a list of centurions belonging to X Fretensis in AD 150, II Traiana in 157 and 194 and the dedication list of all the centurions of III Augusta in AD 162. Funerary epitaphs of centurions can also be utilized in cases where a legion was stationed at a site for a short period of time, giving the analysis a secure chronological basis. The fundamental survey on the origins of legionary centurions is E. Birley (1953a).
35. Summerly (1990) p. 39.
36. On the contrary there is some evidence to suggest that recruits with an Italian background had a better chance of promotion than their provincial comrades; see E. Birley (1989) pp. 127.
37. For example, the scarcity of centurions with a proven British origin among the legions based in the province or indeed elsewhere; see Dessau (1912); Dobson & Mann (1973) p. 204.
38. Tac. *Ann.* 1.32.
39. Tac. *Ann.* 1.23.
40. Ibid. 1.32.
41. Ibid. 1.44.
42. Clemens: Ibid. 1.23, 26, 28.

43. Ibid. 1.23.
44. See Isaac (1995).
45. Goldsworthy (1996) p. 182, Sabin (2000) p. 11.
46. M. P. Speidel (2002) pp. 134–5.
47. Three ranks: Goldsworthy (1996) p. 138. Examples of the high mortality rate of centurions include: Caes. *B. Gal.* 2.25, 7.51. Caes. *B. Civ.* 1.46; Tac. *Hist.* 3.22, 5.20; *Ann.* 12.38.
48. One of the few instances of centurions fleeing battle is that of the *primus pilus* Vibillius who was beaten to death for his desertion; see Vell. Pat. 2.78.3.
49. For example Tac. *Ann.* 12.38.
50. Caes. *B. Gal* 2.25.
51. Ibid. 6.38.
52. [Caesar] *B. Hisp* 23.
53. Caes. *B. Gal.* 6.40; *B. Civ.* 1.46. Note also the episode of Pullo and Vorenus: *B. Gal.* 5.44, see above p. 25.
54. Caes. *B. Gal.* 3.53.
55. Caes. *B Gall.* 3.91, 99.
56. Joseph. *BJ* 6.1.8.
57. *ILS* 7178.
58. Tac. *Ann.* 1.44.
59. There may have been another reason for the behaviour of some of these men, namely psychological trauma caused by prolonged exposure to combat. According to Shay (2003) p. 77: 'A soldier who routs the enemy single-handedly is often in the grip of a special state of mind, body and social disconnection at the time of his memorable deeds.' With regard to the Classical world, the presence of combat trauma in Xenophon's portrait of Clearchus has been explored in Tritle (2004).
60. Plin. *Ep.* 2.13.2.
61. Ibid. 6.25.2.
62. Tac. *Agric.* 19.
63. *P.Mich.* III 164.
64. *BGU* 696.
65. Suet. *Gram.* 24.
66. For example, Caligula dismissed centurions on the grounds of infirmity or old age; Suet. *Cal.* 44. See also: Tac. *Ann.* 1.44 (dismissal of brutal centurions by Germanicus); Caes. *B. Afr.* 54 (dismissal of unworthy centurions by Julius Caesar).
67. Frontin. *Strat.* 4.6.4.
68. HA *Hadr.* 10.6.
69. Eaton (2017)

70. Mrozewicz (1984). Gaetulicius is recorded in Britain after he was promoted from the ranks to the centurionate of XX Valeria Victrix: *RIB* 1725, 2120.
71. *AE* 1928 27. Translated by B. Campbell (2002) p. 36.
72. Maxfield (1981) p. 117 suggests that the provincial governors theoretically had the authority to award *dona*, but the reality was somewhat different: 'The epigraphic evidence for the entire imperial period is unanimous on the point that it was the emperor or a member of the imperial family who granted *dona*, whatever discretionary powers their agents may in theory have had.'
73. Maxfield (1981) pp. 185–6.
74. Bennett (2006) p. 98.
75. *CIL* III 14387/*ILS* 9199.
76. Tac. *Hist.* 1.20.
77. *CIL* III 14387/ *ILS* 9198.
78. *AE* 1998 1435.
79. Presumably the conflict of AD 89 although, as his career encompassed posts in a number of legions, it is not clear in which unit he was serving during the conflict. However, an identical set of decorations were awarded to another centurion, L. Aconius Statura, in the same war and it is possible that these men were serving in the same legion during the conflict. Statura also served in a number of legions but both men served in V Macedonica and XI Claudia. Taking into account the later careers of each man, the former looks more likely as the relevant legion. For L. Aconius Statura see *CIL* XI 5992
80. Published in Bennett (2006) and (2007).
81. Tac. *Hist.* 2.89.

CHAPTER 4

1. Vell. Pat. 2.127. Saddington (2003) p. 28 notes Velleius' interest in, and identification with, the term *adiutor* which he uses to signify the personal assistant of a military leader.
2. Tac. *Ann.* 3.39. A detailed description of his career can be found in Sumner (1970) pp. 265–79.
3. Syme (1939b) pp. 384, 505–6.
4. Most recently A. R. Birley (2000).
5. Syme (1958b) p. 655.
6. E. Birley (1953b) p. 199.
7. Campbell (1975) p. 12.
8. Only one in six of all known consular legati from AD 96–138 had a consular father: Hopkins (1983) p.173.

9. 'So far ahead … a man's attitude, family connections, and resources are unpredictable. Even when nomination is one year before office, men become haughty in the interval – what if they had five years of putting on airs?'; Tac. *Ann.* 2.36.
10. Brunt (1975) p. 141.
11. Saller (1980) p. 57.
12. Dio Cass. 69.13.2. The basis on which Dio made this statement is unknown, but Julius Severus held a number of important commands, including the governorships of Dacia, Lower Moesia, Britain and Judaea, leading the response to the Bar Kokhba revolt in the latter. His career culminated in the prestigious Syrian command. On his career, see A. R. Birley (2005) pp. 129–32 and see below p. 55.
13. For example Avidius Cassius, Pertinax and Ulpius Marcellus: Syme (1988) p. 687.
14. *AE* 1956 124. See Maxfield (1981) pp. 244–5.
15. Brunt (1983) p. 52.
16. Saller (1980) p. 55.
17. Army service did not necessarily bestow relevant military experience, Pliny spent his tribunate auditing financial accounts: Pliny *Ep.* 7.31 .
18. See B. Campbell (1987).
19. Aelius Aristides *Or.* 26.88.
20. For military values under the Republic see Brunt (1990a) pp. 288–323; Rosenstein (2006) pp. 366–8.
21. Stat. *Silv.* 5.2.142–9.
22. Ibid. 4.4.72.
23. A. R. Birley (1981) pp. 222–4.
24. Tac. *Ann.* 12.12.
25. Ibid. 2.52.
26. *ILS* 939. Translation from B. Campbell (1984) p. 320.
27. D'Arms (1988) pp. 56–8; Beard (2008) pp. 206–8.
28. Suet. *Aug.* 46; *Claud.* 25.1.
29. See B. Campbell (1984) pp. 25–6. The governorship of Hispania Tarraconensis had a similar status but presumably for its civic, rather than military, responsibilities.
30. Tac. *Agr.* 40.1.
31. *ILS* 986. Translation from B. Campbell (1984) p. 360. For an analysis of his career under Nero see Conole and Milns (1983).
32. For the decorations available for equestrian and senatorial military service see Maxfield (1981) pp. 145–83.
33. *AE* 1934 176.
34. See above pp. 23–5.

35. Tac. *Hist.* 3.81. See Sidebottom (1993) pp. 245–50 for philosophers' negative attitudes to warfare under the Principate.
36. For competitive tendencies between the army and urban elites, see Ando (2007).
37. Tac. *Agr.* 7; *vulgus*: Kajanto (1970) p. 704; savagery: Tac. *Agr.* 28 (cannibalism); *Hist.* 2.88 (soldier's father killed by soldiers); 3.25 (soldier kills his own father in battle); 3.51 (soldier tries to claim a reward for killing his own brother).
38. See above p. 3.
39. Cornell (1993) p. 167.
40. Evident in Cassius Dio's unsuccessful attempts to converse with Severus' Danubian troops: Dio Cass. 75.2.6.
41. Suet. *Aug.* 24.1.
42. Marshall (1975).
43. Tac. *Ann.* 3.33.
44. Tac. *Ann.* 4.20.4.
45. Ibid. 1.40.3–41.3; Dio Cass. 57.5.6.
46. Vell. Pat. 2.115.3.
47. *RGDA* 1.4; 5.26, 30.
48. Plin. *Pan.* 19.1–2.
49. Suet. *Aug.* 38.1.
50. For a list of holders of the *ornamenta triumphalia*, see Gordon (1952) pp. 312–30.
51. Dio Cass. 51.24.4–25.2.
52. Tac. *Ann.* 3.72, 74.
53. Suet. *Claud.* 24.
54. Dio Cass. 54.11.6, 24.6–8, 31.4. The elder Drusus was awarded triumphal honours and an *ovatio* for his operations in Germany in 11 BC: 54.33.5.
55. Beard (2007) p. 69.
56. Tac. *Ann.* 1.2. The process is explored in an aptly named chapter 'The Doom of the Nobiles' in Syme (1939b) pp. 490–508. For a demographic analysis of the senatorial order under the Principate, see Hopkins (1983) pp. 120–200.
57. Although not with immediate effect: out of forty-two awards of *ornamenta triumphalia* made from Augustus to Hadrian, twelve went to descendants of Republican *nobiles* (almost 29 per cent); B. Campbell (1984) p. 320.
58. Note the interesting case of Vestricius Spurinna, who was awarded a triumphal statue for his exploits in Germany. His young son, who had died during his father's provincial tour of duty, was also honoured with

a statue: Plin. *Ep.* 2.7.1–2, 3.10.6. For a full catalogue of the recipients of honorary statues, see Gordon (1952) pp. 305–30.

59. Plin. *Ep.* 2.7.1;Tac. *Ann.* 4.23, 11.20, 13.53.
60. Note the rivalry between Domitius Corbulo and Suetonius Paulinus over their martial achievements: Tac. *Ann.* 14.29.
61. See above pp. 26–7.
62. Tac. *Ann.* 13.53; see also 11.28.
63. *ILS* 2487 field 30. Reading and translation by M. P. Speidel (2006a). Catullinus' prominence in the extant text can be attributed to his oversight of the epigraphic record of Hadrian's visit, as well as the emperor's desire to reinforce the commander's authority in the eyes of his troops.
64. See Tuck (2005) for a full discussion of Domitian's hunting imagery.
65. Suet. *Dom.* 19; Dio Cass. 67.14.
66. Dio of Prusa 3.135–6.
67. *RIB* 1041.
68. *ILS* 9421.
69. *Tab. Vindol.* II 233; III 593–4, 615.
70. Devijver (1992) pp. 3–4 argues that the army was involved in the supply of animals for games in Rome. If this was the case, incidents like the Moesian hunt must have been a relatively frequent occurrence.
71. See below pp. 189–90. On communication speeds see Millar (1982) pp. 182–3.
72. Austin & Rankov (1995) p. 170.
73. Millar (1977) pp. 314–7.
74. Tac. *Ann.* 2.77.
75. Ibid. 4.73.
76. Ibid. 12.48.
77. Dio Cass. 61.30.4–5; Tac. *Ann.* 11.19. See Potter (1996) p. 52.
78. Joseph. *AJ* 18.4.4.
79. Joseph. *BJ* 7.7.1–3.
80. Joseph. *AJ* 18.124.
81. Tac. *Ann.* 15.17.
82. Cornell (1993) pp. 165–7.
83. Syme (1964).
84. See B. Campbell (1987).
85. See Osgood (2006) pp. 257–60. Tensions between men who held military tribunates on account of family background and those who were promoted for prior military service are evident in Ovid: *Am.* 3.15.6; *Fast.* 4.379–80. In Maecenas' speech, Cassius Dio argues that soldiers from ranks should not be promoted to the Senate: 52.25.6

86. *ILS* 886.
87. Osgood (2006) pp. 276–80.
88. See below pp. 67–9.
89. Plin. *Pan*. 18.
90. Potter (2006) pp. 157–60.
91. Suet. *Dom*. 10.3.
92. Eumenius *Pan*. 8.14.2 (Loeb II p. 251).
93. Suet. *Aug*. 23.
94. Ibid. 25. I have argued elsewhere that emperors often sought to minimize potential casualties for propaganda purposes, see above p. 30.
95. See below pp. 73–6.
96. On the political context of the *Agricola* see Haynes (2006).
97. A. R. Birley (2005) p. 71.
98. A. R. Birley (1981) p. 18 lists 14 examples.
99. Ibid. pp. 30–1. There are 14 former legionary legates and 9 former tribunes on record who governed the same province in which they had previously served.
100. Tac. *Agr*. 7; *contra* Grant (2007) p. 83 who makes the outrageous claim that Agricola was the only candidate capable of taming the legion on the basis of his British tribunate.
101. Tac. *Agr*. 6, 9.
102. Wooliscroft & Hoffmann (2006) p. 196. Note Tac. *Agr*. 19, 21 on his civil activities. The first *iuridicus* in Britain is attested under Agricola: *ILS* 1011.
103. Tac. *Agr*. 18.1.
104. *Britannia* 21 (1990) p. 320; Grant (2007) p. 79.
105. Tac. *Ann*. 14.32.3.
106. Tac. *Agr*. 29–37.
107. Dio Cass. 66.20.2–3.
108. Tac. *Agr*. 35.
109. Cicero *Fam*. 8.5.1. On his persistent attempts to gain a triumph, see Beard (2007) pp. 187–96.
110. Tac. *Agr*. 40.
111. Suet. *Dom*. 10.2–3.
112. Tac. *Agr*. 9.2.
113. Ibid. 24. Epictetus 1.25.15 recalls the boredom of listening to yet another retelling of an old war story. Note also Tac. *Ann*. 14.29 where Quintus Veranius claims that he could have conquered the whole of the province if he had been given two more years.
114. See Lendon (1996) pp. 238–43.
115. For example: Tac. *Hist*. 2.5; Suet. *Vit*. 7.3.

116. Suet. *Dom.* 10.5. On effeminate officers see Phang (2008) pp. 97–9. See below pp. 93–4. for soldierly responses to unmanly emperors.
117. Tac. *Ann.* 2.13; *Hist.* 1.9.
118. Cass. Dio. 52.8.6–7.
119. *ILS* 2311.
120. Pliny *Ep.* 10.87. On appointments through patronage, see Saller (1982) pp. 43–50.
121. Suet. *Vesp.* 4; Dio Cass. 60.33.6. Vespasian's mistress allegedly sold army commands: Ibid. 65.14.
122. HA *Iul.* 1.4.
123. Dio 73.3.1.
124. HA *Sev.* 4.4.
125. *ILS* 4928–9.
126. Cotton (1981) p. 229. See also A. R. Birley (2003).
127. Pliny *Ep.* 7.22.
128. Ibid. 3.8.
129. *CIL* XIII 3162.
130. Lendon (1997) p. 188. A fragmentary text from Vindolanda refers to '… of a good man, there is added also moral progress through love of liberal pursuits and finally moderation': *Tab. Vindol.* III 660.
131. Tac. *Agr.* 5.
132. *Tab. Vindol.* II 225.
133. Suet. *Tib.* 42.
134. A. R. Birley (1981) p. 19.
135. Tac. *Agr.* 7.3; *Hist.* 1.60.
136. Macrob. *Sat.* II 4.5.
137. Suet. *Vesp.* 8.3.
138. Dio Cass. 66.2.2–3.
139. Suet. *Dom.* 1.3.
140. Fronto AD *Amicos* 1.6 (Loeb II pp. 191–3).
141. Syme (1958b) p. 789; (1977).
142. The composition of the so-called Corbulonian group is described in Nicols (1978) pp. 118–24; Vervaet (2003) pp. 443–52.
143. Dio 63.6.3–5. See Vervaet (2002) on Corbulo's unswerving loyalty to Nero.
144. Nicols (1978) p. 119.
145. As a theoretical exercise, a Severan group can be postulated consisting of officers who served under Sex. Julius Severus, a general whose length of service is almost without parallel until the Marcomannic Wars. Three of his officers (Julius Verus, Lollius Urbicus and Statius Priscus) obtained the governorship of Britain, a post which Severus had

previously held. L. Minicius Natalis, a tribune in XIV Gemina during Severus' legionary command, was appointed legate of VI Victrix during Severus' British governorship. Finally, Maenius Agrippa, an equestrian officer who served under Severus in Moesia Inferior appears to have transferred to Britain with his commander as prefect of the British fleet, followed by promotion to the procuratorship of the province. Suffice to say, despite this prosopographical basis, there is no historical evidence for such a group. On Julius Severus' career, see A. R. Birley (1981) pp. 106–9.

146. Pliny *NH* 5.83; Syme (1958b) p. 790.
147. A search was made of the legates catalogued in Franke (1991) from AD 55–67.
148. A. R. Birley (1981) p. 231.
149. B. W. Jones (1993) p. 18.
150. An idea proposed by Nicols (1978) p. 119.
151. There is another possible example in the triumphal honours awarded to Tampius Flavianus by Vespasian for actions in Pannonia, probably accomplished under Nero: *CIL* X 6225.
152. Tac. *Ann.* 6.30.
153. Ibid. 6.27. See B. Campbell (1984) p. 343.
154. Tac. *Ann.* 1.80 referring to Tiberius.
155. Suet. *Aug.* 66.2; Dio Cass. 53.23.5; *ILS* 8995.
156. Tac. *Ann.* 4.18.
157. Tac. *Agr.* 39.2. But note the case of Plautius Silvanus described above pp. 146–7.
158. *SCPP* 35–46.
159. Ibid. 45–7; Vell. Pat. 2.89.3.
160. Potter (1999) p. 82.
161. *SCPP* 163–6.
162. On the role of loyalty in the ideology of military command, we may note the case of Verginius Rufus, who rejected his soldiers' demands to seize power, even though it caused them to hate him: Dio Cass. 63.25.1; Plut. *Galba* 6.1; Tac. *Hist.* 2.68.4. An Italian forester erected an inscription in fulfilment of a vow '*pro salute et victoria L. Vergini Rufi*', after his victory over Vindex: *ILS* 982. Verginius' loyalty formed the basis of his epitaph: Plin. *Ep.* 6.10.4. For an assessment of his actions in AD 69, see Levick (1985).
163. Tac. *Ann.* 14.38.3.
164. Ibid. 13.1; *Hist.* 1.7, 12, 58.
165. Brunt (1983) pp. 63–6. B. Campbell (1984) pp. 404–7 argues that the increased use of equestrians in senior positions during the Severan

period was an *ad hoc* response to crises, probably prompted by a
shortage in senatorial candidates, rather than a deliberate policy of
excluding senators from key posts.
166. Dio Cass. 71.30.1–31.2.
167. Lendon (1997) p. 189: 'Certainly under the Principate the luxurious
express elevator to the highest offices to which those of patrician birth
were entitled usually carried them right past the floors on which the
spears and swords were stored.'
168. Griffin (2001) p. 117.
169. Tac. *Ann.* 15.72.1.
170. Three *coronae* and one *hasta*: *AE* 1951 88.
171. Plin. *Pan.* 14.5.
172. Dio of Prusa 1.31, 44; 3.86–9, 95.

CHAPTER 5
1. Brunt (1988) p. 259.
2. Haynes (2002) 115–25.
3. *SCPP* line 172.
4. *BGU* 140/*Sel. Pap.* 213.
5. *AE* 1937 no. 232. For other texts of a similar date published on bronze
see Corcoran (1996) p. 146.
6. Published with commentary in Fink, Hoey and Snyder (1940).
7. Gradel (2002) p. 341 suggests that the inclusion of Germanicus is a
result of his death in the province. However, as will be discussed below,
the obvious affection which troops from various military units felt for
Germanicus and his family and the official steps taken to appease
the anger of the soldiers after his death indicate that the inclusion of
Germanicus on the military calendar may have stemmed from Tiberius.
8. See above p. 38.
9. Tac. *Ann.* 1.22
10. Ibid. 1.36
11. Tac. *Hist.* 1.67, 2.85, 2.98. During the reign of Commodus, a delegation
of 1500 soldiers from Britain marched to Rome to inform the emperor of
the treasonous activities of Perennis and his sons: Dio Cass. 72.9.2–4;
Herodian 1.9.7.
12. Bowman & Thomas (1991) p. 67.
13. Thomas & Davies (1977) pp 51–2.
14. *Britannia* 17 (1986) pp. 450–2.
15. Maxfield (1986) p. 59.
16. The epigraphic and literary evidence for *vexillationes* are conveniently
collected in Saxer (1967).

17. Tacitus *Hist.* 1.6.
18. Tacitus *Hist.* 2.74.
19. *P. Mich* III 203.
20. Tac. *Hist.* 2.8.
21. Suet. *Tib.* 12.3.
22. For example *P. Mich* VIII 466.
23. *Tab. Vindol.* II 255 (Gaul), 283 (Rome), 310 (London).
24. *Tab. Vindol.* III 650.
25. M. P. Speidel (2006b).
26. A centurion who held a number of different commands, Julius Bassus Sulpicianus, had a brother in the urban cohorts and another who served as a *speculator*; *CIL* VIII 2890.
27. *Tab. Vindol.* II 252, 263, 295, 300.
28. Bowman (1994) pp. 112, 120. See above pp. 44–5.
29. For example Dio Cass. 43.5, 47.48.1, 51.10.2–3.
30. M. A. Speidel (2001) p. 57.
31. *P. Mich.* VIII 465, 466, 562.
32. *P. Mich.* IX 551.
33. *Tab. Vindol.* II 343.
34. *CIL* VIII 278.
35. Ramsay (1925) p. 73. Slow communication speeds undoubtedly had an adverse impact on the ability of the military to respond to external threats. See Amit (1965) and Millar (1982) pp. 7–11.
36. Duncan-Jones (1990) p. 20.
37. M. P. Speidel (1993) p. 112.
38. With two exceptions: New Testament Matthew 22.21; Arrian *Discourses of Epictetus* 4.5.15–17.
39. Jones (1956) pp. 14–5.
40. Sutherland (1959) p. 52.
41. Ibid. p. 55.
42. Kemmers (2006) p. 241.
43. Hekster (2003a) pp. 24–5.
44. Noreña (2001) p. 155.
45. This is particularly well illustrated on a papyrus from Egypt where a recruit from the fleet states that he received his travel expenses from Caesar: *BGU* 423 / *Sel. Pap.* 112.
46. Levick (1982).
47. See above p. 12.
48. Tac. *Hist.* 2.8.
49. Ibid. 1.54.
50. For the use of this motif in classical art see G. Davies (1985).

51. Brilliant (1963) p. 19.
52. *BMCRE* I p. 316 no. 53.
53. *BMCRE* I p. 305–6 nos. 61–3, 65–9.
54. Mattingly (1952) p. 77.
55. Tac. *Hist.* 1.62.
56. Kraay (1952) p. 83.
57. Tac. *Hist.* 1.74. The Praetorians who visited Valens' camp may well have carried the coins back to Rome and distributed them to their comrades.
58. For example *BMCRE* I p. 368 no. 2.
59. Levick (1999) p. 47.
60. Suet. *Galba* 16.2.
61. For example *BMCRE* II p. 184 no. 756, *BMCRE* II p. 74 no. 369.
62. *BMCRE* II p. 258 no. 177
63. *BMCRE* II no. 301.
64. *BMCRE* III p. 19 nos. 102–4.
65. Pliny *Ep.* 9.13.11. *Concordia* was used epigraphically by soldiers to indicate harmony and unity, often at locations where conflict could occur between men from different military units. A slab from Corbridge is dedicated to the concord of two legions, the VI and XX (*RIB* 1125). Presumably, detachments from these legions were working together at the site and this dedication was an attempt to discourage conflict between the soldiers. Alternatively, this inscription may have been erected to celebrate a successful working relationship between soldiers from the two legions. A similar inscription was set up at Carlisle by soldiers from II Augusta and XX Valeria Victrix (*Britannia* 20 (1989) p. 331 no. 4). An altar set up by a *beneficiarius consularis* at Altripp on the Rhine was dedicated to *Concordia variarum stationum* (*ILS* 2401). This was probably aimed at promoting harmony among the different officers stationed at the site. A statue pedestal from Vindolanda was dedicated to the goddess Gallia by soldiers from Gaul in concord with the troops from Britain: *Britannia* 38 (2007) p. 346 no. 2. Like the coinage, it appears that inscriptions dedicated to *Concordia* were aimed at maintaining unity and harmony, both within and between military units.
66. *RIC* II no. 4.39, see Brilliant (1963) p. 108.
67. *BMCRE* IV p. 638 nos. 1495–7.
68. *RIC* III p. 380 nos. 126–7.
69. Brilliant (1963) p. 148.
70. HA *Comm.* 16.2, Herodian 1.10.
71. *BMCRE* V p. 68 no. 284.
72. *RIC* IV. I p. 43.

73. *BMCRR* II p. 529 no. 214.
74. *RIC* I p.194 nos. 5–6, p. 195 no. 18.
75. Hewitt (1983) p. 66.
76. For example *RIC* 4.2 p. 92 nos. 2–8.
77. For example *BMCRE* III p. 498 nos. 1672–3.
78. On the pride taken by a soldier in his association with Hadrian see *ILS* 2558, an epitaph of a soldier recording various physical feats which he performed in front of the emperor.
79. *RPC* 1 p. 71 nos. 16–18.
80. Tac. *Ann.* 14.27.
81. Keppie (1983) p. 205–7.
82. See below pp. 109–10. It should be remembered that the poor quality of the land given to veterans was one of the grievances of the mutineers in AD 14. However, at Aosta the veterans received good land in the valley whereas the remaining inhabitants seem to have been on the mountain slopes. This distribution of good quality land may be linked to the strategic value of the veteran colony or perhaps the fact that their former comrades, as Praetorians, were serving in close proximity to the emperor on a daily basis.
83. Hekster (2007b) p. 339.
84. See above pp. 29–30.
85. For example *RIC* 1 p. 254 no. 467.
86. Scenes 10, 27, 42, 54, 73, 77, 104, 137.
87. Brilliant (1963) p. 119.
88. For example *BMCRE* IV p. 614 no. 1375.
89. Brilliant (1963) p. 95.
90. *BMCRE* III p. 68 no. 257: The depiction of *profectio* and *adventus* in Roman art is examined in Koeppel (1969).
91. *BMCRE* II p. 117 no. 543, *RIC* 4.1 p. 260 no. 315.
92. Wigg (1997) p. 287.
93. Kemmers (2006) p. 209–10.
94. Ibid. p. 227.
95. Kemmers (2006) p. 237.
96. Ibid. p. 255.
97. For example, *ILS* 233.
98. *CIL* VII 2554.
99. M. P. Speidel (1993) p. 110.
100. Fishwick (2004) p. 353.
101. *Feriale Duranum* col. I 2–6.
102. The survival of these altars is due to the fact that they were buried in pits at a later date, perhaps when the fort was finally abandoned.

103. Breeze (1997) p. 68.
104. Explicitly stated on *RIB* 814, 827.
105. Hill (1997) p. 93.
106. Mirković (1994).
107. Tomlin & Annis (1989).
108. Breeze (1997) p. 72.
109. Tac. *Ann*. 1.5.
110. *Fasti Ostienses* frag. 13d.
111. Dio Cass. 69.1.3–4.
112. There is evidence from the trial of Thrasea Paetus that the *diurna populi Romani* was circulated throughout the provinces but it is likely that this underwent some form of official censorship in Rome: Tac. *Ann*. 16.22.3.
113. Ando (2000) p. 45.
114. *Hist*. 1.55, 2.37 The soldiers must also have wondered whether the Senate would give them the donatives and rewards that a new emperor would if they gave them power; see Joseph. *AJ* 19.162.
115. Tac. *Hist*. 1.56.14.
116. *RGDA* 30; *Tabula Siarensis* fr. i, col. a, line 15.
117. Suet. *Claud*. 17; Dio Cass. 60.21. See below p. 116.
118. See above pp. 32–3.
119. Even then the soldiers in Upper Germany, at least, were slow to desert him; Tac. *Hist*. 1.8.
120. Suet. *Nero* 21.1.
121. Champlin (2003) p. 153. There is a conspicuous lack of evidence for the overt coercion of the upper classes to participate in Nero's shows and competitions see ibid. pp. 70–1.
122. Although he planned to deal with Galba's revolt by weeping in front of the soldiers until they pledged their loyalty to him; Suet. *Nero* 43.
123. The Syrian legions were extremely worried by rumours that Vitellius planned to transfer them to Germany and lent their support to Vespasian to avoid this: Tac. *Hist*. 2.80.
124. Herodian 5.2.4–5.
125. Ibid. 5.4.4, 5.8.1.
126. The chaotic events of his reign are described in Syme (1971) pp. 146–62.
127. Herodian 6.9.5.
128. Suet. *Tib*. 48.2.
129. Dio Cass. 60.19.1–22.2.
130. There is a parallel from the modern era in the political opinions of German prisoners of war during the Second World War. Soldierly

confidence in Hitler's abilities as commander-in-chief remained consistently high up until his suicide. Captive soldiers tended to blame military reverses on Hitler's dishonest advisors who kept the true state of affairs from him. See Shils and Janowitz (1948) pp. 304–5.

131. Dio Cass. 54.33.5.
132. Suet. *Cal.* 1.4. See Rich (1999).
133. Dio Cass. 55.2.1.
134. Suet. *Claud.* 1.3.
135. Tac. *Hist.* 1.62.2, 2.59.3.
136. Suet. *Claud.* 1.3; Dio Cass. 55.2.3.
137. *Tabula Siarensis*, fr. i, col. a, lines 26–8, translated with commentary in Crawford (1996) pp. 512–29.
138. Tac. *Ann.* 2.7.
139. For example: Potter (1987), Millar (1988), Griffin (1997), Gónzalez (1999), and Potter (1999). An exception to the lack of modern scholarly interest in the reaction of the army as revealed in these documents is Rowe (2002).
140. Tac. *Ann.* 1.35.4.
141. Ibid. 1.41.
142. Tac. *Ann.* 1.52.
143. Ibid. 1.60, 1.62, 2.25. See above p. 32.
144. Tac. *Ann.* 2.13.
145. Suet. *Cal.* 4.
146. Tac. *Ann.* 3.2.
147. Ibid. 3.29, 5.4, 6.46.
148. Ibid. 1.69.
149. Ibid. 1.7.
150. Tac. *Ann.* 2.83.
151. *Tabula Siarensis*, fr. i, col. a, lines 26–34.
152. Potter (1987) pp. 272–3.
153. Frenz (1989).
154. Ibid. p. 125.
155. *Feriale Duranum*, col. II 12–13.
156. Fink, Hoey & Snyder (1940) p. 138.
157. Griffin (1997) p. 260.
158. Tac. *Ann.* 3.7.
159. Ibid. 3.40.
160. *SCPP* line 172.
161. Tac. *Ann.* 2.79.
162. *SCPP* lines 45–57; Tac. *Ann.* 2.55.
163. *SCPP* lines 52–57.

164. Tac. *Ann.* 2.78.
165. Tac. *Ann.* 3.9.
166. E. Birley (1934) p. 128; Caracalla's fourth consulship began on 1 January AD 213. Caracalla assumed the title of *Germanicus Maximus* on 9 October of the same year. Thus all the inscriptions, with the exception of *RIB* 1235, are likely to have been erected before this date. *RIB* 1235 includes the title *Germanico maximo* and was therefore erected after the emperor's victory in Germany.
167. The phrase *pro pietate* is known from funerary inscriptions. Hope (2001) p. 40 suggested that this phrase was limited on military tombstones to those of XIV Gemina. This is incorrect as it is also found on those of XV Apollinaris; see Mosser (2003) p. 212 no. 94, p. 215 no. 99, p. 219 no. 106.
168. See A. R. Birley (2005) p. 208.
169. There is circumstantial evidence to support this idea. Severus is believed to have visited Carlisle shortly before his death: HA *Sev.* 22.4. Black (1984) has suggested that the Antonine Itinerary records journeys undertaken by Severus and his sons in AD 208–11. Four of the sites where these inscriptions have been found are mentioned in the Itinerary (High Rochester, Netherby, Old Penrith and Ambleside), suggesting the possibility that the troops at these sites received a visit from members of the imperial family. The British section of the Itinerary is discussed in detail by Rivet & Jackson (1970).
170. A. R. Birley (1988) p. 173.
171. Herodian 3.14.9.
172. HA *Carac.* 2.7.
173. Herodian 3.15.5.
174. Dio Cass. 77.1.3.
175. *RIB* 2066.
176. However, note that two of the inscriptions were reused as building stone, in one case barely seven years later, which suggests that the soldiers were not fully reconciled with Caracalla: *RIB* 1705, *Britannia* 16 (1985) p. 325 no. 11.
177. Daniels & Harbottle (1980) p. 71. *CIL* XII 7417, *CIL* VIII 18254.
178. E. Birley (1967) p. 107.
179. *RIB* 1022.
180. *RIB* 1026; *JRS* 57 (1967) p. 205 no. 16; *Britannia* 17 (1986) p. 438 no. 20.
181. Keppie (1994) pp. 47–8.
182. The centurion named at Piercebridge, M. Lollius Venator, could have been the same individual who was a centurion in *Cohors VI Vigilum* in

AD 210: *ILS* 2178. Intriguingly, two other centurions in the province at the same time may also have previously served as centurions in the *vigiles*: L. Apponius Rogatianus (*RIB* 1397, *CIL* VI 1057, vii 28) and Aelius Romanus (*RIB* II.8, 2503.116; *ILS* 2157). These men would presumably have progressed to centurionates in the urban and Praetorian cohorts before being sent to Britain. It is tempting to see their presence as a deliberate attempt to place individuals of proven loyalty in the politically dubious British legions. The careers of these men are discussed in Swan (2008) pp. 71–2, 77.

183. See above pp. 75–6.
184. Dio Cass. 72.9.2–4; Herodian 1.9.7.

CHAPTER 6

1. Most recently: Woods (2000), Malloch (2001), Hind (2003).
2. Suet. *Calig.* 45–8; Dio Cass. 59.25.1.3; Aur. Vict. *Caes.* 3.11–2.
3. Suet. *Calig.* 22.1.
4. Suet. *Galb.* 6.
5. HA *Hadr.* 15.12–3.
6. It was omitted by Hadrian after the Bar Kokhba revolt: Dio 69.14.3. For examples of normal practice, see Reynolds (1982) p. 41 no. 6, p. 101 no.12.
7. Suet. *Aug.* 25.1.
8. B. Campbell (1984) 35–7.
9. Plin. *Pan.* 15.5, 19.3.
10. Herodian 1.5.3.
11. Ibid. 4.7.
12. Syme (1958a) pp. 181–2.
13. Suet. *Claud.* 11.
14. Brunt (1977) p. 106.
15. *SB* VI 9528. Translation from Harker (2008) p. 62.
16. HA *Hadr.* 6.2.
17. Bowman (1970) pp. 23–5.
18. Dio Cass. 71.23.1.
19. *Feriale Duranum* col. I 23–26.
20. According to Josephus, the Praetorians recognised that the emperor ruled because of their protection; *AJ* 19.42. In his accession speech, Otho addressed the Praetorians who elevated him as *commilitones* and reminded them that their fates were now inextricably linked: Tac. *Hist.* 1.37.
21. *P. Bub.* I 4; translation from Harker (2008) p. 55.
22. Rea (1993) pp. 130–1.

23. *Dig.* 29.1.1. This is the first use of *commilitones* in an official document, see B. Campbell (1984) p. 37.
24. Ibid. (1984) p. 26.
25. Veg. *Mil.* 2.5.
26. 1 January: Tac. *Hist.* 1.55, 3 January: Plin. *Ep.* 10.35.
27. Plin. *Ep.* 10.100.
28. Ibid. 10.53, 101, 103, 20 (prison guards).
29. Ibid. 10.22, 28.
30. *AE* 1924 no. 135.
31. Apul. *Met.* 9.41.
32. Tac. *Hist.* 4.31.2.
33. On the soldiers' superstitious nature, see above p. 36.
34. HA *Sev. Alex.* 52.3. This probably reflects a fourth century ideal.
35. Joseph. *AJ* 19.129.
36. The average legionary salary was 900 sesterces annually under Augustus, 1200 sesterces under Domitian, c. 2000 sesterces under Severus and 3000 sesterces under Caracalla.
37. Suet. *Tib.* 48.2.
38. Dio Cass. 62.14.3; 62.27.4; Tac. *Ann.* 15.72.
39. Tac. *Ann.* 1.28.
40. Joseph. *AJ* 19.163.
41. Tac. *Hist.* 1.5.
42. Dio 46.46.7; HA *Sev.* 7.6. It seems unlikely that the amount of money distributed to the soldiers by Augustus was still common knowledge in this period. The soldiers may have learned this from military records. However, it is possible that the soldiers were prompted by an individual with knowledge gleaned from literary accounts or senatorial records.
43. Dio Cass. 76.15.2.
44. Ibid. 77.10.4.
45. Ibid. 74.11.2. See above p. 13.
46. The legal benefits available to soldiers are discussed in B. Campbell (1994) pp. 207–99; Alston (1995) pp. 53–68.
47. See above p. 31.
48. *BGU* 140.
49. Phang (2001) p. 382.
50. *CJ* 9.16.1.
51. Ibid. 1.18.1.
52. The importance of this diploma and further awards of the title *pia fidelis* are discussed in Holder (1999).
53. *AE* 1993 1572–3.

Notes

54. Dio Cass. 73.15.2. On the epigraphic evidence see M. P. Speidel (1993) p. 113.
55. For example *III Parthica Severiana* (*ILS* 484, 2653), *VIII Augusta Severiana Alexandriana* (*ILS* 1179, 3156).
56. *BGU* 628 / *FIRA* 1. 56.
57. Osgood (2006) 369.
58. Dio Cass. 55.4.2; Suet. *Aug.* 56.4.
59. Macrob. *Sat.* 2.4.27.
60. *CIL* V 890, 2389, 2839; *ILS* 2243, 2336; *AE* 1997 685. See Keppie (1983) pp. 111–2.
61. Plin. *NH* 33.82.
62. *RGDA* 15.3–17, 28.
63. Keppie (1983) pp. 114–22. Note also Augustus' advice to his veteran colonists at Firmum on selling all of their unsurveyed land: *CIL* IX 5420; Keppie (1983) pp. 182–3.
64. HA *Hadr.* 17.6–7.
65. Junius Gallus was disgraced by Tiberius for proposing new privileges for the Praetorian Guard: Tac. *Ann.* 6.3; Dio Cass. 58.18.3–4.
66. Ibid. 77.3. See also 77.10.4.
67. See Lendon (1997) pp. 252–66 on honour and military loyalty.
68. *BGU* 423/ *Sel. Pap.* 112.
69. Val. Max. 7.8.6; *CIL* II 6058. On his career, see Linderski (2002) pp. 578–9; Osgood (2006) pp. 272–3.
70. Suet. *Calig.* 38.2; Dio Cass. 59.15.2.
71. Joseph. *AJ* 19.365–6.
72. Plin. *Ep.* 10.107.
73. M. P. Speidel (1970) p. 146.
74. See Eaton (2017).
75. Tac. *Hist.* 3.44.
76. Roxan (1996) p. 253. Trajan awarded full citizenship rights to members of an auxiliary cohort who had served with distinction in Dacia (but not to their children): *CIL* XVI 160. On diplomas issued as a reward for special services, see Phang (2001) p. 64.
77. *SCPP* lines 159–63. For the charges against Piso, see above pp. 74–5. There is a strong correlation between the sentiments expressed here and in civic oaths of loyalty made to Augustus and his family. In the words of the oath from Conobaria (*AE* 1988 723): 'I will establish as my enemies those whom I observe are enemies of their party. And if anyone thinks or does anything against them, I will pursue them on

land and sea all the way to extermination.' The civic oath to Caligula from Aritium in Lusitania (*ILS* 190) similarly pledges a 'war of extermination' against the emperor's enemies. On the Conobaria oath, see Gónzalez (1988). Oaths of loyalty to the Julio-Claudian emperors are conveniently collected in Herrmann (1968) pp. 122–6.

78. Tac. *Ann.* 14.7.
79. See above pp. 94–100.
80. Suet. *Claud.* 27.2. On Caligula's childhood exposure to the soldiers, see above p. 103.
81. Tac. *Hist.* 2.59.
82. Rich (1999) p. 555.
83. See Phang (2001) pp. 350–1, 361–6.
84. Dio 71.10.5 (Faustina); *CIL* VIII 22689 (Crispina). On Julia Domna's adoption of the title, see Levick (2007) pp. 42–3.
85. See above p. 22.
86. Galinsky (1996) p. 329.
87. Severy (2003) p. 86.
88. Tac. *Ann.* 1.69.
89. Suet. *Calig.* 25.3.
90. Tac. *Ann.* 12.27.
91. Lucilla, Bruttia Crispina (wife of Commodus), Anna Faustina (great niece of M. Aurelius): Levick (2007) p. 56.
92. *RIB* 1791; *CIL* XIII 6671.
93. Levick (2007) pp. 43, 140–1.
94. *Feriale Duranum* col. i. 10; col. ii 7, 19, 26, 28; col. iii. 7.
95. Galinsky (1996) p. 329.
96. Kuttner (1995) p. 187.
97. Ibid. (1995) p. 189.
98. Nicolay (2007) pp. 140–1.
99. Ibid. p. 149.
100. Information received from V. Stokes (Project Manager, University of Leicester Archaeological Services) pers. comm.
101. Dolmans & Thunissen (2002) p. 20.
102. Maxfield (1981) p. 92.
103. Catalogued in Boschung (1987).
104. Rose (1997) p. 35.
105. Henig (1974) nos. 748, App. 80. I disagree with Henig, who believes they represent the children of Germanicus. They more closely resemble those of Claudius in Boschung (1987) p. 251.
106. See Severy (2003) pp. 80–2 for the military campaigns led by Augustus' relatives.

107. But note criticism of Tiberius for delegating Drusus and Germanicus to suppress the mutinies in AD 14 rather than deal with them himself: Tac. *Ann.* 1.46–7.
108. Vell. Pat. 2.104.
109. Tac. *Ann.* 1.17.
110. Note the loan of 400 *drachmae* obtained by the cavalryman L. Caesilius Secundus using a silver helmet, military decoration and silver scabbard with ivory inlay as security: *P. Vindob.* L 135.
111. Marcus Valerius Maximianus was rewarded with a horse, decorations and weapons by Marcus Aurelius for having personally killed an enemy chief: *AE* 1956 124.
112. Helmet ACA 04 (Xanten), Rheinisches Landesmuseum Bonn.
113. *RIC* I p. 52 no. 165a. The Boscoreale Cups, a pair of silver drinking goblets from the Augustan period, also juxtapose Augustus, Drusus and Tiberius. On one, Drusus is shown in military costume presenting barbarian children to Augustus. On the second, Tiberius is shown sacrificing prior to war and triumphing after his victory.
114. Kuttner (1995) p. 173.
115. Nicolay (2007) p. 170.
116. Hekster (2001) pp. 39–40.
117. Joseph. *AJ* 19.217. The title of Germanicus was awarded to the male descendants of Drusus in perpetuity: Suet. *Claud.* 1.3.
118. Herodian 1.8.3; HA *Marc.* 20.6–7; *Pert.* 4.11; *Did. Iul.* 8.3.
119. Uzzi (2005) pp. 98–9.
120. Plut. *Galba* 9.1–2.
121. *Feriale Duranum* col. i 14–16; Herodian 3.9.1–2; HA *Sev.* 16.3–4.
122. Dio Cass. 76.7.4, 77.9.4; HA *Sev.* 10.7.
123. Hekster (2003b) pp. 189–90.
124. Lőrincz (1982) pp. 142–4.
125. HA. *Elag.* 1.4; Herodian 5.4.4, 5.7.3. See Potter (2006) p. 155.
126. Dio of Prusa 1.28–9.
127. Suet. *Claud.* 17. He organized re-enactments of key scenes from the conquest of Britain on the Campus Martius, clad in a general's cloak: 21.6.
128. *BMCRE* III 425, 433–4.
129. Bennett (2001) pp. 49–52. Pliny claimed that Trajan's lengthy inspection tour was for the purposes of restoring discipline, meeting the incumbent legates and assessing the military situation on the ground; *Pan.* 18.1.
130. HA *Hadr.* 10; Dio Cass. 69.9.3–4. Note Plutarch *Mar.* 7.3: 'It is a most agreeable spectacle for a Roman soldier when he sees a general eating common bread in public.'

131. HA *Pesc. Niger* 11.
132. Suet. *Tib.* 18.2; *Herodian* 2.11.2; HA *Sev. Alex.* 51.5.
133. Tac. *Hist.* 1.31.
134. Dio Cass. 68.12; HA *Sev. Alex.* 47.
135. Dio Cass. 77.13; Herodian 4.7.4–7. Septimius Severus also enthusiastically participated in routine military chores: ibid. 2.11. On imperial *labor* in general, see Phang (2008) pp. 239–42.
136. Joseph. *BJ* 5.349–51, 7.13–6. See Goldsworthy (1999) pp. 203–6.
137. *CIL* XVI 69. See A. R. Birley (2001) p. 127.
138. See above p. 86.
139. Pseudo-Hyginus *de munitionibus castrorum* 11. See above p. 87.
140. See Harto Trujillo (2008) pp. 28–32 for a useful summary of military speeches in Roman literature.
141. The historicity of battle exhortations in antiquity is discussed in Hansen (1993).
142. Dio Cass. 71.24.1–26.4.
143. Herodian 1.5.3–8.
144. Herodian 2.10.2–8.
145. Ibid. 3.6.1–7.
146. *ILS* 2487. I use the edition of M. P. Speidel (2006a).
147. M. P. Speidel (2006a) p. 5.
148. Field 30.
149. Field 29.
150. B. Campbell (1984) p. 79.
151. Field 2. I disagree with Speidel's interpretation that this passage refers to one of the legionary battle lines. The details discussed are relevant to the senior centurions as 'managers' rather than the soldiers themselves.
152. Field 26.
153. M. P. Speidel (2006a) p. 88.
154. Pseudo-Hyginus, *de munitionibus castrorum* 7–10, 23, 33.
155. Tac. *Ann.* 2.13.
156. Suet. *Aug.* 10.4. At the battle of Philippi, Octavian fled his camp shortly before it was captured: App. *B Civ.* 4.110.
157. Herodian 3.7.3.
158. Dio Cass. 75.6.7.
159. Levithan (2008) cites a number of emperors who were wounded during sieges: Joseph. *BJ* 3.226–9 (Vespasian); Dio 65.5.1 (Titus), 68.31.3 (Trajan), 76.11.3 (Septimius Severus); HA *The Two Gallieni* 4.3 (Gallienus); Amm. Marc. 24.5.6 (Julian).
160. Herodian 7.2.6.
161. HA *Max.* 12.
162. Dio Cass. 77.13.2.

163. B. Campbell (1984) pp. 68–9.
164. Trajan's Column: scenes 24 and 72; Great Trajanic Frieze: slab 6; Column of Marcus Aurelius: scene 66.
165. Lepper & Frere (1988) p. 70; Goldsworthy (1996) p. 276; Fields (2005) p. 60; Shotter (2007) p. 107.
166. Diod. Sic. 5.29.4–5; Livy 10.26.11, 23.24; Cunliffe (2002) pp. 552–3, (2003) p. 151.
167. *CIL* XII 1077.
168. Coulston (2003) p. 405. The descriptions of the relevant Column casts in the *Museo della Civiltà Romana* in Rome carry the same assertion.
169. See Bonfante (1984).
170. Crawford (1974) no. 286.
171. P. J. E. Davies (1997) pp. 62–3.
172. Frontin. *Strat.* 2.9.2–5.
173. I am entirely unconvinced by the argument that the Roman heads displayed on a Dacian fortification in Scene 25 symbolised that the invasion of Dacia was undertaken in response to 'barbarian' crimes: Coulston (2003) pp. 407–8. The presentation of Dacian heads to Trajan occurs a scene earlier, and therefore it is more logical that the Roman heads displayed by Dacians were a retaliatory gesture for a Roman 'atrocity', if such a schematic reading of the monument is necessary.
174. Dio Cass. 43.24.3–4.
175. Isserlin (1997) p. 94.
176. Dio Cass. 67.11.3.
177. Dio Cass. 74.8.3, 75.7.3; HA *Sev.* 9.1, 11.6; *Niger* 6.1; *Clod.* 9.6.
178. Herodian 3.8.1.
179. Plut. *Galb.* 28. The heads were used to terrify the Senate into submission: Dio Cass. 63.7.5.
180. The victims are usefully collected in Voisin (1984).
181. Suet. *Iul.* 85.
182. Dio Cass. 72.6.
183. Ibid. 16.1.
184. App. *B Civ.* 4.20. It appears that there is a clear literary *topos* of tyrannical rulers gazing at the decapitated heads of their enemies. According to Seneca, Marcus Antonius enjoyed gazing at the heads of his enemies while he dined: *Ep.* 83.25. Caligula enjoyed watching criminals being beheaded (also while he dined): Suet. *Calig.* 32. Nero mocked the grey hair and nose on the heads of Cornelius Sulla Felix and Rubellius Plautus respectively: Tac. *Ann.* 14.57, 59. Poppaea personally viewed the head of Octavia: ibid. 14.64. Otho gazed at Galba's head 'with insatiable eyes': Tac. *Hist.* 1.44. On the other hand,

Marcus Aurelius refused to see Avidius Cassius' decapitated head and ordered it to be buried: Dio Cass. 71.28.1.

185. Plut. *Galb.* 28; Tac. *Hist.* 1.47. The heads had previously been prominently displayed alongside the military standards: ibid. 1.44.

186. Suet. *Galb.* 20.2. The transportation of severed heads was a perennial problem. The tombstone of Insus (discussed below) shows one being carried by its conveniently long hair. In scene 23 on Trajan's Column, a soldier carries a head with the hair clasped in his teeth. Galba's baldness prohibited either of these approaches.

187. Plut. *Galb.* 27.3.

188. Caes. *B Hisp.* 32.

189. Silberberg-Peirce (1986) p. 314.

190. This is not solely an ancient phenomenon. American troops collected enemy skulls to take home in both the Pacific and Vietnam conflicts: Weingartner (1992), Harrison (2006), Boorstein (2007). In 1944 *Life* magazine published a photograph showing a female war worker admiring a Japanese skull sent by her boyfriend, whose description ('a big, handsome Navy lieutenant') implies masculine and sexual connotations concerning his gift. The previous year, a mother petitioned the authorities to allow her to nail a Japanese ear, sent by her son, to her front door: see Ferguson (2006) pp. 546–7.

191. Curle (1911) p. 129; Clarke (2000) p.24.

192. *Britannia* 37 (2006) p. 468 no. 3. A fragmentary tombstone from Chester (*RIB* 522), also belonging to a cavalryman, may depict a severed head.

193. Caes. *B Gall.* 3.14, 6.8, 7.62.

194. Dio Cass. 56.13.

195. Joseph. *BJ* 6.133–4, 6.245.

196. Dio Cass. 67.10.1.

197. Plin. *Pan.* 15.5. There is a clear parallel with the importance of the emperor watching the games in Rome: see Hekster (2005) on the emperor as a 'viewer' of the arena.

198. *ILS* 2558.

199. Livy 24.15.

200. Lib. *Orat.* 18.45. Valens used the same tactic: Zos. 4.11.

201. See M. P. Speidel (1970) for an analysis of his career.

202. Touati (1987) p. 49. They are the only dismounted cavalrymen depicted on the monument.

203. Dio Cass. 68.14.

204. *SEG* IX 101.

205. Described in M. P. Speidel (1970) p. 183.

206. Dio Cass. 68.14.3; *Fasti Ostienses* AD 106. Octavian sent Brutus' head to be thrown at the feet of Caesar's statue in Rome: Suet. *Aug.* 13.1.The abuse of the head was a means of further punishing the victim after death. Caesarian soldiers used the head of one of his assassins as a ball, throwing it between themselves until it smashed: App. *B Civ.* 3.26. Galba's head was given to the servants of one of his victims, who outraged it further: Suet. *Galb.* 20.3, Plut. *Galb.* 28
207. In a similar way, the consul Gaius Flaminius had a helmet adorned with a Suebic scalp: Sil. 5.133–4.
208. Slim (1999) p. 188, quoted in Coulston (2003) p. 405.
209. The use of enemy body parts as an affirmation of the chain of command is illustrated in the following incident from the Second World War. In 1944 President Roosevelt was presented with a letter opener made from the arm bone of a Japanese soldier by a congressman. The president later returned the gift after a public outcry from religious groups: Weingartner (1992) pp. 60–1.
210. Tac. *Hist.* 1.4.

CONCLUSION
1. Strabo 17.3.25.
2. Dio Cass. 53.11.5.
3. Cic. *Phil.* 13.24.
4. Dio Cass. 77.15.2.
5. Dio Chrys. *Or.* 1.28. On this concept see Dio Cass. 56.16.3: 'You Romans are to blame for this, for you send as guardians of your flocks, not dogs or shepherds, but wolves.'

APPENDIX
1. Keppie (1996) pp. 120–1. On the Guard in general, see Durry (1938), Passerini (1939), Rankov (1994).
2. Tac. *Ann.* 16.27; *Hist.* 1.38.
3. Suet. *Aug.* 49.1; *Tib.* 37.1.
4. *AE* 1978 286; Tac. *Ann.* 4.5.
5. Tac. *Hist.* 2.93.
6. Tac. *Ann.* 4.5.
7. Dio Cass. 75.2.5.
8. Durry (1938) pp. 246–7.
9. Inscriptions concerning these individuals are listed in Kennedy (1978) pp. 288–92.
10. See Breeze & Dobson (1969).
11. Dio Cass. 24.25.6; 55.23.1.

12. Ibid. 53.11.5; Tac. *Ann.* 1.17.
13. Ibid. 1.17.
14. Tac. *Hist.* 1.23; 2.21. The same sentiments are evident in Dio Cass. 74.16.3; Herodian 2.10.6.
15. HA *Did. Jul.* 5.9.
16. Praetorian Guard and *equites singulares Augusti*: Scheidel (2007) p. 427; *Germani*: Bellen (1981) p. 103.
17. Scheidel (1996) p. 128.
18. Vitruvius 6.1.4; Tac. *Hist.* 2.93.
19. On the urban cohorts, see Freis (1967).
20. Suet. *Aug.* 101.
21. See Freis (1967) pp. 48–9.
22. Ibid. pp. 55–9.
23. On the *vigiles* in general, see Baillie Reynolds (1923).
24. The most detailed study of the deployment of the *vigiles* is Rainbird (1986).
25. See Mann (1983a).
26. *Corp. Glossar. Latin.* III p. 31.
27. On the *Germani corporis custodes*, see Bellen (1981).
28. Bellen (1981) p. 53.
29. Suet. *Galba* 12.2, *Cal.* 43.
30. For example: Joseph. *AJ* 19.119.
31. Roymans (2004) p. 56.
32. M. P. Speidel (1984b) pp. 43–5, (1994a) p. 29.
33. Suet. *Cal.* 43.
34. Dio Cass. 56.23.4.
35. Caligula: Joseph. *AJ* 19.122; Nero: Suet. *Nero* 30.2, 47.3. Reward for popularity: Bellen (1981) p. 67.
36. Joseph. *AJ* 19.121.
37. On the *equites singulares Augusti*, see M. P. Speidel (1994a).
38. Speidel (1994a) p. 83.
39. See above p. 45.
40. Tac. *Hist.* 1.6.
41. See Ashby & Baillie Reynolds (1923), Sinnigen (1962), Mann (1988), Rankov (1990), (2006).
42. For example: HA *Hadr.* 11.4–6; *Comm.* 4.5; *Did. Jul.* 5.8; *Pesc. Nig.*2.6; Herodian 3.5.4–5; Dio Cass. 79.15.1.
43. Mann (1988). Sheldon (2005) pp. 250–60 discusses the *frumentarii* in a chapter dramatically entitled 'The Roman secret service'.
44. Rankov (1990) pp. 178–80.

Index